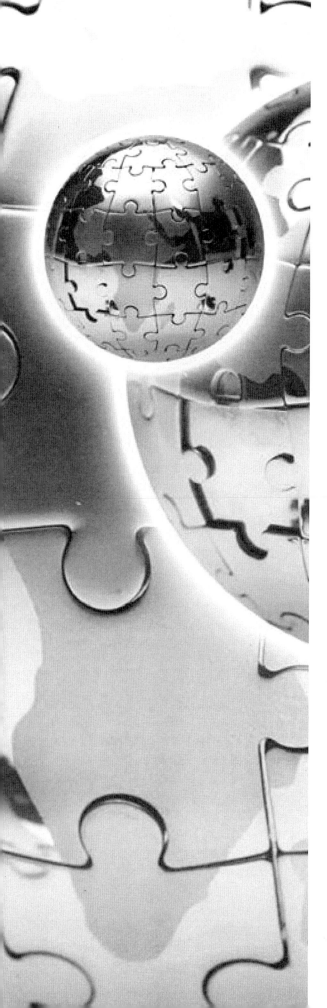

Investment Operations Certificate (IOC)

IT in Investment Operations

Edition 7, August 2014

This learning manual relates to syllabus version 7.1 and will cover exams from **11 November 2014 to 10 May 2017**

APPROVED WORKBOOK

Welcome to the Chartered Institute for Securities & Investment's IT in Investment Operations study material.

This manual has been written to prepare you for the Chartered Institute for Securities & Investment's IT in Investment Operations examination.

Published by:
Chartered Institute for Securities & Investment
© Chartered Institute for Securities & Investment 2016
20 Fenchurch Street
London
EC3M 3BY
Tel: +44 20 7645 0600
Fax: +44 20 7645 0601

Email: customersupport@cisi.org
www.cisi.org/qualifications

Author:
Andrew Bradford

Reviewers:
Paul Taylor
Kevin Sloane

This is an educational manual only and Chartered Institute for Securities & Investment accepts no responsibility for persons undertaking trading or investments in whatever form.

While every effort has been made to ensure its accuracy, no responsibility for loss occasioned to any person acting or refraining from action as a result of any material in this publication can be accepted by the publisher or authors.

All rights reserved. No part of this publication may be reproduced, stored in a retrieval system, or transmitted, in any form or by any means, electronic, mechanical, photocopying, recording or otherwise without the prior permission of the copyright owner.

Warning: any unauthorised act in relation to all or any part of the material in this publication may result in both a civil claim for damages and criminal prosecution.

A learning map, which contains the full syllabus, appears at the end of this manual. The syllabus can also be viewed on cisi.org and is also available by contacting the Customer Support Centre on +44 20 7645 0777. Please note that the examination is based upon the syllabus. Candidates are reminded to check the Candidate Update area details (cisi.org/candidateupdate) on a regular basis for updates as a result of industry change(s) that could affect their examination.

The questions contained in this manual are designed as an aid to revision of different areas of the syllabus and to help you consolidate your learning chapter by chapter.

Learning manual version: 7.3 (October 2015)

Learning and Professional Development with the CISI

The Chartered Institute for Securities & Investment is the leading professional body for those who work in, or aspire to work in, the investment sector, and we are passionately committed to enhancing knowledge, skills and integrity – the three pillars of professionalism at the heart of our Chartered body.

CISI examinations are used extensively by firms to meet the requirements of government regulators. Besides the regulators in the UK, where the CISI head office is based, CISI examinations are recognised by a wide range of governments and their regulators, from Singapore to Dubai and the US. Around 50,000 examinations are taken each year, and it is compulsory for candidates to use CISI learning manuals to prepare for CISI examinations so that they have the best chance of success. Our learning manuals are normally revised every year by experts who themselves work in the industry and also by our Accredited Training Partners, who offer training and elearning to help prepare candidates for the examinations. Information for candidates is also posted on a special area of our website: cisi.org/candidateupdate.

This learning manual not only provides a thorough preparation for the examination it refers to, it is also a valuable desktop reference for practitioners, and studying from it counts towards your Continuing Professional Development (CPD). Mock examination papers, for most of our titles, will be made available on our website, as an additional revision tool.

CISI examination candidates are automatically registered, without additional charge, as student members for one year (should they not be members of the CISI already), and this enables you to use a vast range of online resources, including CISI TV, free of any additional charge. The CISI has more than 40,000 members, and nearly half of them have already completed relevant qualifications and transferred to a core membership grade. You will find more information about the next steps for this at the end of this manual.

With best wishes for your studies.

Lydia Romero, Global Director of Learning

It is estimated that this workbook will require approximately **70** hours of study time.

What next?
See the back of this book for details of CISI membership.

Need more support to pass your exam?
See our section on Accredited Training Partners.

Want to leave feedback?
Please email your comments to learningresources@cisi.org

Chapter One

Information Technology in the Securities Industry

This syllabus area will provide approximately 4 of the 100 examination questions

1. Introduction

There are ten chapters to this workbook, corresponding to the syllabus areas of the examination.

Chapter 1 introduces the reader to the industry participants and financial instruments that are relevant to the syllabus. It also introduces the reader to the different elements of a securities trade and explains the concept of 'straight-through processing' (STP). The achievement of STP is one of the goals of the IT department in most investment firms.

Chapter 2 describes the regulatory environment in which securities firms operate. It outlines how investment firms are regulated, and the effect of regulation on the business applications that are used by an investment firm and also on the way that the firm's IT infrastructure is managed.

Chapter 3 describes the roles of investment exchanges, clearing houses and information vendors in the investment industry.

Chapters 4 to 7 inclusive take us through the process of a securities trade, beginning with the order and ending with the position that results from the settled trade.

Chapters 8 to 10 inclusive deal with IT management issues, covering the management of day-to-day operations, the management of business change, the selection of suppliers of new applications, and the impact of outsourcing and offshoring.

2. Financial Services Industry Participants

Learning Objective

1.1   Know the role of the following participants within the financial services industry: retail banks and building societies; investment banks; pension funds; insurance companies; fund managers; stockbrokers; wealth managers, platforms and financial advisers; custodians; third party administrators (TPAs)

2.1   Retail Banks and Building Societies

Retail (or high street) banks provide services such as taking deposits from, and lending funds to, retail customers, as well as providing payment and money transmission services. They may also provide similar services to business customers. Historically, these banks have tended to operate through a network of branches located on the high street. They also provide internet and telephone banking.

In the UK, the sector has gone through a period of consolidation and, increasingly, integration with non-bank institutions such as insurance companies, as well as providing traditional banking services.

Larger retail banks also offer products such as investments, pensions and insurance.

As well as retail banks, most countries also have savings institutions that started off by specialising in offering savings products to retail customers, but now tend to offer a similar range of services as banks. In the UK, these are usually known as building societies. They were established in the 19th century when small numbers of people would group together locally and pool their savings, allowing some members to build or buy houses. Building societies are jointly owned by the individuals that have deposited or borrowed money from them – the 'members'. It is for this reason that such savings organisations are often described as mutual societies.

Over the years, many smaller building societies have merged or been taken over by larger ones. In the late 1980s, legislation was introduced allowing building societies to become companies or banks – a process known as **demutualisation**. Some large building societies remain as mutuals, such as the Nationwide Building Society. They continue to specialise in services for retail customers, especially the provision of deposit accounts and mortgages.

2.2   Investment Banks

Investment banks provide advice to, and arrange finance for, companies who want to float on the stock market, to raise additional finance by issuing further shares or bonds, or carry out mergers and acquisitions. They also provide services for those institutions who might want to invest in shares and bonds, for example pension funds and asset managers.

The financial crisis of 2007–10 saw the disappearance of many well-known investment banks, which were either taken over by other banks or converted into bank holding companies; for example, Merrill Lynch was taken over by Bank of America.

Typically, an investment banking group provides some or all of the following services, either in divisions of the bank or in associated companies within the group:

- **Corporate finance and advisory work**, normally in connection with new issues of securities for raising finance, takeovers, mergers and acquisitions.
- **Banking**, for governments, institutions and companies.
- **Treasury dealing** for corporate clients in foreign currencies, with financial engineering services to protect them from interest rate and exchange rate fluctuations.
- **Investment management** for sizeable investors such as corporate pension funds, charities and private clients. This may be either via direct investment for the wealthier, or by way of collective investment schemes. In larger firms, the value of funds under management runs into many billions of pounds.
- **Securities trading** in equities, bonds and derivatives and the provision of broking and distribution facilities.

Only a few investment banks provide services in all these areas. Most others tend to specialise to some degree and concentrate on only a few product lines.

2.3   Pension Funds

Pension funds are one of the key planning methods by which individuals can make provision for retirement. There is a variety of pension schemes available ranging from ones provided by employers to self-directed, or personal, pension schemes.

Pension funds themselves are large, long-term investors in shares, bonds and cash. Some also invest in physical assets such as property. In addition, some pension funds are allowed to use derivative instruments to protect, or hedge, their other assets against market falls. To meet their aim of providing a pension on retirement, the sums of money invested by pension funds are substantial.

2.4   Insurance Companies

One of the key functions of the financial services industry is to allow risks to be managed effectively. The insurance industry provides solutions for much more than the standard areas of life and general insurance cover. Protection planning is a key area of financial advice, and the insurance industry provides a wide range of products to meet many potential scenarios. These products range from payment protection policies designed to pay out in the event that an individual is unable to meet repayments on loans and mortgages, to fleet insurance against the risk of an airline's planes crashing.

Insurance companies collect premiums in exchange for the cover provided. This premium income is used to buy investments such as shares and bonds and, as a result, the insurance industry is a major player in the London stock market. Insurance companies will subsequently realise these investments to pay any claims that may arise on the various policies.

2.5   Fund Managers

Fund management is the administration of portfolios for pension funds, insurance companies and collective investment schemes. It is also known as asset management, or investment management.

This sector also includes hedge funds, which are aggressively managed portfolios of investments that use advanced investment strategies such as leveraged, long, short and derivative positions in both domestic and international markets with the goal of generating high returns.

Fund managers run portfolios of investments for others. They invest money for institutions, such as pension funds and insurance companies, as well as for collective investment schemes, such as unit trusts and open-ended investment companies (OEICs), and for wealthier individuals. Some are organisations which focus solely on this activity; others are divisions of larger entities, such as insurance companies or banks.

Investment managers who buy and sell shares, bonds and other assets in order to increase the value of their clients' portfolios can conveniently be sub-divided into **institutional** and **private client** fund managers. Institutional fund managers work on behalf of institutions, for example, investing money for a company's pension fund, or an insurance company's fund, or managing the investments in a unit trust. Private client fund managers invest the money of relatively wealthy individuals. Institutional portfolios are usually larger than those of private clients.

Investment managers charge their clients for managing their money; their charges are often based on a small percentage of the fund being managed, and sometimes on the performance of the portfolio.

2.6 Stockbrokers, Wealth Managers, Platforms and Advisers

There are three broad types of stockbrokers: institutional, corporate and private client. Institutional brokers typically execute trades on behalf of institutional clients, such as fund managers, pension funds, companies and local authorities. Corporate brokers advise companies on fund raising (eg, new issues of shares) and work to generate interest among investors for the company's securities.

Private client stockbrokers (who are also known as wealth managers) arrange stock market trades on behalf of their private investors and charities. They may **advise** investors about which individual shares, bonds or funds they should buy or, alternatively, they may offer **execution-only** services, where instructions are carried out but advice is not offered. When they act in an advisory capacity, these firms usually charge the client a percentage of the portfolio's value, but when they provide execution-only services, they usually charge by the transaction.

Like fund managers, firms of stockbrokers can be independent companies, but often they are divisions of larger entities, such as investment banks or other asset managers.

Financial advisers offer the private investor financial planning services, such as creating and managing pension plans, and other tax-sheltered investments, such as individual savings accounts (ISAs).

Their role is to establish the client's investment objectives and attitude to risk, and then to recommend suitable investments that will meet the client's requirements. For smaller customers, they often recommend that the majority of the portfolio is invested in collective investment schemes because such schemes are the easiest way to diversify a small portfolio. For larger customers, they often appoint a discretionary wealth manager to manage their portfolios in a mixture of collective investment schemes, equities and bonds, according to parameters specified by the adviser, who then charges the client an annual oversight fee.

Platforms are online services designed to enable both financial advisers and retail investors to manage their investment portfolios. They offer their users the ability to:

- view and monitor all their investments on a single computer application;
- research information about individual investments that they have invested in or are considering investing in;
- place buy and sell orders online;
- keep track of income due and income received;
- monitor their tax liabilities;
- perform **portfolio modelling**, such as 'what-if' scenario analysis;
- compare the actual return on investment of the portfolio to that of a **benchmark** portfolio.

Both advisers and platforms usually charge the client a percentage of the portfolio's value for the services that they provide.

2.7   Custodians

Custodians are banks that specialise in safe custody services looking after portfolios of shares and bonds on behalf of others, such as fund managers, pension funds and insurance companies.

The core activities they undertake include:

- holding assets in safekeeping, such as equities and bonds;
- arranging settlement of purchases and sales of securities;
- collecting income from assets, namely dividends in the case of equities and interest in the case of bonds;
- providing information about the underlying companies and their annual general meetings;
- managing cash transactions;
- performing foreign exchange transactions where required;
- providing regular reporting on all their activities to their clients; and
- managing stock-lending activity on behalf of their clients.

Cost pressures have driven down the charges that a custodian can make for its traditional custody services and have resulted in consolidation within the industry. The custody business is now dominated by a small number of global custodians which are often divisions of investment banks.

2.8   Third Party Administrators (TPAs)

Third party administrators (TPAs) undertake investment administration on behalf of other firms and specialise in this area of the investment industry. The number of firms and the scale of their operations have grown with the increasing use of outsourcing by firms. Outsourcing is explained in detail in Chapter 10.

3.   Financial Instruments Covered by this Workbook

The financial instruments and transaction types that the workbook is concerned with in Chapters 3 to 7 inclusive are: currencies, securities including bonds and equities, and listed derivatives, including futures, options and OTC derivatives. It is assumed that most examination candidates will be familiar with the basic characteristics of these instruments as a result of taking the *Introduction to Securities & Investment* Investment Operations Certificate (IOC) paper.

For the benefit of any *IT in Investment Operations* candidate who is not taking the introduction examination, this section briefly summarises the characteristics of these instruments. More detailed information about them may be found in the *Introduction to Securities & Investment* workbook.

3.1   Currencies

The foreign exchange market, which is also known as the Forex or FX market, refers to the trading of one currency for another. It is by far the largest market in the world. In the 1970s, trading in currencies became 24-hour as it could take place in the various time zones of Asia, Europe and America. Of the $4 trillion daily global turnover in October 2010, trading in London accounted for around $1.36 trillion, or 34% of the total, making London by far the largest global centre for foreign exchange. In second and third places respectively, trading in New York accounted for over 16%, and Tokyo accounted for 6%.

Trading of foreign currencies is always done in pairs. These are **currency pairs** where one currency is bought and the other is sold, and the prices at which these take place make up the **exchange rate**. When the exchange rate is being quoted, the name of the currency is abbreviated to a three-digit reference; so, for example, sterling is abbreviated to GBP, which you can think of as an abbreviation for GB pounds. The most commonly quoted currency pairs are:

- US dollar and Japanese yen (USD/JPY);
- Euro and US dollar (EUR/USD);
- US dollar and Swiss franc (USD/CHF);
- British pound and US dollar (GBP/USD).

When currencies are quoted, the first currency is the base currency and the second is the counter or quote currency. The base currency is always equal to one unit of that currency, in other words, one pound, one dollar or one euro. For example, at the time of writing the EUR:USD exchange rate is 1:1.2378 which means that €1 is worth $1.2378.

When currency pairs are quoted, a market maker or foreign exchange trader will quote a **bid and ask price**. Staying with the example of the EUR:USD, the quote might be 1.2377/79. So if you want to **buy** €100,000 then you will need to pay the higher of the two prices and deliver $123,790; if you want to **sell** €100,000 then you get the lower of the two prices and receive $123,770.

The Forex market is an over-the-counter (OTC) market where brokers and dealers negotiate directly with one another. The main participants are large international banks which continually provide the market with both bid (buy) and offer (sell) prices. Central banks are also major participants in foreign exchange markets, which they can use to try to control money supply, inflation, and interest rates. There are several types of FX transactions commonly used:

- **Spot transactions** – the 'spot rate' is the rate quoted by a bank for the exchange of one currency for another with immediate effect (spot trades are 'settled' – that is, the currencies actually change hands and arrive in recipients' bank accounts, two business days after the transaction date).
- **Forward transactions** – in this type of transaction, money does not actually change hands until some agreed-upon future date. A buyer and seller agree on an exchange rate for any date in the future, for a fixed sum of money, and the transaction occurs on that date, regardless of what the market rates are then. The duration of the trade can be a few days, months or years, as agreed between the parties.
- **FX swaps** – the most common type of forward transaction is the currency swap. In a swap, two parties exchange currencies for a certain length of time and agree to reverse the transaction at a later date.

3.2 Securities

Securities include bonds (also known as debt instruments) and equities. Securities may be bought and sold – the subject of much of Chapters 3 to 7 of this workbook – but they may also be borrowed and lent. Stock borrowing and lending is covered in Chapter 6.

3.2.1 Bonds

Bonds are essentially IOUs; the issuer of the bond receives money from the initial buyer of the bond, and undertakes to pay the holder of the bond regular interest and then return the money (the capital) at a particular future date. The regular interest rate that is paid by the issuer is known as the **coupon** rate, and the date on which the interest is paid is known as the coupon date.

Although bonds rarely generate as much attention as shares, they are the larger market of the two in terms of global investment value. Bonds are issued by governments, supranational institutions and companies.

- **Government bonds** are issued by national governments (eg, Japan, the US, Italy, Germany, and the UK).
- **Supranational bonds** are issued by agencies such as the European Investment Bank and the World Bank.
- **Corporate bonds** are issued by companies, such as the large banks and other large corporate listed companies.

Traditionally, bonds have been regarded as less risky than shares, provided their issuers remain solvent. This is because the issuer of a bond is obliged to pay the coupon irrespective of market conditions. Government bonds have, until recently, been regarded as being of particularly low risk, as it was thought unlikely that a government will **default**, ie, fail to pay the interest or repay the capital on the bond, although at the time of writing there is real concern about the abilities of some Eurozone countries to service their high levels of debt. Corporate bonds, however, can face the risk of complete default; in other words the issuing company could go bust. Both carry **interest rate risk**, which means that the price of the bond could fall substantially if interest rates rise sharply.

3.2.2 Equities

Equities, or 'shares', are the other form of securities. Holding shares in a company is the same as having an ownership stake in that company. So a shareholder in, say, technology giant Apple Corporation is a part-owner of Apple.

Shares are, however, riskier than bonds as:

- At the extreme end of the spectrum, there is always the risk that the company could go into liquidation (but of course in this case the holder of a bond issued by the same company may also be likely to lose out). However, substantial companies such as Apple (known as 'blue chip' companies) are highly unlikely to go bust.
- More likely, is the chance that the shares may go down in value instead of up – as the investor hopes.
- In addition, there is the risk that the issuing company will have a poor trading year: if it makes little or no profit it may be unable to pay a dividend (a profit distribution to shareholders) – or may pay a lower one than in previous years. This is a serious risk for an investor relying on dividends as a major source of income.

The major reason an investor would prefer equities over bonds is from the potential benefits that can arise from owning shares, namely **dividends** and the prospect of **capital growth**. Traditionally, equity investments have outperformed bonds and cash over the longer term – that is, periods of ten years or more.

3.2.3 The Issuance of Securities

Stock exchanges and investment firms play a role in the issuance of both debt and equity securities, ie, they play a role in creating the security in the first instance. This activity is known as **primary market activity**. The most common process of securities issuance is known as the **Initial Public Offering (IPO)**.

IPOs are usually **underwritten**, that is to say that a group of banks will (in exchange for a fee) commit to purchasing any shares that are not bought by investors at the end of the offer period. Underwriting therefore provides a guarantee to the issuer that all the shares will be sold.

An IPO is the first sale of a corporation's shares to investors on (one or more) public stock exchanges. The main purpose of an IPO is to raise capital for the corporation. While IPOs are effective at raising capital, being listed on a stock exchange imposes heavy regulatory compliance and reporting requirements.

Example

Facebook filed for an IPO in the spring of 2012. The shares were offered at $38 each, pricing the company at $104 billion, the largest valuation to date for a newly public company. On 16 May, one day before the IPO, Facebook announced that it would sell 25% more shares than originally planned owing to high demand. The IPO raised $16 billion, making it the third largest in US history.

Trading in the stock began on May 18, but was delayed that day due to technical problems with the NASDAQ exchange. The stock struggled to stay above the IPO price for most of the day, forcing underwriters to buy back shares to support the price. At closing bell, shares were valued at $38.23, only $0.23 above the IPO price and down $3.82 from the opening bell value.

The opening was widely described by the financial press as a 'disappointment'. The stock nonetheless set a new record for trading volume of an IPO. On 25 May 2012, the stock ended its first full week of trading at $31.91, a 16.5% decline.

The term IPO refers only to the first public issuance of a company's shares. If a company later sells newly issued shares (again) to the market, it is called a **'follow-on' offering**.

When a shareholder sells shares it is called a **secondary offering** and the shareholder, not the company who originally issued the shares, retains the proceeds of the offering. These terms are often confused. In distinguishing them, it is important to remember that only a company which issues shares can make a primary offering.

3.2.4   The Secondary Market in Securities

Learning Objective

1.2   Know the elements of a secondary market equity trade

1.3   Know the elements of a secondary market bond trade

Once the security has been created on the primary market, investors may buy and sell that security without the involvement of the issuer. This is also known as **secondary market activity**. This workbook is primarily concerned with secondary market trades; therefore we begin by providing two example trades and introducing the candidate to the terminology that will be used throughout the learning manual.

Example – Shares

On 7 April 2007, Investor A buys 100 shares of ICI plc at a price of £10.00 per share, for value date 11 April 2007. Investor A will pay the broker £1,000.00 (ie, 100 shares at £10 each) plus commission of £50.00, making a total of £1,050.00.

This book uses the following terminology to describe each of the elements of this trade:

Term	Explanation of term	Example
Trade date	The date that the trade is carried out.	7 April 2007
Instrument	The identity of the instrument being bought or sold.	ICI plc shares
Trade price	The price of the instrument being bought or sold.	£10.00 per share
Trade quantity	The amount of the instrument being bought or sold.	100 shares
Instrument currency or trade currency	The currency in which the trade price is expressed.	GBP
Settlement currency	The currency in which the investor will pay for the instrument (usually, but not necessarily, the same as instrument currency).	GBP
Principal amount	The number of shares multiplied by the price.	£1,000.00 (100 x £10)
Fees	Commissions and any other charges paid by the investor.	£50.00
Consideration	Principal amount + fees and charges.	£1,050.00
Value date	The date on which the investor should pay the consideration of the trade, and take legal ownership of the instrument.	11 April 2007
Settlement date	The date on which the investor actually does pay the consideration of the trade, and takes legal ownership of the instrument. Settlement date should be the same as value date, but there may be a delay in the process. Possible causes of such delays are examined in Chapters 4, 5 and 6 of this workbook.	11 April 2007

The trade elements of a bond trade are slightly more complicated, because of:

- the effect of interest or coupon on the trade elements. Bond issuers usually pay coupons annually or semi-annually, but sometimes at more frequent intervals. The coupon is paid to the investor who holds the bond on the **record date**, which is usually one business day before the coupon date. Even if that investor only bought the bond a few days before record date, they will receive from the issuer the coupon for the entire coupon period, and the investor that held the bond for the earlier part of the coupon period will receive nothing. For this reason, when bonds are bought and sold on the secondary market, the **accrued interest** on the bond for the coupon period is also bought and sold at the same time.
- the fact that bond prices are usually quoted as a percentage of the trade quantity.

Example – Bonds

The Cable and Wireless 4% Convertible Bond maturing 16 July 2016 last paid a coupon on 16 January 2012. On trade date 5 February 2012, for value date 8 February 2012, Investor A sells £100,000 face value of this bond to Investor B at a trade price of 96% of face value. Assuming that there are no commissions or fees, then the consideration that B has to pay A will be calculated as follows:

Principal amount:	£100,000 face value @ trade price 96%	£96,000.00
Accrued interest:	£100,000 face value x 4% for 23 days	£252.05
Consideration		£96,252.05

The elements of this trade are therefore as follows:

Term	Explanation of term	Example
Trade date	The date that the trade was carried out.	5 February 2012
Instrument	The identity of the instrument being bought or sold.	Cable and Wireless 4% Convertible Bond maturing 16 July 2016
Trade price	The price of the instrument being bought or sold.	96% (of trade quantity)
Trade quantity	The amount of the instrument being bought or sold.	£100,000
Instrument or trade currency	The currency in which the trade price is expressed.	GBP
Settlement currency	The currency in which the investor will pay for the instrument (usually, but not necessarily, the same as instrument currency).	GBP
Principal amount	Face value multiplied by the price.	£96,000.00 (£100,000 x 96%)
Fees	Commissions and any other charges paid by the investor.	Nil
Interest days	The number of days interest that has been used to calculate the interest amount.	16 Jan to 8 Feb 2012 (ie, 23 days)
Accrued interest amount	The amount of interest that has been bought and sold on this trade.	£252.05
Consideration	Principal amount + accrued interest + fees.	£96,252.05 (£96,000 + £252.05)
Value date	The date on which the investor should pay the consideration of the trade, and take legal ownership of the instrument.	8 February 2012
Settlement date	The date on which the investor actually does pay the consideration of the trade, and takes legal ownership of the instrument. Settlement date should be the same as value date, but there may be a delay in the process.	8 February 2012

3.2.5 Consideration – An Inclusive Definition

By combining the above two examples, we can provide an inclusive definition of the term 'consideration' that applies to all forms of securities trades – both bond trades and equity trades:

Consideration = principal amount + accrued interest + commission + fees and charges

The calculation of interest, commissions, fees and charges is covered in Chapter 4.

3.3 Derivatives

A derivative is a financial instrument whose price is derived from that of another asset such as a bond, an equity, an equity index or a currency. The asset on which the derivative instrument is based on is known as the 'underlying asset', or sometimes 'underlying' for short.

Broadly speaking, there are two distinct groups of derivatives, which are differentiated by how they are traded. They are exchange-traded derivatives (ETD) and OTC derivatives.

3.3.1 Exchange-Traded Derivatives

Futures and options are examples of exchange-traded derivatives. Both futures and options have standardised features which are defined by the exchange on which they are listed. The role of the exchange is to provide a marketplace for trading to take place. The process of trading these instruments is examined in Chapter 3.

Futures and options are derived from cash instruments such as currency exchange rates, interest rates, government bonds, equity indices (such as the FTSE 100 index) individual equities, as well as physical commodities such as metals and agricultural products.

Definitions

- A **future** is a standardised, transferable, exchange-traded contract that requires delivery of the underlying instrument at a specified price, on a specified future date. Unlike options, futures convey an obligation to deliver or take delivery of the underlying instrument.
- A **call option** gives the buyer (or holder) the right (but NOT the obligation) to purchase the underlying instrument at a specified price on or before a given date.
- A **put option**, on the other hand, gives the buyer (or holder) the right (but NOT the obligation) to sell the underlying instrument at a specified price on or before a given date.

3.3.2 OTC Derivatives

OTC derivatives are ones that are negotiated and traded privately between parties without the use of an exchange. In other words they are traded 'over-the-counter'. Products such as interest rate swaps, forward rate agreements and other exotic derivatives are mainly traded in this way. The OTC market is larger than the exchange-traded market in terms of the value of contracts traded daily.

OTC derivatives are complex instruments (more complex than ETDs), and are not dealt with at length in this workbook. A more comprehensive explanation can be found in the *Introduction to Securities & Investment* workbook. The following subsections provide brief descriptions of the most common forms of OTC contracts.

Interest Rate Swaps

Interest rate swaps are the most common form of swaps. They involve an exchange (or 'swap') of interest payments and are usually constructed whereby one leg of the swap is a payment of a fixed rate of interest and the other leg is a payment of a floating rate of interest. They are usually used to hedge exposure to interest rate changes and can be most easily appreciated by looking at an example.

Example

Company A is embarking on a three-year project to build and equip a new manufacturing plant and borrows funds to finance the cost. Because of its size and credit status, it has to borrow at variable rates.

It can reasonably estimate what additional returns its new plant will generate but, because the interest it is paying will be variable, it is exposed to the risk that the project may turn out to be uneconomic if interest rates rise unexpectedly.

If the company could secure fixed rate finance, it could remove the risk of interest rate variations and more accurately predict the returns it can make from its investment. To do this, Company A could enter into an interest rate swap with an investment bank.

As part of the swap, it pays a fixed rate to the investment bank and in exchange receives an amount of interest calculated on a variable rate. With the amount it receives from the investment bank, it then has the funds to settle its variable rate lending.

In this way, it has hedged its interest rate exposure risk.

The two exchanges of cash flow are known as the **legs** of the swap and the amounts to be exchanged are calculated by reference to a **notional amount**. The notional amount in the above example would be the amount that Company A has borrowed to fund its project.

Typically, one party will pay an amount based on a fixed rate to the other party, who will pay back an amount of interest that is variable and usually based on LIBOR (London Inter-Bank Offered Rate). The variable rate will usually be set as LIBOR plus, say, 0.5% and will be reset quarterly.

Currency Swaps

A currency swap occurs when two parties exchange two payment streams in different currencies, calculated at a different interest rate, and also agree to return the original principal amount to each other at an exchange rate agreed at the start of the contract.

Credit Default Swaps

A credit default swap (CDS) is a contract under which two trade parties agree to isolate and separately trade the credit risk of one or more securities or other obligations issued by a third party.

Under a credit default swap agreement, a protection buyer pays a periodic fee to a protection seller in exchange for a contingent payment by the seller upon a credit event (such as a default or failure to pay) happening to the underlying securities. When a credit event is triggered, the protection seller either takes delivery of the defaulted security for the par value (physical settlement) or pays the protection buyer the difference between the par value and recovery value of the bond (cash settlement).

Credit default swaps resemble an insurance policy, as they can be used by debt owners to hedge against credit events. However, because there is no requirement to actually hold any asset or suffer a loss, credit default swaps can be used to speculate on changes in credit spread. Also, it is important to remember that they are not regulated as insurance policies, and investors do not have the same level of regulatory protection as do policyholders.

Credit default swaps are the most widely traded credit derivative product. The typical term of a credit default swap contract is five years, although, being an over-the-counter derivative, credit default swaps of almost any maturity can be traded.

The excessive issuance and trading of CDS contracts was considered to be a major cause of the credit crunch of 2008. At the time, these contracts could be traded – or swapped – from investor to investor without any regulator overseeing the trades to ensure the buyer had the resources to cover the losses if the security were to default. As a result of the lessons learned from this turbulent year, regulators in the US and Europe have introduced radical new regulations for the oversight of the OTC derivative markets. These new regulations are examined in Chapter 2 of this workbook.

Equity and Equity Index Swaps

This is where one of the payment streams is based on the return from holding an equity or equity index instead of being based on an interest rate.

Equity Contracts for Difference

A contract for difference (CFD) is a contract between two parties, buyer and seller, stipulating that the seller will pay to the buyer the difference between the current value of an equity and its value at a future date. If the difference is negative, then the buyer pays instead to the seller. CFDs allow investors to speculate on share price movements, without the need for ownership of the underlying shares.

Contracts for difference allow investors to take long or short positions, and unlike futures contracts have no fixed expiry date or contract size. CFDs are often used by UK investors to gain exposure to the growth potential of an individual equity without the requirement to pay stamp duty.

Contracts for difference are sometimes referred to as spread bets, especially in the UK.

4. The Concept of Straight-Through Processing (STP)

Learning Objective

1.4   Understand the concept of straight-through processing

4.1   STP Principles

Straight-through processing (STP) is a set of working practices and systems that enable transactions to move seamlessly through the processing cycle, without manual intervention or redundant handling.

STP enables the entire trade process for capital markets and payment transactions to be conducted electronically without the need for rekeying or manual intervention, subject to legal and regulatory restrictions.

The key principles of STP are the following:

- The transaction (such as an order or trade) is entered into the firm's systems only once – it should never have to be rekeyed into another of the firm's systems.
- As most investment firms need to record the transaction into more than one system, there need to be automated interfaces between all systems that need to store records of the order or trade.
- Trade processing should consist of a set of logical stages, each one being dependent on the satisfactory conclusion of the previous stage. No stage should commence until the previous stage has completed successfully.
- Clerical intervention should be avoided as far as possible, but clerical staff should be enabled to manage by exception – that is to say that if one of the processing stages fails to complete satisfactorily, the fact that this has happened should be presented to skilled staff in a form in which they can deal with the exception in the most efficient manner.
- Principles one to four above apply not just within the individual firm but also between the various firms involved in the transaction. This means that the industry needs to have common message standards when information needs to be exchanged between different organisations. These standards are described in Chapter 6.

Historically, STP solutions were needed to help financial markets firms move towards one-day trade settlement of securities transactions, as well as to meet the global demand resulting from the explosive growth of online trading. Now the concepts of STP are applied in order to:

- reduce systemic and operational risk;
- improve the certainty of settlement;
- minimise operational cost;
- improve customer service.

As a result, investment firms' IT departments are often involved in process improvements that are designed to improve the STP rate.

4.2   To What Extent is STP Actually Achieved in Practice?

The STP-compliant environment described above is an ideal, and not all firms achieve 100% STP for all financial instruments. There is evidence that the more complex the instrument, the lower the STP rate.

ISDA Benchmarking Survey

Each year the International Swaps and Derivatives Association (ISDA) conducts an operations benchmarking survey of its member firms. Some of the findings of the 2011 survey included the following details.

While over 90% of currency option trades and 80% of interest rate swap trades automatically led to the production of a confirmation message on trade date, the figure dropped to 60% for trades in commodity options.

'Large' firms reported that the average amount of days it took to agree a confirmation for various asset classes was as shown in the table below. 2005 figures are shown for comparison, and you will see that, while significant improvements have been made in six years, the picture is still patchy. The STP performance of equity derivatives in this area still lags behind that of other instruments.

Average Monthly Levels of all Outstanding Confirmations (in Business Days) for Large Firms

Instrument Class	2005 survey result	2011 survey result	% Improvement
Interest rate derivatives	11.4	2.1	81.58%
Credit derivatives	23.5	0.5	97.87%
Equity derivatives	16.7	6.7	59.88%
Currency options	5.3	1.8	66.04%
Commodity derivatives	20.2	0.9	95.54%

End of Chapter Questions

Think of an answer for each question and refer to the appropriate section for confirmation.

1. Which types of market participant deal with private individuals?
    Section 2

2. How does an investment bank differ from a retail bank?
    Sections 2.1 and 2.2

3. What is the role of the custodian?
    Section 2.7

4. What is the difference between value date and settlement date?
    Section 3.2.4

5. What is the difference between the 'principal amount' of a bond or equity trade and the 'consideration' of that trade?
    Section 3.2.4

6. What are the five key principles of straight-through processing?
    Section 4.1

Chapter Two
The Regulatory Framework for IT

This syllabus area will provide approximately 6 of the 50 examination questions

1. UK and European Regulation

Many candidates will be familiar with the fundamentals of regulation as a result of taking one of the regulatory Investment Operations Certificate papers. For the benefit of any *IT in Investment Operations* candidate who is not taking one of these papers, this section briefly summarises the scope of the regulations that affect securities firms, and discusses their IT implications.

1.1 The Need for Regulation

Learning Objective

2.1 Understand the need for regulation

The risk of monetary loss that can arise from dealing in all types of financial transactions has meant that financial markets have always been subject to the need for rules and codes of conduct to protect investors and the public. As markets developed, there grew a need for market participants to be able to set rules so that there were agreed standards of behaviour, and to provide a mechanism so that disputes could be settled readily. This need developed into what is known as 'self-regulation', where, for example, a stock exchange, as well as providing a secondary market for shares, would also set rules for its members and police their implementation.

As markets, financial institutions and financial services developed, and the potential impact that they could have on both the economy and society grew, self-regulation became increasingly untenable, and most countries moved to a statutory approach and established their own regulatory bodies.

The development of global markets, and a series of crises ranging from Barings Bank to Enron and WorldCom, emphasised not only the need for improved regulation and standards, but for international co-operation to develop a common approach in a whole range of areas. This was hugely exacerbated in 2008 as the global community battled against the effects of the credit crunch. With the increasing globalisation of financial markets there is a demand from governments and investment firms for a common approach to regulation in different countries.

The main purposes and aims of regulation, in all markets globally, are to:

- maintain and promote the fairness, efficiency, competitiveness, transparency and orderliness of the securities and futures industry;
- promote understanding by the public of, and trust in, the operation and functioning of the securities and futures industry;
- provide protection for members of the public investing in, or holding, financial products;
- minimise crime and misconduct in the securities and futures industry;
- reduce systemic risks in the securities and futures industry; and
- assist in maintaining the market's financial stability by taking appropriate steps in relation to the securities and futures industry.

1.2　Regulation in the UK

1.2.1　The Financial Services and Markets Act 2000 (FSMA)

Modern regulation in the UK began with the passing of the Financial Services and Markets Act 2000 (FSMA), which introduced a new structure for the regulation of the financial services industry in the UK. FSMA established a new single regulator for the UK – the Financial Services Authority (FSA). It empowered the FSA with broad responsibility for both the prudential and business conduct regulation of firms within the financial services industry. To explain these terms:

- **Prudential** regulation is concerned with the financial soundness of firms, making sure that they are not about to become bankrupt. The purpose of prudential regulation is to prevent investors and the economy in general from suffering losses as a result of the failure of individual firms or, at worst, multiple firms.
- **Business conduct** regulation is concerned with the way in which business is done, particularly the way products are marketed and sold. Its purpose is to protect investors from losses that may arise from ethically dubious illegal practices, or poor management of business processes.

Part II of FSMA, 'Regulated and Prohibited Activities', details the general prohibition which states that no person can carry on a regulated activity in the UK, or purport to do so, unless they are either authorised or exempt. **Authorisation** is brought about by the relevant person applying to the regulator for permission to perform particular regulated activities, and the FSA giving such permission. The 'person' in this context is the firm, which could be incorporated as a company or could be an unincorporated entity such as a sole trader or partnership.

Regulated activities under FSMA are defined by the type of investment (such as shares, bonds or deposits) and the range of activity (there are 15 regulated activities in the act including dealing, managing, and accepting deposits).

All regulated forms are expected to adhere to the following 11 principles:

1. A firm must conduct its business with integrity.
2. A firm must conduct its business with due skill, care and diligence.
3. A firm must take reasonable care to organise and control its affairs responsibly and effectively, with adequate risk management systems.
4. A firm must maintain adequate financial resources.
5. A firm must observe proper standards of market conduct.
6. A firm must pay due regard to the interests of its customers and treat them fairly.
7. A firm must pay due regard to the information needs of its clients, and communicate information to them in a way which is clear, fair and not misleading.
8. A firm must manage conflicts of interest fairly, both between itself and its customers and between a customer and another client.

9. A firm must take reasonable care to ensure the suitability of its advice and discretionary decisions for any customer who is entitled to rely upon its judgement.
10. A firm must arrange adequate protection for clients' assets when it is responsible for them.
11. A firm must deal with its regulators in an open, co-operative way, and must disclose to the regulator appropriately anything relating to the firm of which the regulator would reasonably expect notice.

The UK regulator also monitors its member firms' compliance with three sets of rules that originate from European Union legislation – the Markets in Financial Instruments Directive (MiFID), the Capital Requirements Directive and, from 2012, the European Market Infrastructure Regulation (EMIR). **MiFID** is examined in Section 1.3 of this chapter; the **Capital Requirements Directive** (the EU's specific implementation of Basel II) and EMIR are described in Section 1.4.

When the European Union (EU) legislates for Europe as a whole, the legislation enacted by the EU is known as **Level 1 legislation**. Level 1 legislation is often at a high level; the detailed instructions that have to be complied with are usually found in the individual legislation of the member states. This is known as **Level 2 legislation**. The UK government and the regulators are responsible for the enactment and enforcement of Level 2 legislation concerning MiFID, EMIR and Basel II in the UK. The process can be explained by the following diagram:

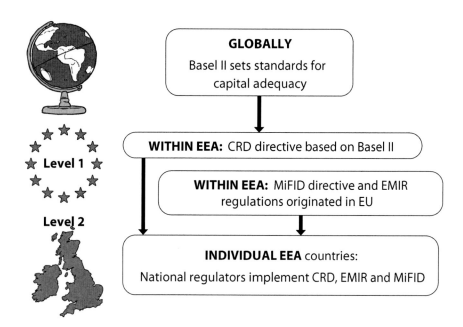

1.2.2   The Financial Services Act (FSA) 2012

This act abolished the FSA and replaced it by three new bodies:

Financial Policy Committee (FPC)

The Financial Policy Committee is a new committee which was established within the Bank of England, with responsibility for 'macro-prudential' regulation, or regulation of the stability and resilience of the financial system as a whole. Its role is: *'Contributing to the Bank's objective to protect and enhance financial stability, through identifying and taking action to remove or reduce systemic risks, with a view to protecting and enhancing the resilience of the UK financial system.'*

Prudential Regulation Authority (PRA)

The Prudential Regulation Authority is responsible for prudential regulation of financial firms that manage significant risks on their balance sheets – in other words, it will be responsible for the regulation and supervision of 'significant' individual firms including all deposit-taking institutions, insurers and other prudentially significant firms. Its statutory objectives are: *'to promote the safety and soundness of these firms and, specifically for insurers, to contribute to the securing of an appropriate degree of protection for policyholders.'*

The PRA has the primary objective of enhancing financial stability by promoting the safety and soundness of PRA-authorised firms in a way which minimises the disruption caused by any firms which do fail. In fulfilling its objective, it will take an intrusive approach to regulation and supervision. Both regulators still use the principles that were originally laid down by the FSA when it was founded.

Financial Conduct Authority (FCA)

The Financial Conduct Authority focuses on regulation of all firms in retail and wholesale financial markets, as well as the infrastructure that supports these markets. It has responsibility for firms that do not fall under the PRA's scope (approximately 25,000 firms). The FCA's role includes:

- supervision of investment exchanges and monitoring firms' compliance with the Market Abuse Directive;
- powers to investigate and prosecute insider dealing;
- responsibility for overseeing the Financial Ombudsman Service (FOS), the Consumer Financial Education Body (CFEB) and the Financial Services Compensation Scheme (FSCS);
- working closely with the FPC and PRA.

Its statutory objective is to ensure that the relevant markets function well.

Its role also includes: *'Enhancing confidence in the UK financial system by facilitating efficiency and choice in services, securing an appropriate degree of consumer protection, and protecting and enhancing the integrity of the UK financial system.'*

Timescale

The FCA and PRA began work in January 2013. Certain chapters in this workbook make references to specific FCA rules. Unless otherwise stated, students should assume that the PRA has an identical rule.

1.3 Europe-Wide Regulation – The Markets in Financial Instruments Directive (MiFID)

Learning Objective

2.2   Know the function of UK and European regulators in the financial services industry

The European System of Financial Supervision is an institutional architecture of the EU's framework of financial supervision created in response to the financial crisis of 2007/08. First proposed by the European Commission in 2009, it replaced three existing Committees of Supervisors with three new authorities called European Supervisory Authorities (ESAs): a European Banking Authority (EBA); a European Insurance and Occupational Pensions Authority (EIOPA); and a European Securities and Markets Authority (ESMA).

ESMA's mission is to enhance the protection of investors and reinforce stable and well-functioning financial markets in the European Union. As an independent institution, ESMA achieves this mission by building a single rulebook for EU financial markets and ensuring its consistent application and supervision across the EU.

ESMA contributes to the supervision of financial services firms with a pan-European reach, either through direct supervision or through the active co-ordination of national supervisory activity.

ESMA's role is becoming increasingly relevant to UK financial firms. The idea behind ESMA is to establish a 'EU-wide financial markets watchdog'. One of its main tasks is to regulate **credit rating agencies**. In 2010' credit rating agencies were criticised for the lack of transparency in their assessments and for a possible conflict of interest.

ESMA also supervises and makes the rules for the trade repositories that are mentioned in Section 1.4 of this chapter and in Chapter 3.

1.4 Know the Regulatory Objectives of MiFID/MiFID II

Learning Objective

2.3   Know the regulatory objectives of MiFID/MiFID II

The Markets in Financial Instruments Directive (MiFID) was enacted in 2004 and came into force on 1 November 2007, replacing the previous Investment Services Directive (ISD) which was introduced in 1993. The legislation is detailed, prescriptive and wide-ranging – MiFID's physical presence is twice the size of any of its predecessors.

MiFID applies to all firms in the European Economic Area (EEA), comprising 27 EU states plus Iceland, Norway and Liechtenstein, and is concerned primarily with:

* classification of clients (see Section 4.2);
* conflicts of interest;
* handling of client money and client assets;
* handling of client orders, including pre-trade and post-trade transparency, plus best execution.

1.4.1 Conflicts of Interest

MiFID recognises that conflicts of interest may occur when an investment firm may be acting, for example:

- for both investors in and issuers of the same security at the same time;
- for more than one investor that has an interest in a particular security;
- for investors that have an interest in a particular security at the same time that the firm itself has an interest in the same security.

MiFID requires firms to have a conflict management policy that requires them to:

1. take steps to prevent conflicts of interest giving rise to the material risk of damaging clients' interests;
2. identify, proactively, business areas where conflicts are likely to arise;
3. document each potential conflict and describe how its effect should be mitigated; and
4. disclose its policy to clients on request.

1.4.2 Handling of Client Orders and Trade Execution

This is by far the most complex area of MiFID. It imposes different rules on different types of industry participants. It also introduces two new terms that were not in common use before MiFID:

- **Multilateral Trading Facility (MTF)** – a system that brings together multiple parties (eg, retail investors or other investment firms) that are interested in buying and selling financial instruments, and enables them to do so. These systems can be stock exchanges, crossing networks or matching engines that are operated by an investment firm or a market operator. Instruments may include shares, bonds and derivatives. An investment exchange is a form of MTF. For more on these terms, see Chapter 3, Section 2.
- **Systematic Internaliser (SI)** – a firm which on a frequent and systematic basis deals on its own account by executing client orders which are outside the scope of any MTF or regulated market.

MiFID requirements are as follows:

Pre-Trade Transparency

MiFID establishes minimum standards of pre-trade transparency for shares traded on regulated markets and MTFs.

Investment exchanges, other multilateral trading facilities and systematic internalisers that operate continuous **order-matching systems** must make aggregated order information available at the five best price levels on the buy and sell side.

For **quote-driven markets** – see Chapter 3 – the best bids and offers of all market makers must be made available.

MiFID also obliges an investment firm that is a systematic internaliser to undertake what is effectively a public market-making obligation. That is, the firm must provide definite bid and offer quotes in liquid shares for orders below 'standard market size'.

Post-Trade Transparency

Investment exchanges and MTFs must publish the details of all trades executed in their systems. The exact detail of what information is to be published is left to the regulator of the country concerned.

Additionally, investment firms must publish details of trades in relevant instruments executed in the OTC markets.

Publication must be **close to real time**, and in any event within **three minutes** of trade execution. Exceptions are made for trades taking place outside a venue's normal trading hours, when publication must be made **prior to the start of the next trading day**. The full text of the rule about the timeliness of publication states:

'Information which is required to be made available as close to real time as possible should be made available as close to instantaneously as technically possible, assuming a reasonable level of efficiency and of expenditure on systems on the part of the person concerned. The information should only be published close to the three-minute maximum limit in exceptional cases where the systems available do not allow for a publication in a shorter period of time.'

National regulators receive all the published post-trade details from all the publishers within their jurisdiction and enter them into a database that they use to monitor market abuse and insider dealing.

Best Execution

Broadly speaking, best execution places an obligation on the sell-side firm to get the lowest available price for its customer when the customer is buying, and the highest available price when the customer is selling. There are, however, factors other than price that will be taken into account. Section 3 of Chapter 4 of this workbook provides examples of how best execution is achieved under different scenarios.

Article 21 of the MiFID regulations requires firms that execute orders on behalf of clients to:

1. establish an execution policy, which must contain information on the venues used to execute client orders. Those venues must allow it to obtain consistently the best possible result for execution for their clients;
2. disclose the policy to clients and obtain their consent to that policy;
3. monitor the effectiveness of arrangements in order to identify and correct any deficiencies and review the appropriateness of the venues in its execution policy at least yearly; and
4. upon client request, be ready to demonstrate that the client's order has been executed in line with its execution policy.

1.4.3   The IT Implications of MiFID

When MiFID became operational, investment firms were faced with a major change programme, the characteristics of which were:

* The individual firm had to take part. It could not opt out.
* There was a 'drop-dead' date (1 November 2007) for completion of the changes – the firm had to be ready by that date. This was known as the 'implementation date'.

- The changes needed to be made by a large number of industry participants at the same time. This added to risk, because there was a danger that, for example, one firm might be ready but a major counterparty or settlement agent might not.
- Within each individual firm there were potentially a large number of individual applications and/or business processes that required amendment or complete replacement. At the beginning of the change programme it might not have been clear which applications were affected or to what extent.
- At the beginning of the change process, firms had to base the detail of the changes on interpretation of complex legal documents, whose ramifications and consequences were often the subject of debate, or even initial confusion within the industry.

MiFID and Business Applications

The front office dealing applications that are concerned with order execution have to base their decisions about how trades are to be executed for different classes of client and different instruments on the firm's execution policy. As part of the STP philosophy, these decisions need to be automated; therefore the firm's execution policy rules need to be designed into these applications.

1.4.4   MiFID II

In October 2011, the European Commission (EC) published its proposals to amend MiFID, referred to as MiFID II.

In summary form, the changes are as follows:

Scope
- The scope of MiFID will be extended to more firms, such as certain commodity firms, data providers and non-EU firms operating in the EU (known as 'third-country firms').
- Additional instruments will be brought into the scope of MiFID, such as structured deposits and emissions allowances.

Electronic Trading
- Derivatives which are sufficiently liquid and eligible for clearing will need to be traded on eligible platforms.
- A new category of trading venue, called Organised Trading Facilities (OTFs), will be introduced. An OTF is described as *'any facility or system that is not an MTF or regulated market, operated by an investment firm or market operator, in which multiple third-party buying and selling interests in financial instruments are able to interact in the system in a way that results in a contract'*.
- Requirements will be imposed on operators of OTFs and the operation of OTFs will be introduced as a separate permission.

Transparency and Transaction Reporting
- Transparency requirements will be extended to additional instruments, such as bonds and derivatives.
- Trade reports will need to be published through Approved Publication Arrangement (APA) firms, which will also be subject to authorisation and certain organisational requirements. APAs are a proposed market infrastructure mechanism for collecting and publishing market data; approval will be given by ESMA or a member state regulator on the basis of criteria which had not been defined when this workbook was published.
- Transaction reports will need to capture additional information.

Third Country Firms

- An equivalence decision will need to be made by the EC in respect of third countries before firms from these jurisdictions can request to provide services.
- As a minimum, third-country firms seeking to access the retail market will be required to establish branches in the countries they are offering services.

Investor Protection

- Receipt of monetary inducements by certain firms, such as portfolio managers and firms giving independent investment advice, will be banned.
- Advice must meet certain criteria in order to be classified as 'independent', and additional information will need to be provided to clients.
- Definition of non-complex instruments will be updated to remove 'structured UCITS', which will prevent these funds from being sold without an assessment of their appropriateness for the client.

Product Intervention

- National regulators will have powers to permanently ban products, in co-ordination with ESMA, and ESMA will also be able to temporarily ban products.
- Position limits for products such as commodity derivatives will be introduced. This will include powers for regulators to require existing positions to be reduced.

Implementation Timetable

The proposals are now with the European Parliament and the Council of the European Union for discussion. Implementation of the new measures is not expected until at least 2016.

1.5   European Market Infrastructure Regulation (EMIR)

Learning Objective

2.9   Know the regulatory objectives of the European Markets Infrastructure Regulation (EMIR)

In 2010, the European Commission published its final proposal for the European Market Infrastructure Regulation (EMIR), which was designed to improve transparency and reduce the risks associated with the derivatives market. EMIR also establishes common organisational, conduct of business and prudential standards for central counterparties (CCPs) and trade repositories. The scope of the regulation is very similar to that of the US Dodd-Frank legislation which is covered in Section 5.2 of this chapter.

The regulation introduces:

- a reporting obligation for OTC derivatives; this involves the use of trade repositories which are discussed in Chapter 4;
- a clearing obligation for eligible OTC derivatives;
- measures to reduce counterparty credit risk and operational risk for bilaterally-cleared OTC derivatives;
- common rules for CCPs and for trade repositories; and
- rules on the establishment of interoperability between CCPs.

1.6 Global Regulation – Basel II

Learning Objective

2.6   Know the regulatory objectives of Basel II/III

1.6.1 Background

The **Bank for International Settlements (BIS)** is an international organisation (located in the Swiss city of Basel) that fosters international monetary and financial co-operation. It also serves as a bank for central banks. One of its key aims is to promote international monetary and financial stability. It was instrumental in setting up what is now known as the **Basel Committee on Banking Supervision**.

The Committee was formed in response to the messy liquidation of a German bank in 1974. On 26 June 1974, a number of banks had released Deutschmarks to Bank Herstatt in Cologne in exchange for dollar payments deliverable in New York. On account of differences in the time zones, there was a lag in the dollar payments to the counterparty banks and, during this gap, and before the dollar payments could be effected in New York, Bank Herstatt was liquidated by German regulators. As a result, those banks that had paid Deutschmarks to Herstatt never received the dollars in exchange.

This event contributed to the process by which the Basel Committee later published a set of minimal capital requirements for banks in 1988. This was known as the 1988 Basel Accord, or Basel 1. The aim of the Basel Accord was to ensure that bank regulators throughout the world applied similar prudential standards to the banks that they regulated.

Since 1988, operational risk has grown to assume a level of importance approaching that of credit and market risk. Because of the dramatic changes in financial markets, products, management practices, technological innovations and supervisory approaches, banks are beginning to use increasingly sophisticated processes to measure and assess their operational risk exposure. Basel I is now widely viewed as outdated, as it is risk-insensitive and can easily be circumvented. A more comprehensive set of guidelines, known as Basel II, was therefore published in 2004, and was implemented by over 100 countries in 2007. Operational risk is addressed for the first time in the revised Accord.

1.6.2 The Basel II Accord in Operation

To promote greater stability in the financial system, Basel II uses a 'three pillars' concept:

1. Minimum capital requirements (Pillar 1);
2. Supervisory review (Pillar 2); and
3. Market discipline (Pillar 3).

The Basel I Accord dealt only with parts of each of these pillars. For example, as explained above, of the key Pillar 1 risks, credit risk was dealt with in a simple manner, market risk was an afterthought, and operational risk was not dealt with at all.

Although there are other definitions, the most widely accepted definition of operational risk today is: *'The risk of loss resulting from inadequate or failed internal processes, people and systems or from external events.'* This is the formal definition which has been drawn up by the Basel Committee.

1.6.3   Pillar 1

The first pillar provides improved risk-sensitivity in the way that capital requirements are calculated for three major components of risk that a bank faces: credit risk, market risk and operational risk. In turn, each of these components can be calculated in two or three ways of varying sophistication. Other risks are not considered fully quantifiable at this stage.

The minimum overall capital ratio is between 8% and 15% depending on which approach to risk measurement the firm chooses to adopt, but the methods of measuring market, credit and operational risk exposure are now more elaborate.

$$\text{Capital ratio} = \frac{\text{Capital requirement}}{\text{(Credit risk exposure + market risk exposure + operational risk exposure)}}$$

The **market risk** element, dealing with trading losses, is unchanged from Basel 1, which was amended for this purpose in 1997.

The **operational risk** part is new – it says that banks' capital should reflect the risk of mistakes and wrongdoing. The Basel Committee provides seven examples of where banks and investment firms may be exposed to operational risks; these are listed in Section 1.4.6.

Acceptable Methods of Measuring Risk

Pillar 1 requires a more detailed explanation. It lays down a new means of measurement acceptable to international regulators. In seeking to provide common standards, it outlines three different measurement approaches of increasing complexity for calculating risk exposure:

- The **Basic Indicator Approach** – as the name implies, this is the most basic approach and requires a bank to hold a fixed percentage (denoted '**alpha**') of its gross income as operational risk capital. This fixed percentage is set by the Basel Committee at a level of 15%. It is anticipated that smaller, domestic institutions that do not possess sophisticated risk management tools and techniques will use the basic indicator approach.
- The **Standardised Approach** – this approach is more refined than the basic indicator approach because it divides a firm's activities into a number of standardised business lines, allowing different risk profiles to be allocated to each. In other words, it introduces the concept of risk-weighted assets (RWAs). This is intended to provide a more representative reflection of an organisation's overall operational risk. Like the basic indicator approach, it uses gross income as a broad indicator that reflects the scale of business operations within each business line and therefore the likely scale of operational risk. It splits a firm's gross income between a number of defined business lines and then multiplies this by a factor (denoted '**beta**') specific to each business line to produce the amount required to be held as operational risk capital for that particular business. The overall amount of operational risk capital is then the sum of all these calculations.

The different factors reflect the assumed riskiness of each business and range from 12% to 18%. The standardised approach relies on indicators and factors set by the regulators and recognises that many institutions do not yet have sufficient loss data and analytical risk processes to calculate their own capital charge. It provides a basis for moving towards a more sophisticated methodology and encourages better operational risk management. In order to qualify to use this approach, a firm must convince its regulator that it has the necessary management structure, expertise and systems to measure and control its operational risk.

- The **Advanced Measurement Approach (AMA)** – this is the most risk-sensitive of the three approaches. It allows banks to use their own internal measurement system and loss data as a basis for calculating the capital charge. The primary motive for a firm to move from the standardised approach to AMA is to reduce its capital allocation requirement which rewards more sophisticated risk management. AMA can cover a range of measurement techniques, providing that the regulators approve them. Approval will mean the inclusion of quantitative and qualitative measures. Where qualitative measures are used, they must have the potential to be objectively validated.

Banks that adopt AMA are allowed to use their own **value-at-risk (VaR) models** for calculating market risk exposure, providing they pass a review process. The objective of the review process is to ensure integrity and consistency in the market risk calculation. The basic standards demanded by the Directive are:

○ the VaR estimate must be to a 99% confidence level;
○ losses must be calculated on the basis of a ten-day holding period; and
○ historic data must cover a minimum period of 250 days.

Value-at-risk is covered in more detail in Chapter 4.

In order to qualify to use the advanced measurement approach, the regulators require banks to comply with more stringent criteria than the standardised approach. They list generic qualitative and quantitative criteria aimed at ensuring that a bank has satisfactory risk management processes, risk measurement systems and risk infrastructure in place to be able to use AMA.

1.6.4   Pillar 2

This pillar requires **supervisors** to ensure that each bank has sound internal processes to assess capital adequacy based on a thorough evaluation of its risks. It provides a framework for dealing with all the other risks that a bank faces, such as **reputational risk**, **liquidity risk** and **legal risk**, which the Accord combines under the title of **residual risk**.

1.6.5   Pillar 3

The third pillar greatly increases the **disclosures** that the bank must make. This is designed to allow the market to have a better picture of the overall risk position of the bank and the capital adequacy of its positions, and to allow the counterparties of the bank to price and deal appropriately.

1.6.6   The IT Implications of Basel II

Basel II has three different sets of implications for the IT department. Firstly, like MiFID, it was a major change programme in its own right that needed to be managed appropriately. Chapter 8 deals with these issues. Secondly, it affects the content of business applications. For example, firms that have decided to use either the standardised approach or the advanced measurement approach for calculating their capital requirements must ensure that they have the business applications in place to perform these calculations.

Applications that are affected by Basel II are discussed in detail elsewhere in this workbook. They include:

- applications that are able to calculate VaR (these are discussed fully in Chapter 4, Section 2);
- applications that can mark positions to market (these are discussed fully in Chapter 4, Section 2);
- applications that can perform interest accruals (these are discussed fully in Chapter 6, Section 4.1.1);
- applications that can perform both internal and external reconciliations of cash and securities (these are discussed fully in Chapter 6, Sections 6.2 and 6.3).

Finally, the emphasis on operational risk affects the way that the IT department manages its activities. Poor management and processes can contribute to the occurrence of the **seven operational risk events** identified by the Basel Committee. For example:

1. **Internal fraud** – misappropriation of assets, tax evasion, intentional mismarking of positions and bribery. *These activities can be facilitated by practices that allow, inter alia, unauthorised access to applications and underlying data. They may be mitigated by the use of application password control and the deployment of systems that support the concept of segregation of duties.*
2. **External fraud** – theft of information, hacking damage, third-party theft and forgery. *As for (1) above, but in addition, these problems can be mitigated by the deployment of anti-virus software, anti-spyware software, firewalls, etc.*
3. **Employment practices and workplace safety** – discrimination, workers, compensation, employee health and safety. *There are no specific IT-related issues to this event; it is a company-wide issue.*
4. **Clients, products, and business practice** – market manipulation, anti-trust, improper trade, product defects, fiduciary breaches and account churning. *'Product defects' in this context includes defects in the software and hardware that is used to process the firm's data. Good IT practice involves the use of standardised, reliable methodologies to discover and document business requirements, select software vendors and packages, build, test and deploy software and manage projects. It also involves the use of configuration management and change control procedures to ensure that the right software versions are deployed.* These topics are examined more deeply in Chapters 9 and 10.
5. **Damage to physical assets** – natural disasters, terrorism and vandalism. *See (6).*
6. **Business disruption and systems failures** – utility disruptions, software failures and hardware failures. *These risks may be mitigated by proper Business Recovery Plans, which are examined in Chapter 8. Software failures may also arise as a result of product defects (Basel II Event no.4).*
7. **Execution, delivery, and process management** – data entry errors, accounting errors, failed mandatory reporting and negligent loss of client assets. *These events, in turn, may be caused by product defects.*

1.6.7 Basel III

In December 2010, Basel Committee members agreed a new standard, Basel III, to replace Basel II.

Basel III will require banks to hold 4.5% of common equity (up from 2% in Basel II) and 6% of Tier I capital (up from 4% in Basel II) of risk-weighted assets (RWAs). Basel III also introduces additional capital buffers:

1. A mandatory capital conservation buffer of 2.5%.
2. A discretionary countercyclical buffer, which allows national regulators to require up to another 2.5% of capital during periods of high credit growth.

In addition, Basel III introduces a minimum 3% leverage ratio and two required liquidity ratios. The Liquidity Coverage Ratio requires a bank to hold sufficient high-quality liquid assets to cover its total net cash outflows over 30 days; the Net Stable Funding Ratio requires the available amount of stable funding to exceed the required amount of stable funding over a one-year period of extended stress.

The following tables show the expected implementation dates for the transition from Basel II to Basel III.

Capital Requirements

Date	**Milestone** – Capital Requirement
2013	**Minimum capital requirements** – start of the gradual phasing-in of the higher minimum capital requirements.
2015	**Minimum capital requirements** – higher minimum capital requirements are fully implemented.
2016	Conservation buffer – start of the gradual phasing-in of the conservation buffer.
2019	Conservation buffer – the conservation buffer is fully implemented.

Leverage Ratio

Date	**Milestone** – Leverage Ratio
2011	**Supervisory monitoring** – developing templates to track the leverage ratio and the underlying components.
2013	**Parallel run I** – the leverage ratio and its components will be tracked by supervisors but not disclosed and not mandatory.
2015	**Parallel run II** – the leverage ratio and its components will be tracked and disclosed but not mandatory.
2017	**Final adjustments** – based on the results of the parallel run period, any final adjustments to the leverage ratio.
2018	**Mandatory requirement** – the leverage ratio will become a mandatory part of Basel III requirements.

Liquidity Requirements

Date	Milestone – Liquidity Requirements
2011	**Observation period** – developing templates and supervisory monitoring of the liquidity ratios.
2015	**Introduction of the LCR** – introduction of the Liquidity Coverage Ratio (LCR).
2018	**Introduction of the NSFR** – introduction of the Net Stable Funding Ratio (NSFR).

2.   Data Protection

Learning Objective

2.4   Know the significance of the Data Protection Act 1998: principles; non-compliance

The **Data Protection Act 1998** details how personal data should be dealt with to protect its integrity and to protect the rights of the persons concerned. Any firm holding and processing personal data must register with the **Information Commissioner** as a **data controller**.

2.1   Principles

The Data Protection Act lays down eight principles of good data protection practice. It states that personal data shall:

1. be processed fairly and lawfully;
2. be obtained for one or more specified and lawful purposes, and shall not be further processed in any manner that is incompatible with those purposes;
3. be adequate, relevant and not excessive in relation to the purpose or purposes for which it is processed;
4. be accurate and, where necessary, kept up-to-date;
5. not be kept for longer than is necessary for its purpose or purposes;
6. be processed in accordance with the rights of the subject under the Act;
7. be safeguarded by the use of appropriate technical and organisational measures to prevent unauthorised or unlawful processing of personal data, and against accidental loss or destruction of, or damage to, the personal data;
8. not be transferred to a country or territory outside the EEA, unless that country or territory ensures an adequate level of protection in relation to the processing of personal data.

2.2   Penalties for Non-compliance with the Act

An individual who suffers damage by reason of any contravention by a data controller of any of the requirements of this Act is entitled to compensation from the data controller for that damage.

In addition to the compensation that a data owner may claim under the provisions of the Act itself, regulated firms may face additional sanctions. The Information Commissioner has the power to impose fines.

Example

In 2007 the FSA fined Nationwide Building Society £980,000 for failing to have effective systems and controls to manage its information security risks. The failings came to light following the theft of a laptop from a Nationwide employee's home in 2006. During its investigation, the FSA found that the building society did not have adequate information security procedures or controls in place, potentially exposing its customers to an increased risk of financial crime. The FSA also discovered that Nationwide was not aware that the laptop contained confidential customer information and did not start an investigation until three weeks after the theft.

2.3   Practical IT Issues

IT managers need to consider the following practical issues concerning protection of client and employee data:

- **Encryption** – is sensitive data encrypted where its loss or leakage would cause financial loss or embarrassment to its subjects? If data is encrypted, is the key stored in a secure place?
- **Password protection** – is sensitive data password-protected where its loss or leakage would cause financial loss or embarrassment to its subjects? Are there adequate controls over which employees are given passwords to access it?
- **Portable devices** – are there controls over what data may be copied to external drives and memory sticks? Are there controls about what data may be held on laptops and other mobile devices (such as iPads and smartphones) that may be taken out of the office? How is this data protected?
- **Outsourcing arrangements** – do the controls that apply to the firm's own employees also apply to any organisations to whom functions have been outsourced? What procedures are in place to ensure that these external organisations comply with these controls?

Note that the **European Union Data Protection Directive** of 1995 states that data may only be transferred to a country outside the European Union if that country provides an adequate (ie, similar to EU-standard) level of protection. Some exceptions to this rule are provided, for instance when the data controller themselves can guarantee that the recipient will comply with the data protection rules.

2.4   Specific FCA Rules Which Affect How IT is Organised

Learning Objective

2.5   Know the significance to IT of the following rules: Senior Management Arrangements, Systems and Controls (SYSC); Conduct of Business Sourcebook (COB); Client Asset Sourcebook (CASS)

Both the FCA and the PRA have three identical sets of rules covering conduct of business, the management of customer assets and the responsibilities of senior management. These rules affect both the way that the IT function is organised in regulated firms, and also they prescribe the way that some of the applications in those firms work. The individual rules are examined, where relevant, in later chapters of this workbook. In this chapter we shall simply describe the purpose of each of the three sets of rules.

Senior Management Arrangements, Systems and Controls (SYSC)

There are 21 individual rules. The purpose of these rules, according to the regulators is to:

1. encourage firms' directors and senior managers to take appropriate practical responsibility for their firms' arrangements on matters likely to be of interest to the appropriate regulator because they impinge on the appropriate regulator's functions;
2. increase certainty by amplifying Principle 3, *('A firm must take reasonable care to organise and control its affairs responsibly and effectively, with adequate risk management systems')* under which a firm must take reasonable care to organise and control its affairs responsibly and effectively, with adequate risk management systems;
3. encourage firms to vest responsibility for effective and responsible organisation in specific directors and senior managers; and
4. create a common platform of organisational and systems and controls requirements for all firms.

Conduct of Business Sourcebook (COBS)

The FCA has 21 COBS rules. Rule 2.1 states the purpose of the rule set as a whole, which is to ensure that firms always act honestly, fairly and professionally in accordance with the best interests of their clients.

Client Asset Sourcebook (CASS)

The CASS rules set out how assets (including cash and securities) that belong to clients must be managed. The rules are examined in detail in Chapter 6 of this workbook but, in summary form, they insist that if a firm is physically holding assets that belong to clients then these assets must be:

1. segregated from assets that belong to the firm itself – so that, for example, there is no danger that assets belonging to clients could be used to deliver a trade conducted by the firm itself;
2. regularly reconciled and, if a shortfall is found, then the firm has to rectify it.

3.   Know Your Customer (KYC)

Learning Objective

2.9   Know the purpose of 'know your customer'

There are three reasons why banks and investment firms need to take positive steps to know their customers.

Firstly, the Basel Committee on Banking Supervision published its approach to KYC policies for banks in 2001. These published safeguards went beyond simple account-opening and record-keeping and required banks to formulate a **customer acceptance policy** and a tiered **customer identification programme** which involves more extensive diligence for higher risk accounts. It also included a recommendation for proactive **account monitoring** for suspicious activities.

Secondly, in the UK, the Money Laundering Regulations 2010 and the regulatory rules legally required firms to adopt **identification procedures for new clients** (to 'know your customer') and keep records in relation to this proof of identity. The obligation to prove identity is triggered as soon as reasonably practicable after contact is made and the parties resolve to form a business relationship. Failure to prove the identity of a client could lead to an unlimited fine and a jail term of up to two years.

Finally, MiFID regulations require firms to **classify their clients** as one of the following:

- **eligible counterparty** – eg, another regulated bank or stock exchange member firm;
- **professional client** – eg, a pension fund;
- **retail client** – eg, a private individual.

These classifications have increasing levels of protection. Clear procedures must be in place to classify clients and assess their suitability for each type of investment product, the appropriateness of any investment advice given, and the suitability of any transaction suggested to them.

By using the collected customer information, investment advisers can establish who they are authorised to do business with and understand their client's risk tolerance, investment knowledge and financial position. This information will allow informed decisions to be made regarding what can and cannot be included in a client's portfolio.

3.1   Verification Checks

Client Due Diligence (CDD)

The Money Laundering Regulations insist that CDD procedures are carried out when the regulated firm:

- establishes a business relationship;
- carries out an occasional transaction;
- suspects money laundering or terrorist financing;
- doubts the integrity of information previously obtained for CDD purposes.

Enhanced Due Diligence (EDD)

The Money Laundering Regulations require that, under certain circumstances, regulated firms must employ EDD. The types of clients that require EDD are:

- persons who were not personally present when the CDD identity checks were made; and:
- 'Politically Exposed Persons (PEPs)' – who are in turn defined by the regulations as '*individuals (and their immediate family members) who, in the preceding year, have exercised a prominent public function in a state or institution outside the UK.*'

Under CDD the types of acceptable documentary evidence to prove the identity of a new client would include the following:

For an individual:

- an official document with a photograph will prove the name, eg, passport, international driving licence;
- a utilities bill with name and address will prove that the address supplied is valid.

For a corporate client (a company):

- proof of identity and existence would be drawn from the constitutional documents (Articles and Memorandum of Association) and sets of accounts;
- for smaller companies, proving the identity of the key individual stakeholders (directors and shareholders) would also be required.

For a trust:

- the identity of the settlor (the person putting assets into trust), the trustees and the controller of the trust (the person who is able to instruct the trustees) would all be verified, along with a copy of the trust deed.

Case Study – Coutts & Co

In March 2012 the Financial Services Authority fined Coutts & Co (a subsidiary of RBS) £8.75 million for failing to take reasonable care to establish and maintain effective anti-money laundering (AML) systems and controls relating to high-risk customers, including politically exposed persons (PEPs).

In 2010, the FSA visited Coutts as part of its review into banks' management of high-risk money laundering situations. The FSA's investigation identified that Coutts did not apply robust controls when starting relationships with high-risk customers and did not consistently apply appropriate monitoring of those high-risk relationships. In addition, the FSA determined that the AML team at Coutts failed to provide an appropriate level of scrutiny and challenge.

The FSA identified deficiencies in nearly three-quarters of the PEP and high-risk customer files reviewed. Specifically, in one or more of each inadequate file Coutts failed to:

1. gather sufficient information to establish the source of wealth and source of funds of its prospective PEP and other high risk customers;
2. identify and/or assess adverse intelligence about prospective and existing high-risk customers properly and take appropriate steps in relation to such intelligence;
3. keep the information held on its existing PEP and other high-risk customers up-to-date; and
4. scrutinise transactions made through PEP and other high-risk customer accounts appropriately.

Coutts agreed to settle at an early stage and therefore qualified for a 30% discount. Were it not for this discount, the FSA would have imposed a financial penalty of £12.5 million.

3.2 An IT Perspective on KYC

There are very few roles within the securities industry where interaction with an external end client is required. The verification information given above describes the process for taking on new clients or maintaining existing clients and would typically be handled by dedicated operations or sales teams.

An exception to this generalisation might be where IT resources are supporting a system used by external clients. In these cases, the type of information that is required to validate a client would be driven by the nature of the request. For example, a customer reporting a bug in a piece of code – ie, providing information – might not need to be fully authenticated in the same way as someone asking for system access or password administration.

The typical IT role associated with KYC activities is to support and build the underlying systems. In the securities industry there is a requirement to track, consolidate and report on client-related activity at a greater level of detail and frequency than before this legislation was put in place. Many organisations have purchased or built **customer relationship management (CRM)** systems that act as a central repository for client information. These CRM systems allow relevant functions to authenticate using KYC procedures and to have access to a central system with the latest record of the verification information that has been captured, including, where required, scanned images of ID and paperwork. Fully implemented CRM systems should also contain a history of all client contact; eg, a record of all letters, emails, trades, calls, cash flows, etc.

A further point to consider is that the greater the level of automation and STP there is in a firm, the fewer chances there are for manual checking. This means that client information must be validated as soon as it is entered into the system.

4. US Regulation with a Global Footprint

Some regulatory requirements of the US government and regulators have significant effects on the operations of securities and investment firms located outside the US. These requirements can be said, therefore, to have a 'global footprint'. The two main acts and their effects are discussed in this section.

4.1 The Dodd-Frank Act

Learning Objective

2.12   Know the features and characteristics of Dodd-Frank: background

4.1.1 Introduction and Background

The **Dodd-Frank Wall Street Reform and Consumer Protection Act (DF)** is a US law that was signed in July 2010 and implementation began in stages in 2012. It is the most significant change to financial regulation in the US since the 1930s, affecting all the US regulatory agencies and almost every aspect of the nation's financial services industry.

The events that led to the passing of DF were the shocks to the financial system caused by the credit crunch in 2007 and 2008 and, in particular, the bankruptcy of Lehman Brothers in September 2008. When the liquidators began their work they found it very difficult to unwind the firm's OTC derivative positions. These were worth over $60 billion and involved over 8,000 trading counterparties. One year after the bankruptcy the liquidator was still employing over 300 people to reconcile and unwind these transactions

DF is an enormous piece of legislation covering many aspects of the financial markets, regulation and corporate governance. There are too many individual sections to cover in depth in this workbook, but many readers will find themselves having to deal with specific and far-reaching DF requirements concerning transaction reporting in general, and the post-trade treatment of OTC derivatives in particular.

4.1.2 Overview of the Dodd-Frank Legislation

The main provisions include:

1. **Consumer protection** – DF creates a new independent watchdog within the Federal Reserve (known as the 'Fed'), with the authority to ensure consumers get the clear, accurate information they need to shop for mortgages, credit cards and other financial products, and protect them from hidden fees, abusive terms and deceptive practices.
2. **Investor protection** – DF provides tough new rules for transparency and accountability for credit rating agencies to protect investors and businesses.
3. **Ends 'too big to fail' bailouts** – DF aims to end the possibility that taxpayers will be asked to bail out financial firms whose collapse would threaten the economy. It is designed to:
   ○ establish a safe way to liquidate failed financial firms;
   ○ impose tough new capital and leverage requirements that make it undesirable to get too big;
   ○ update the Fed's authority to allow system-wide support but no longer prop up individual firms.
4. **Advance warning system** – DF creates a **council** to identify and address systemic risks posed by large, complex companies, products and activities before they threaten the stability of the economy.
5. **Executive compensation and corporate governance** – DF provides shareholders with a say on pay and corporate affairs with a non-binding vote on executive compensation and golden parachutes.
6. **Regulatory enforcement** – DF strengthens oversight and empowers regulators to aggressively pursue financial fraud, conflicts of interest and manipulation of the system.
7. **Technical expertise** – DF creates a new Office of Financial Research within the Treasury to be staffed by economists, accountants, lawyers, former supervisors, and other specialists, with the aim of supporting the council's work by collecting financial data and conducting economic analysis.
8. **Making risks transparent** – through the Office of Financial Research and member agencies, the council will collect and analyse data to identify and monitor emerging risks to the economy and make this information public in annual reports to Congress.

4.1.3 IT Implications of Dodd-Frank

Items 3, 4, 7 and 8 in the above list have led the existing US regulators, in particular the Commodity Futures Trading Commission (CFTC) which regulates most derivative trading in the US, to impose new regulatory requirements which will require significant business application upgrades over the next few years. DF is not the only driver for these changes; similar requirements have arisen from the European Markets Infrastructure Regulations (EMIR). EMIR is dealt with in Section 5.4 of this chapter. The application changes introduced as a result of DF include the following:

Transaction Reporting Changes

- Swap trades will have to be reported within 15 minutes of trade execution. Regulatory transaction reporting is discussed more fully in Chapter 5.
- The counterparty of the trade will need to be identified by a new code, the Legal Entity Identifier (LEI). The significance of this new code is discussed more fully in Section 1 of Chapter 5.

Clearing and Settlement of OTC Derivative Transactions

Historically, most OTC derivative trades have been settled directly between participants, without the involvement of a clearing house. Regulators are insisting that where suitable clearing arrangements are in place, OTC derivative trades should be cleared through a recognised clearing house. The clearing process is examined in detail in Chapter 3.

The Use of OTC Derivative Trade Repositories

One of the reasons that the liquidators of Lehman Brothers found the task so complex was that there was no single database containing all the firm's OTC derivative trades. As a result, the CFTC is now insisting that all such trades are entered into a trade repository maintained by an independent third party. Trade repositories are examined in Chapter 3. Note that the EU's EMIR regulations – see Section 1.4 of this chapter – has an almost identical requirement.

4.2   The Foreign Account Tax Compliance Act (FATCA)

Learning Objective

2.8   Know the features and characteristics of the Foreign Account Tax Compliance Act (FATCA)

4.2.1   Introduction and Timetable

FATCA was enacted in March 2010 and comes into force in January 2013. It is an important development in US efforts to combat tax evasion by US persons holding investments in offshore accounts. FATCA requires certain US taxpayers holding financial assets outside of the US to report certain information about financial accounts held by US taxpayers, as well as foreign entities in which US taxpayers hold a substantial ownership interest to the Internal Revenue Service (IRS), the US tax authority.

FATCA also affects some non-US financial institutions known as **foreign financial institutions (FFIs)**, such as UK securities and investment companies.

The original IRS rules stated that an FFI would need to register with the IRS between 1 January and 30 June 2013 and sign an agreement with the IRS by 1 July 2013 to ensure that it avoids a 30% withholding tax on income generated by US investments after 1 January 2014. However, the UK government (as well as several other governments including France and Spain) is currently negotiating an agreement with the IRS whereby the FFI will make its reports to its own national tax authority, Her Majesty's Revenue and Customs (HMRC) in the case of the UK, instead of the IRS. HMRC will then forward the required information to the IRS.

4.2.2   Implementation of the Act

Existing Accounts

FFIs will be required to investigate all existing accounts to determine whether the owner of the account is a US resident, a US citizen, or a US-registered company. Accounts of **less than $50,000 for an individual and less than $250,000 for an entity** can be treated as non-US accounts, but all other client information must undergo a search for evidence or indications of US status. The aim of the electronic search is to find US data without initially having to personally contact the client. Where the search results indicate that the account owner is of interest to the US authorities, the FFI needs to check whether all the appropriate IRS documents are on file for that client. An FFI can rely on KYC documents that it has already collected, provided that these contain the level of detail and are in the format demanded. Client relationships for which there is not yet sufficient documentation available need to be further scrutinised and requests made for documents from the account holders.

There are special due diligence arrangements for accounts of **more than $1m** that are more onerous and anticipate that a relationship manager could know the status of his/her account holders, irrespective of the documentation held. Their knowledge of the account must be taken into consideration as part of the review.

If an FFI does not receive the requested documentation from a client, then the client is considered a **recalcitrant account holder**, which ordinarily would result in the application of a 30% FATCA withholding tax and reporting to the IRS; however UK FFIs will report to HMRC.

New Accounts

When new accounts are opened, FFIs must obtain and examine documentary evidence establishing the US or non-US status of individual account holders. For new individual accounts that are identified as held by US persons, the FFI will obtain **Form W-9** from the individual holders of the accounts. All the client onboarding information collected in connection with a new individual financial account will be examined to identify the possibility of potential US status.

Accounts need to be scrutinised where the following arises:

- documentation suggesting that account holders are US residents or US citizens;
- a US address associated with an account holder of the account (whether a residence address or a correspondence address);
- a US place of birth for an account holder of the account;
- any other details of potential US status, including a 'care of' address, holding address, or PO box;
- a power of attorney or signatory authority granted to a person with a US address;
- standing instructions to transfer funds to an account maintained in the US or directions received from a US address; or
- a US telephone number.

4.2.3   Withholding and Reporting

In general, a withholding agent (a US or foreign person that has control, receipt, custody, disposal or payment of any item of income of a foreign person that is subject to withholding) is required to withhold 30% on a withholdable payment made to an FFI, unless the FFI meets the requirements we have already covered. In addition, an FFI must withhold 30% on any payment it makes to a recalcitrant account holder, as well as any payment it makes to another FFI, unless that FFI meets certain requirements. However, none of these procedures for withholdings will apply to UK FFIs that are subject to the agreement between the US and UK.

UK FFIs are likely to need to report the following information about their US accounts to HMRC:

- The name, address, and taxpayer identification number (TIN) of each account holder that is a specified US person and, in the case of any account holder which is a US-owned foreign entity, the name, address, and TIN of each substantial US owner of such entity.
- The account number.
- The account balance or value at year-end.
- Gross dividends, interest and other income paid or credited to the account (timing will be determined in the FFI agreement).

Reporting of gross receipts and gross withdrawals or payments from US accounts will not be required for the first year of reporting in 2013. However, an FFI will be required to identify any US account holder by 30 June 2014 as a recalcitrant account holder and then report them to HMRC by 30 September 2014.

The UK/US Agreement

The UK (along with France, Germany, Italy, and Spain) took part in joint discussions with the US government to explore an intergovernmental approach to FATCA, supporting the overall aim to combat tax evasion, while reducing risks and burdens on financial institutions. An intergovernmental agreement was signed in September 2012 which provides a mechanism for UK financial institutions to comply with their obligations without breaching the data protection laws. Under the agreement, financial institutions pass information to HMRC who will then automatically exchange this information with the IRS.

Because of the very complex due diligence requirement of FATCA, many financial firms in the UK are not accepting US citizens or residents as clients.

4.2.4 IT Implications

The process of examining existing accounts for evidence of US ownership of accounts and contacting customers for clarification and further information may require special enquiries and workflow processes to be developed, tested and implemented.

5. The Impact of Regulation on an Investment Firm's IT Operations

The impact of the regulatory environment upon an investment firm's IT functions may be summarised as follows.

5.1 Impact On The Application Configuration

The following diagram shows a simplified example of the application configuration of a typical investment bank.

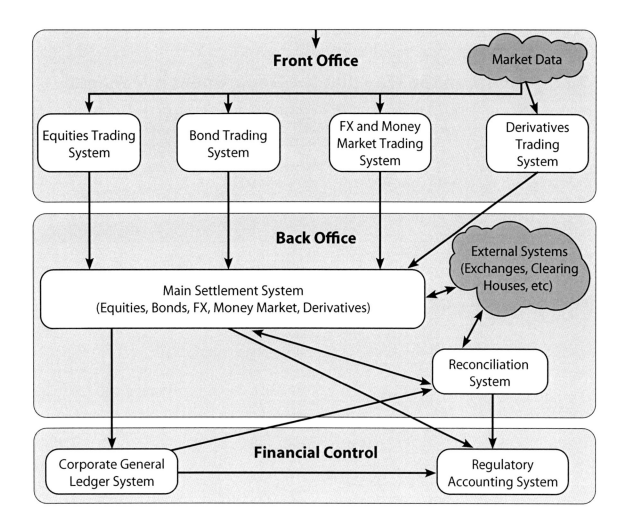

The reason that the Regulatory Accounting System is present in the configuration is that regulators require firms to produce a statutory **Capital Adequacy Report** each month – if this were not required or if the requirements were to change substantially, the nature and form of this application would be very different from what it is.

In this chapter we have mentioned that there are rules concerning, *inter alia*:

- **Best execution** – therefore the design of the front office systems (the applications that are primarily concerned with the management of order flow) has to take these rules into account in its business logic if these regulations are to be complied with.
- **Pre-trade publication of bid and offer prices** – if the firm concerned was a systematic internaliser, then it would need to build in the ability to broadcast these prices to its customers in the relevant front-office systems.
- **Post-trade publication of trade details within three minutes of execution** – again, business logic needs to be built into the front office systems concerned in order to comply with this requirement.
- **Client assets need to be reconciled** – this is one of the reasons for the existence of the reconciliation application. Another reason for the existence of this application is that it used to detect problems that can lead to operational risk – specifically those risks caused by internal fraud and errors in execution, delivery and process management.

5.2   Impact on the Way that the Department is Managed

Poor management of the IT function is a major contributor to an unacceptable level of operational risk. Basel II identifies seven operational risk events. Poor IT practice can increase operational risk, while good practice can mitigate it.

Good practice is examined in Chapters 8 to 10 of this workbook.

End of Chapter Questions

Think of an answer for each question and refer to the appropriate section for confirmation.

1. In 2013, which UK regulator will be responsible for supervision of investment exchanges?
    Section 1.2.2

2. What are the three main MiFID requirements for firms that handle customers' orders?
    Section 1.4.2

3. What are the seven operational risk events defined by the Basel Committee?
    Section 1.6.6

4. What are the eight principles of good data protection practice?
    Section 2.1

5. Which two pieces of legislation introduced the concept of repositories?
    Sections 1.3, 1.5 and 4.1.3

6. Which group of FCA/PRA rules requires regulated firms to 'vest responsibility for effective and responsible organisation with directors and senior management'?
    Section 2.4

7. Under the UK 'know your customer' rules, what types of documentary evidence are suitable to prove the identity of a new corporate client?
    Section 3.1

8. What is the definition of a recalcitrant account holder, and which piece of legislation introduced this term?
    Section 4.2.2

9. What are the main ways that financial regulation affects the work of the IT department?
    Section 5

Chapter Three

IT and the Functional Flow of Financial Instruments

This syllabus area will provide approximately 4 of the 50 examination questions

1. Introduction

Section 2 of this chapter describes the roles of investment exchanges, and the types of trading platforms they provide for their member firms. Section 3 describes the role of clearing houses and provides examples of the trade flows between exchange member firms, exchanges and clearing houses – all of whom play a part in processing the trade. Section 3 goes on to look at changes to the competitive landscape of exchanges and clearing houses, and looks at the role of external real-time information sources.

2. The Roles and Functions of Investment Exchanges

Learning Objective

3.1   Understand the function and connectivity of investment exchanges, multilateral trading facilities and broker crossing networks: classification; economic functions; order handling systems; connectivity

2.1   Definitions of Terms

A **multilateral trading facility (MTF)** is any type of system or service that brings together multiple parties that are interested in buying and selling financial instruments, and enables them to do so. The term was first used in the MiFID directive of 2004. Prior to MiFID there was no generic term to describe such systems and services. Under MiFID rules, both investment exchanges and broker crossing networks are forms of MTF.

An **investment exchange** (also known as a stock exchange, share market, stock market, bourse or derivatives exchange) is a corporation or mutual organisation which provides facilities for stockbrokers and traders to trade company stocks and other securities, including bonds, derivatives and physical commodities such as precious metals and agricultural products.

Crossing occurs when a broker acts as agent on both sides of a given transaction. If the broker has a buy order and an equivalent sell order, it can 'cross' the orders. Under MiFID rules, crossing is only permitted if it results in best execution. **Broker crossing networks** are a form of MTF.

Many investment banks provide their institutional clients with access to broker crossing networks. These networks allow the bank's clients to match up and conduct crossing transactions without going through an exchange. Crossing networks allow traders to gain large blocks of liquidity while keeping transaction costs down.

In the UK, investment exchanges are presently regulated by the FCA, which has classified them as follows:

*   A **Recognised Investment Exchange (RIE)** is one that is based in the UK and is recognised by the FCA – see Section 2.2 for a list of these exchanges and a brief description of their business.

- A **Recognised Overseas Investment Exchange (ROIE)** is one that is based outside the UK but admits UK banks and securities firms as members, and is recognised by the FCA. There are currently 8 exchanges in this category, including NASDAQ in the US and the Australian Securities Exchange Limited.
- A **Designated Investment Exchange (DIE)** is an overseas exchange that does not carry on a regulated activity in the UK and is not a regulated market. Designation allows securities firms to treat transactions effected on a designated investment exchange in the same way as they would treat transactions effected on an RIE. Overseas exchanges may apply to the FCA to be included on the FCA's list of designated investment exchanges. Before adding an investment exchange to the list of designated investment exchanges, the FCA will look at whether the investment exchange provides an appropriate degree of protection for consumers. The FCA will also undertake a public consultation prior to adding the investment exchange to the list of designated investment exchanges.

2.2   Recognised Investment Exchanges (RIEs)

- **NYSE Euronext Liffe** (usually known as **NYSE Liffe**) is the largest derivatives exchange in the UK, offering a wide range of financial and commodity products.
- The **London Stock Exchange plc (LSE)** is the largest formal market for securities in the UK and facilitates deals in equities, bonds and some derivatives such as exchange-traded funds and covered warrants.
- The **London Metal Exchange Limited (LME)** trades a wide variety of futures and options contracts based on non-ferrous metals.
- **ICE Futures Europe** trades futures and options on a wide range of energy products.
- **CME Europe** trades a wide range of derivative contracts.
- **BATS Chi-X Europe** offers trading in more than 3,600 securities across 15 major European markets.
- **ICAP Securities & Derivatives Exchange Limited** is an equity market for ssmall- and medium-sized companies who want to raise money from investors to finance and grow their businesses. It allows companies to come to the public markets for the first time to raise equity finance, or for existing listed companies to raise further finance.

2.3   Economic Functions of an Investment Exchange

There are three economic functions of an investment exchange:

1. To provide a means for companies to raise new capital in the form of equities and bonds.
2. To provide facilities for investors to trade company stocks and other securities.
3. To create standardised derivative instruments such as futures and options which are based on the underlying securities, and to provide facilities for investors to trade in these derivative instruments.

Investors who wish to trade instruments that are listed on an investment exchange have to route their orders to a stock exchange member firm. That member firm's IT department will need to organise connectivity to a large number of exchange computer systems to facilitate trading. The following sections describe the major systems used by the two largest UK investment exchanges – the LSE and NYSE Liffe.

In principle, there are three types of exchange order-handling systems used throughout the world.

An **order-driven** system has no designated or official market makers. A member firm which wishes to buy a given investment at a given price submits an order to the relevant exchange system, while at the same time other member firms which wish to sell the same product submit sell orders to the system. When a buyer's bid meets a seller's offer (or vice versa), the exchange's matching system will decide that a deal has been executed. The identity of the buyer is not known to the seller, and vice versa.

A **quote-driven** system is one where some of the exchange's member firms take on the obligation of always making a two-way price in each of the products (typically, stocks) in which they make markets. These firms are, therefore, known as **market makers**. If another member firm wishes to buy or sell then they approach the market maker directly, either by telephone, or more likely electronically, by using the exchange system concerned. In a quote-driven market, the identity of the buyer and seller are known to each other.

Order-driven systems are most suitable when the products concerned are highly liquid; that is to say that on every trading day there will be large volumes of trading activity. Quote-driven systems on the other hand are most suitable for products which are illiquid; that is to say that on most trading days there are usually low volumes of trading activity.

Hybrid systems offer both facilities – most orders are fulfilled through the order queue, but market makers exist side by side to guarantee trade execution if there is not enough liquidity in the order queue.

2.4   LSE Systems

2.4.1   Trading Systems

The LSE offers the following trading systems to its member firms:

- **SETS (hybrid platform)** – SETS (Stock Exchange Electronic Trading Service) is used to trade all securities in the FTSE All Share Index as well as the more liquid of the AIM securities and the major Dutch stocks. It is the London Stock Exchange's hybrid trading service that combines electronic order-driven trading throughout the day with integrated market maker liquidity provision, delivering guaranteed two-way prices.
- **SETSqx (hybrid platform)** – SETSqx (Stock Exchange Electronic Trading Service – quotes and crosses) supports four electronic auctions a day (at 08:00, 11:00, 15:00 and 16:35) along with continuous stand-alone, quote-driven market making. It is used to trade all UK domestic equities not traded on SETS.
- **SEAQ (quote-driven platform)** – SEAQ (Stock Exchange Automated Quotations) is the quote-driven platform for the fixed-interest market and those AIM securities not traded on either SETS or SETSqx.
- **Order Book for Retail Bonds (hybrid platform)** – in February 2010 the exchange launched this new trading platform for UK gilts (government bonds) and a selection of sterling-denominated corporate bonds. The trading day is made up of an initial opening auction phase followed by continuous trading supported by market makers until market close. There is no closing auction.

The LSE's trading systems are based on its Millennium Exchange software platform, which went live in 2011. This system was built by Millennium IT, the Sri Lankan software and services company that the LSE bought for £18 million in 2009.

2.4.2　Other LSE Systems

As well as the exchange's trading systems, there are a number of other LSE systems that the member firm may need to arrange connectivity to. The word 'may' is used in this context because some of the services are also provided by other organisations that compete with the LSE to provide these services.

- **Regulatory News Service (RNS)** – companies whose shares or bonds are listed on the exchange have a legal duty to make announcements about price-sensitive information as soon as possible. Price-sensitive information includes, *inter alia*, details of P&L forecasts, changes in major shareholders, appointments and resignations of directors, plus any other major announcements. The RNS allows the listed companies to make these announcements, and investors to view them and take action. The RNS is, therefore, made available to listed companies, LSE member firms, professional investors and the media.
- The **Corporate Events Diary** is an online calendar for tracking upcoming corporate events affecting UK securities traded on the LSE. It offers advance warning of both stock situation notices and ex-dividend status in a simple, easy-to-use calendar format that allows users to:
  - keep up-to-date with corporate events;
  - anticipate the pricing impact of key events on securities; and
  - prepare both front and back offices for impending announcements.
- The **SEDOL Masterfile** is a database of securities that provides a common, unique identification code (the SEDOL code) that all market participants may use to identify an individual security. It covers securities listed on all the world's major markets, not just those listed on the LSE.
- **European regulatory trade reporting** – broker-dealers in Europe have a legal obligation to report all trades to their regulators electronically. The reason that a regulatory trade report is required is so that the regulators can monitor the markets to track insider dealing and other forms of market abuse (see Chapter 2, Section 3). The LSE, among other organisations, provides facilities for firms to make regulatory trade reports.
- **Participant services** are designed to supply member firms with information about their market share, quality of execution, etc.

2.5　NYSE Liffe Trading Systems and Connectivity

2.5.1　Introduction

NYSE Liffe specialises in trading futures and options. The underlying instruments on which NYSE Liffe's futures and options are based include currency exchange rates, interest rates, government bonds, equity indices such as the FTSE 100 index and individual equities, as well as physical commodities such as softs and agricultural products.

2.5.2　Trading System

By definition, futures and options markets are highly liquid – the volume of trading in derivative instruments more often than not exceeds the volume of trading in the underlying instruments. Therefore, the exchange provides a single, order-driven trading system for all contracts – the Universal Trading Platform (UTP). A member firm that wishes to buy a given futures or options contract at a given price submits an order to LIFFE UTP, while at the same time other member firms who wish to sell the same contract submit sell orders to the system. When a buyer's bid meets a seller's offer (or vice versa), LIFFE UTP will decide that a deal has been executed. The identity of the buyer is not known to the seller, and vice versa.

2.6 Providing Connectivity to Investment Exchanges' Systems

The member firm's IT department is responsible for providing connectivity to those investment exchange systems that users need to carry out their business. In a large firm, this will probably include all the LSE systems and LIFFE UTP, but a smaller firm may need to use only some of the systems described in this chapter. Many firms will also require connectivity to other exchanges which may be located in the UK or overseas.

Connectivity to trading systems, of course, needs to be real-time and capable of processing data at high speeds in a robust manner. Hardware, software and interface connection failures at times when the markets are under pressure from volatile prices and/or high trading volumes can cost the member firm very dearly.

Member firms' IT departments may be involved either in developing front office applications that include real-time interfaces to exchange systems, or in implementing package systems that include these interfaces.

2.6.1 In-House Development

If the firm is developing in-house, then the developers will need access to the following types of publications and facilities that are provided by all the relevant exchanges:

- **Data exchange specifications** – these cover the message formats for data that is to be sent to or received from the exchange. DESs also explain the sequence of messages.
- **Data dictionaries** – most messages are based on data dictionaries. A data dictionary is a defined as a centralised repository of information about data such as meaning, relationships to other data, origin, usage, and format.
- **Data security standards** – these cover the rules for data encryption (if required).
- **Service level standards** – these cover a variety of standards that the member firm must meet, including:
  ○ the normal working days and hours of business of the service to which you are communicating;
  ○ any rules about the timeliness of a message: for example, regulatory trade reporting messages must be sent not later than three minutes after the trade was executed;
  ○ specific rules about non-standard conditions, such as trade cancellation and amendment.
- **Testing facilities** – all exchanges offer testing facilities so that the firm can test its new developments; some exchanges insist that a level of mutual testing has been carried out before a new application or new member firm is allowed to connect to its systems.

Details of all the publications and services that each individual exchange offers are usually to be found on its website, sometimes in a secure area.

2.6.2 Packages

Because of the cost of the initial development and then the cost of the day-to-day maintenance, many member firms do not build their own trading systems; instead they implement packages that (as well as providing other facilities) provide the connectivity required to all the exchanges that the user firm requires.

The next two illustrations show the functionality of package systems. The first diagram is kindly provided by Linedata Group. The Linedata package is widely used by **buy-side** firms (fund management institutions that take investment decisions on behalf of investors) and provides features such as portfolio modelling and pre-trade compliance, as well as the necessary connectivity to sell-side firms.

The second diagram is kindly provided by Fidessa plc. The Fidessa package is widely used by **sell-side** firms (exchange members and other firms that quote prices) and provides connectivity to over 200 exchanges and other venues as well as the necessary connectivity to buy-side firms that is examined in chapter 4. It communicates with buy-side firms using the FIX protocol which is examined in chapter 6.

The reasons why such systems may be bought as packages rather than built in-house are examined in chapter 9.

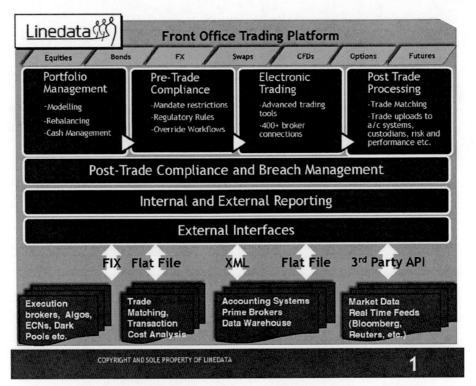

Linedata Buy-side Front Office Platform

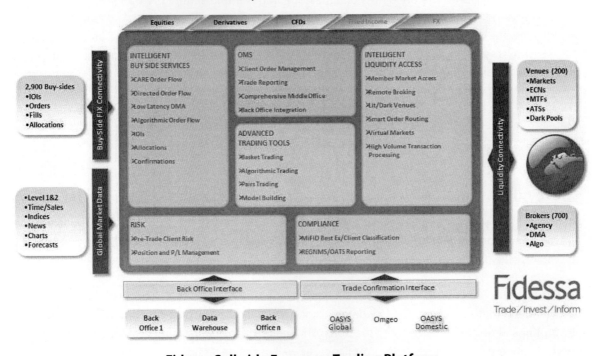

Fidessa Sell-side European Trading Platform

3. Clearing Houses

Learning Objective

3.2   Understand the function and connectivity of clearing houses: recognised clearing houses; settlement and custody services; central counterparty services

3.1   Introduction

Clearing houses provide one or both of two services to their customers. These are:

- settlement and custody services and;
- central counterparty (CCP) services.

In the UK markets, the settlement and custody services are provided by Euroclear UK & Ireland (EUI) and the central counterparty services are operated by a number of different organisations, depending on the exchange where the trade is executed. Sections 3.3 and 3.4 of this chapter describe the two services in more detail.

3.2   Recognised Clearing Houses

Following the passing of the Financial Services Act 2012, clearing houses are now recognised by the Bank of England. The Bank recognises the following five clearing houses in the UK:

- LME Clear Limited;
- Euroclear UK & Ireland Ltd (EUI);
- LCH.Clearnet Ltd (London Clearing House);
- ICE (InterContinental Exchange) Clear Europe Ltd;
- CME (Chicago Mercantile Exchange) Clearing Europe Ltd.

Following the implementation of the EU's EMIR regulations, clearing houses within the EU can also choose to be recognised by the pan-European regulator ESMA. Two clearing houses, at the time of writing (June 2014), have so far chosen this route:

- European Central Counterparty Ltd (EuroCCP);
- NasdaqOMX Clearing AB (SE).

3.3   Settlement and Custody Services

These services are provided for the securities market only; there is no direct equivalent for derivatives trades. For the UK securities markets they are provided by Euroclear UK & Ireland Ltd (EUI).

Although EUI is regulated as a recognised clearing house, its role is quite different from that of the CCP. Membership of EUI is open to stock exchange member firms, institutional investors, custodians and registrars.

EUI and its equivalent institutions in other countries are often described as **central securities depositories (CSDs)**. The services that EUI provides are described below.

3.3.1 The Settlement Service

The principal function of EUI is to settle all transactions in UK- and Irish-registered equities, and it uses its CREST system to carry out these functions. Trades are usually settled against payment in GBP, EUR and USD, but may be settled free of payment, in certain circumstances.

In the EUI environment, investors are able to hold their securities either in dematerialised form, where there are no share certificates and evidence of ownership is in the form of an accounting entry in the EUI system itself; or in certificated form.

EUI offers settlement throughout the day with effective **Delivery-versus-Payment (DvP)** occurring between 05:30 and 13:00 each business day. At that point the buyer of securities takes delivery of the securities, and the buyer's payment bank guarantees to pay the seller's payment bank, which in turn is obliged to pay the seller.

When a trade is originated in the SETS system, the trade will have been novated by a CCP, which will take on the obligations of both parties to the trade and enable multilateral settlement netting. The role of CCPs is examined in the next section.

As part of the settlement process of registered securities, EUI has automated interfaces to the systems used by registrars; as settlement occurs, the registrars are provided with the necessary information to update the register and, if required, issue share certificates.

3.3.2 Other Services

Other services provided by EUI to its members include the following:

1. **Regulatory trade reporting** – like the LSE, EUI can provide broker-dealers with the facilities to report their trades to European regulators in real time. EUI competes with the LSE in this respect.
2. **Custody services** – stock belonging to members is held in accounts on their behalf.
3. **Payment of dividends** to members.
4. **Processing of corporate action entitlements** to members.
5. **Specialised facilities for stock lending and borrowing** – Euroclear UK & Ireland's services in this area are described in Chapter 6, Section 2.2.4.

3.3.3 Communicating with EUI

Most packaged equity settlement systems contain all the necessary interfaces to communicate with EUI. In the event that the firm is building its own equity settlement system, then EUI publishes a Data Exchange Manual (DEX) which contains descriptions of all the necessary message formats. The DEX may be downloaded from www.euroclear.com.

3.4 Central Counterparty Services

Central counterparty services are provided to firms which carry out trades in:

- securities;
- exchange-traded futures and options;
- over-the-counter (OTC) derivatives.

The principle is as follows. When an order to buy from Party A is matched with an order to sell from Party B in order-driven market systems such as SETS or LIFFE UTP, neither of the parties is aware of the identity of the other party. As soon as the exchange has matched the orders, its systems inform a clearing house. The clearing house then takes over the obligations to make payments and/or deliver the relevant securities or derivatives.

This process – the substitution of one party to a contract by another party – is known as **novation**. As a result of novation, the clearing house has become the central counterparty (CCP) – every other counterparty settles its obligations with the clearing house and not with each other.

The advantages to an exchange and its member firms in having a CCP include the following:

- **Post-trade anonymity** – it is not necessary for the exchange to divulge the identity of Party A to Party B or vice versa, so there is no danger of one party learning the other party's commercial secrets as a result of discovering its trading pattern.
- **Netting of positions** – Party A may have carried out many trades in an identical futures or options contract. The CCP nets these into a single position.
- **A reduction in credit risk** – because Party A and Party B are unaware of each other, they are, by definition, unaware of each other's credit status. Once the CCP has novated the contract, Party A no longer has to worry about Party B's ability to meet its obligations throughout the life of the futures or options contract or during the settlement period for the cash equity. The CCP's ability to meet its obligations is monitored by the FCA. However, the CCP has to monitor the ability of its member firms to meet their obligations. It does this by requiring them to place collateral with the CCP to meet margin requirements.

3.4.1 Margin and Collateral

It is beyond the scope of this workbook to give a comprehensive and accurate description of margin requirements; the following is a simplified example:

Example

1. On 1 February 2011 Party A buys a futures contract that obliges it to take delivery of 1,000 shares in ABC plc on 30 March 2011 in return for payment by Party A of £10 per share. So the total amount it has to pay to the CCP if it still holds the contract on 30 March would be £10,000.
2. However, by 7 February the price of ABC plc shares is only £8 per share. Party A stands to lose £2,000 if it still holds the position on 30 March. The CCP, therefore, requires Party A to make a margin payment of £2,000 to cover the CCP's risk.
3. If, at some time between 8 February and 30 March, the price of ABC shares rises to £9 per share, then the CCP will refund £1,000 to Party A. If, however, it falls to £7 per share, then the CCP will demand another £1,000 from Party A.

To summarise, whenever a member firm's positions show potential losses it must make a margin payment to the clearing house. In this way the clearing house is protected against default by the member firm.

The actual calculations performed by the CCP are much more complicated than this and cover two aspects of margin – **initial margin** and **variation margin**. Most clearing houses use a methodology known as SPAN (Standardised Portfolio Analysis of risk) in order to calculate initial margin. This is a leading margin system which has been adopted by most options and futures exchanges around the world. SPAN is based on a sophisticated set of algorithms that determine initial margin according to a global (total portfolio) assessment of the one-day risk for a trader's account.

Margin calls do not have to be paid in cash. As an alternative, the CCP accepts the deposit of a wide variety of government bonds and other collateral as cover for initial margin. The cash or securities used to meet the call are known as **collateral**.

3.4.2 Multilateral Settlement Netting

Clearing houses that act as central counterparties to securities trades are also in a position to provide Multilateral Settlement Netting (MSN). MSN was introduced in the UK markets in 2002 as a secondary phase after LCH.Clearnet began offering this service to members of the LSE.

Prior to the introduction of the netting service, each trade at EUI settled individually. If Party A made 100 trades on a given day – each trade buying 100 shares of ABC plc from 100 different other parties – there would have been 100 settlements of ABC shares with Party A.

With the advent of the netting service, Party A now has only one settlement of its obligations in ABC plc shares; therefore, the CCP service provides the additional benefit of reduced settlement costs to member firms (see Section 3.5.1 for a worked example of multilateral settlement netting).

3.4.3 Competition Between Clearing Houses

The different clearing houses compete with one another to win CCP business from the various exchanges and their member firms.

Other LCH.Clearnet Clearing Services

LCH.Clearnet also offers CCP services for OTC derivatives and repos. These services have been available for many years, but the use of such services for OTC derivatives will shortly be mandated as a result of the Dodd-Frank act in the US and EMIR in Europe. These legal changes were discussed on Chapter 2.

3.4.4 SwapClear

Swaps are not traded on exchanges, but on the OTC market. See Chapter 1 for more information. SwapClear is LCH.Clearnet's service for centralised clearing of these instruments.

In 2011, SwapClear cleared more than 50% of the OTC interest rate swap market. Currently the one million trades in SwapClear have an aggregate notional principal amount of over $290 trillion, with a further $80 trillion of cleared transactions removed through multilateral trade compression.

Launched in 1999, SwapClear initially cleared plain vanilla interest rate swaps in four major currencies. Today, it clears swaps in 17 currencies:

- USD, EUR, and GBP out to 50 years;
- AUD, CAD, CHF, SEK and vanilla JPY out to 30 years; and
- the remaining nine currencies out to ten years.

It also clears overnight index swaps (OISs) out to two years in USD, EUR, GBP and CHF.

To submit a trade for clearing, the client and executing broker both affirm the trade via MarkitSERV2, a third-party trade matching service. The trade is then 'given up' or 'novated' by both sides to the client's chosen SwapClear clearing member, who clears the trade through LCH.Clearnet.

The execution and subsequent give-up process are governed by the documents between the executing broker, client and SwapClear clearing member. All subsequent trade events, such as novations and partial novations, will be handled by the SwapClear clearing member without any involvement from the executing broker.

Other CCPs also offer clearing services for the OTC markets.

3.4.5   RepoClear

Repos – sale and repurchase agreements – are transactions where Party A lends money to Party B providing that Party B provides Party A with collateral in the form of government bonds. The mechanism of the exchange of cash and collateral is that Party B 'sells' the securities to Party A under an agreement where A can repurchase them at a later date. The concept is examined in more detail in Chapter 6.

Repos are not traded on an exchange; they are traded on the OTC market.

LCH.Clearnet operates a CCP service for repo trades. The benefits to participants are as follows:

- credit risk reduction;
- balance sheet netting;
- multilateral settlement netting; and
- post-trade anonymity.

3.4.6   Types of Clearing House Membership

Not all members of NYSE Liffe are members of the clearing house. An NYSE Liffe member may elect also to become a member of the clearing house, or it may elect to have its trades cleared by another firm, known as a **general clearing member (GCM)**.

When a firm has elected to have its trades cleared by a GCM, the GCM will manage the margin requirements of its clients in the same way that the clearing house manages the margin requirements of the GCM.

A firm that does not clear its own trades is known as a **non-clearing member (NCM)**, or dealer member. An NCM needs connectivity to the exchange's systems, but not to the clearing house's systems; a GCM, however, needs connectivity to both entities' systems.

Sometimes a firm may be a clearing member of one exchange, where it does a substantial volume of business, but a non-clearing member of another exchange. This may be because its trading volumes on the second exchange are lower, or because the second exchange is located overseas, perhaps in a different time zone, and the firm feels that its clearing arrangements are better handled by a local agent. In other words, it has outsourced the clearing of trades on the second exchange.

3.4.7 Communicating with Central Counterparties

There are several package software applications dedicated to the futures and options market that contain all the necessary interfaces with the CCP's systems.

All the details of the interface specifications are available from clearing houses' websites.

3.5 Trade Flows from Exchange to Clearing House to Final Settlement

3.5.1 Equities Traded on SETS

Example

On 12 February an investor placed an order to buy 5,000 ABC shares with Exchange Member A for £5 per share for value date 15 February. Exchange Member A placed this order on the SETS queue and it was matched with a sell order from another member.

Exchange Member A also placed four additional orders for ABC shares on the SETS queue on 12 February, all for value date 15 February, and all the orders were matched by other member firms. The summary for all five additional orders is, therefore, as follows:

Trade No	Operation	Share Quantity	Share Price £	Trade Value £
1 (described above)	Buy	+5,000	5.0	−25,000
2	Buy	+7,500	5.10	−38,250
3	Buy	+4,000	5.05	−20,200
4	Sell	−6,000	5.05	+30,300
5	Sell	−2,000	5.00	+10,000
Net Securities due to Member A	+8,500	Net Cash Payable by Member A	−43,150

When the orders are matched, the SETS system reports them to Member A, to the CCP chosen by Member A, and to EUI. Remember from Section 3.4.3 that Member A has the choice of nominating either LCH.Clearnet or SIX x-clear as its chosen CCP.

EUI will then automatically generate settlement instructions on behalf of both Member A and the CCP in the early evening (after SETS has closed for the day, but before EUI closes) of 15 February – the contractual value date of all five trades. Providing that the CCP has 8,500 ABC shares to give to Member A, and Member A is in a position to pay £43,150.00, the five trades will settle as a single item.

Member A still has to arrange the settlement of the five individual trades with the client(s) concerned.

From 12 February until the final settlement, the CCP will monitor Member A's margin position. The average price of the 8,500 shares that the firm has to settle is approximately £5.08 per share. If the market price of ABC shares falls below this level at any time between 12 February and the date on which settlement occurs, the CCP will call Member A to deposit collateral to cover the difference.

Diagrammatically, the process can be represented in the following way:

**SETS Trade Flows –
Exchange Member is also a Clearing Member**

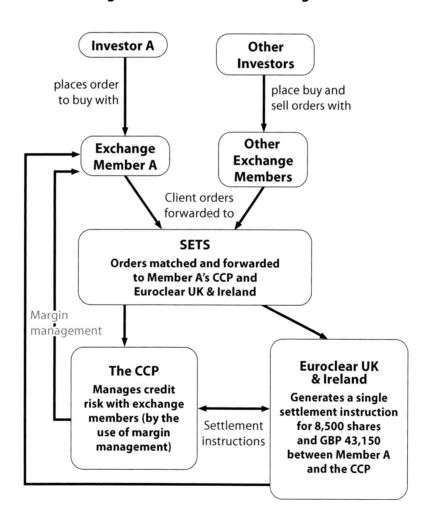

3.5.2 Equities Traded on SEAQ

When equities are traded on SEAQ (a quote-driven market) the following process applies:

1. There is no central counterparty and, therefore, novation and netting are not involved. No CCP is involved with the transaction.
2. When the exchange member receives a report from SEAQ, it is up to that member to send settlement instructions to EUI.
3. EUI will then settle the trades individually on the agreed value date, providing that:
    a. both Exchange Member A and the relevant market maker have instructed EUI, and their settlement instructions agree with each other – this is covered in Chapter 6.
    b. the buyer has the cash to pay for the securities, and the seller has the securities to deliver.

Diagrammatically, the trade flow may be expressed in the following manner:

SEAQ Trade Flows

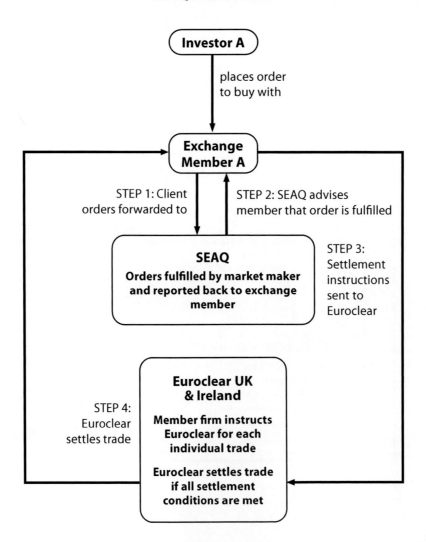

3.5.3   Futures or Options Traded on LIFFE UTP

**Liffe Member Trade Flows –
Exchange Member is also a Clearing Member**

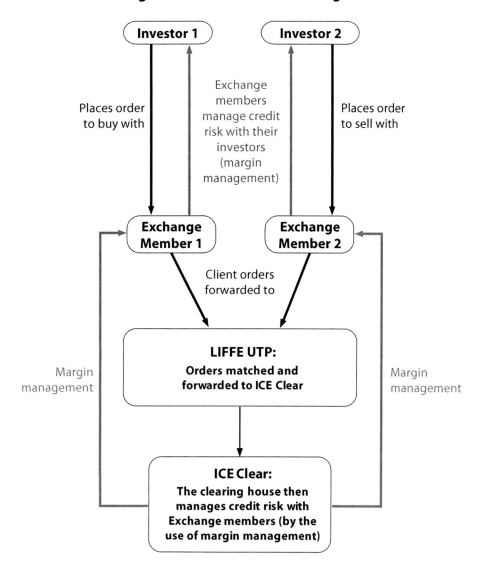

The above diagram shows the flow of client orders to exchange member firms that are also clearing members of the exchange. Once the LIFFE UTP system has matched the orders, then the exchange reports the matched trades to ICE Clear and the transactions are novated.

The clearing house then manages its credit risk with the member firms by the use of margin management. If the member firm were not itself a clearing member, then two exchange members who are also clearing members would be involved and the diagram would then look like this:

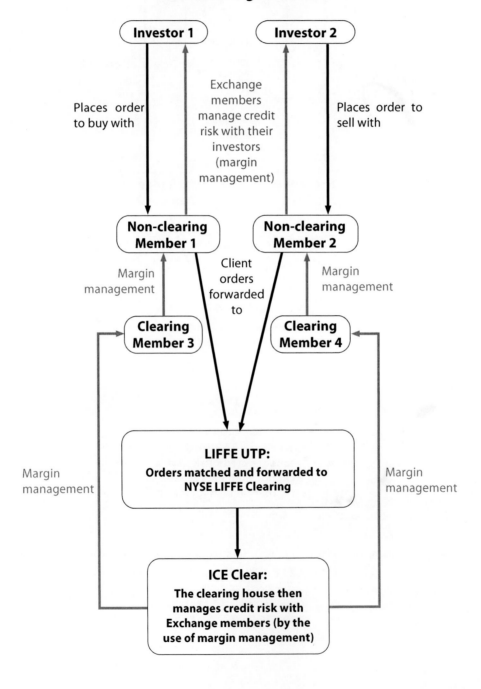

3.6 Trade Repositories

Learning Objective

3.3   Know the function and connectivity of Trade Data Repositories

A **trade repository** or **swap data repository** is an entity that centrally collects and maintains the records of over-the-counter (OTC) derivatives. These electronic platforms act as authoritative registries of key information regarding open OTC derivatives trades.

The purpose of trade repositories is to provide regulators with visibility into risk exposures by firm and counterparty. Repositories are supervised in Europe by the European Securities and Markets Authority (ESMA) under the EMIR regulations. Similar regulatory initiatives are conducted in the United States where the Commodity Futures Trading Commission (CFTC) has developed the Dodd-Frank Act regulation, under which swap data repositories are regulated. In Europe, it became compulsory to report OTC trades to repositories in February 2014.

In Spring 2014, ESMA recognised the following repositories:

Trade Repository	Derivative Asset Class
DTCC Derivatives Repository Ltd (DDRL)	All asset classes
Krajowy Depozyt Papierów Wartosciowych S.A. (KDPW)	All asset classes
Regis-TR S.A.	All asset classes
UnaVista Ltd	All asset classes
CME Trade Repository Ltd (CME TR)	All asset classes
ICE Trade Vault Europe Ltd (ICE TVEL)	Commodities, credit, equities, interest rates

All of these publish data exchange manuals specifying the inputs and outputs that are necessary to use their services.

4. Real-Time Information Sources

Learning Objective

3.4   Understand the functionality of external real time information sources: pre-trade price and liquidity discovery; analytics; post-trade information dissemination

4.1   Introduction

Securities industry firms depend on high-quality, fast and robust feeds of real-time information covering market prices, company announcements and corporate actions, and economic and political events, in order to make investment decisions. Without accurate and up-to-date market information sources, the financial markets would be unable to trade in the volumes that they do, nor to trade in highly innovative and complex instruments.

This section describes the major services that are offered by the two market-leading suppliers of real-time market data – Thomson Reuters and Bloomberg – and also deals with some of the technology implications of using and distributing this data throughout the firm.

The original missions of both Reuters, starting in the 1970s, and Bloomberg, in the early 1980s, were to deliver market data to securities professionals. Since then, both companies have expanded enormously and diversified widely, and they both offer a very wide range of information services, media content and packaged software that is far beyond their original scope. However, this section is limited to the primary functions of both information providers: providing market information to the securities industry. Reuters was acquired by Thomson Financial in 2007.

4.2   Functionality Provided by the Information Vendors

There are a number of information vendors available in the market, with Bloomberg and Thomson Reuters being two of the most popular. However all facilities provided can be broken down into three groups – namely:

1. **Pre-trade – liquidity and price discovery** – both vendors act as 'consolidators' of market information; and as a result a securities firm can use the vendors' screens to discover the best price across a number of exchanges. In addition, both vendors display relevant data from the OTC and FX markets. Thomson Reuters supplies round-the-clock news and real-time prices from over 2,000 market makers and brokers, covering 175 currencies. Pre-built calculators allow for complex analysis. Thomson Reuters provides official daily market fixings for over 50 currencies.
2. **Pre-trade – analytics** – both vendors supply analytical tools to perform 'what if' scenario analysis and to price complex derivative instruments and strategies.
3. **Trade execution and post-trade services** – both firms provide facilities for conversational dealing (ie, dealing using instant-messenger type services) and also link traders, brokers, dealers and execution venues through an order-routing hub. Order-routing hubs are discussed in Chapter 4. Thomson Reuters' Trade Notification Service is a real-time messaging hub for confirming FX trade information back to counterparties.

End of Chapter Questions

Think of an answer for each question and refer to the appropriate section for confirmation.

1. Which type of investment exchange is based outside the UK but admits UK firms as members?
   Section 2.1

2. Which three of the London Stock Exchange's trading systems are hybrid platforms?
   Section 2.4.1

3. 'Millennium Exchange' replaced which exchange's trading system technology in 2010?
   Section 2.4.1

4. What is the technical term for 'the substitution of one party to a contract by another party'?
   Section 3.4

5. What benefits does the use of a central counterparty provide to members of a derivatives exchange?
   Section 3.4

6. What additional benefit (to those in Question 5) does the use of a central counterparty provide for members of a securities exchange?
   Section 3.4.2

7. Is it necessary for a NYSE Liffe member firm to also be a clearing member of ICE Clear?
   Section 3.4.6

8. Which regulator is responsible for the supervision of trade repositories serving the UK markets?
   Section 3.6

9. What is the purpose of a trade repository and what are the main regulatory drivers behind it?
   Section 3.6

10. What services does Thomson Reuters provide to FX traders?
    Section 4

Chapter Four
The Role of IT in the Front Office

This syllabus area will provide approximately 4 of the 50 examination questions

1. Introduction

Chapter 4, together with Chapters 5 and 6, follows the flow of a client order through the various stages of execution and settlement.

Using the STP principles that were described in Chapter 1, the process from the issuance of an order, its subsequent execution, and finally the issuance of the settlement instructions can be summarised in this diagram:

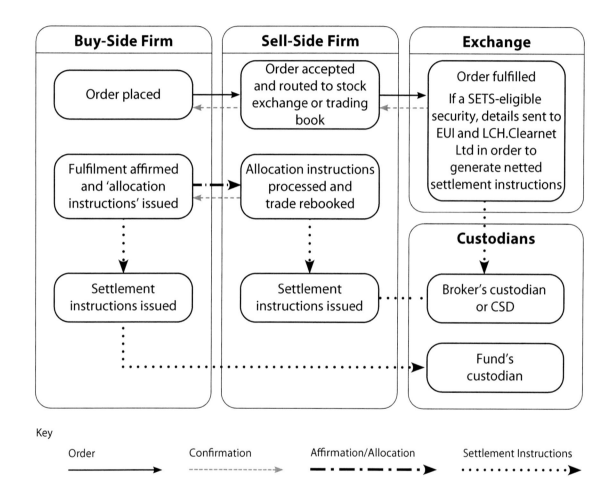

The order flow steps are examined in more detail in Section 3.3 of this chapter.

2. The Investment Decision Process

Learning Objective

4.1   Understand the investment decision support process

Before an order to buy or sell securities is placed, there has, of course, to be a decision to buy or sell. This section explains the investment decision processes used by buy-side firms.

It is generally accepted that there are four stages to the portfolio management process:

1. **Determining the investment objectives of the client** – it is important to establish the objectives of the client prior to offering investment advice or investment management services.
2. **Formulating an investment policy and strategies to meet those objectives** – portfolio construction and management – this stage would include determining how much the client has to invest, how much income they require from the portfolio, over what timescale the client wishes to invest and any financial protection needed for any dependants.
3. **Stock selection** – based on the details provided by the client, it would then be necessary to apportion the amount to be invested into the four broad asset classes – cash, equities, fixed income products and property – in accordance with the client's objectives.
4. **Performance measurement** – it is very important to review how the investments are performing on a regular basis and to make sure that they continue to meet the clients' objectives. Changes in the portfolio can be made should they be required.

Using equities as an example, buy-side firms will generate **buy orders** under the following circumstances:

1. if their clients have cash available for investment; and
2. they anticipate that the price of a given stock will rise; or
3. they anticipate that the price of stocks quoted on given exchanges will rise; or
4. they anticipate that the price of stocks issued by companies in a given sector, (eg, pharmaceuticals, motors) will rise; or
5. some combination of 2 to 5 above.

Equally, they will generate **sell orders** if:

6. their clients need to raise cash that is currently invested (for example to pay pensioners); or
7. they anticipate that the price of a given stock will fall; or
8. they anticipate that the price of stocks quoted on given exchanges will fall; or
9. they anticipate that the price of stocks issued by companies in a given sector, (eg, pharmaceuticals, motors) will fall; or
10. some combination of 7 to 9 above; or
11. the portfolio does not match the investment objectives and constraints (eg, it is too heavy in one particular sector).

In order to make these decisions, buy-side firms therefore need to have the following information to hand, and one of the roles of the IT department is to provide the applications and services that the investment decision-makers need.

- **Cash flow forecasts**
  - predicted cash inflows and outflows;
  - cash that has been earmarked for a purpose – eg, for an alternative investment, as collateral;
  - cash that is genuinely free which can be invested.
- **Economic and financial forecasts and research recommendations** – the decision-makers use these tools to decide which countries, sectors and individual companies have the highest growth potential or the highest potential to lose money. These types of data may be presented on paper, in person at conferences and briefings or online in a variety of private and public websites.
- **Market data** – the trading systems of the various exchanges, as well as the applications provided by market data suppliers such as Thomson Reuters and Bloomberg, supply information about current market prices and liquidity on the various exchanges where the instruments are listed. These facilities were discussed in more detail in chapter 3.
- **Performance measurement software applications** – these applications measure the performance of the firm's investment portfolios and usually:
  - compare the performance achieved to industry peer groups and stock market indices;
  - attribute the performance to factors such as stock selection, currency selection, etc.

The investment manager would also have access to the various modelling ('what-if') tools to help shape his or her decisions, as well as details of his or her funds' investment restrictions, objectives and constraints to ensure they trade correctly.

3. The IT Support Requirements of Order Placing and Filling

Learning Objective

4.2 Understand the IT support requirements of order placing and filling, including: order entry (agency, principal and third party orders); pre-trade compliance; best execution; Treating Customers Fairly; transaction capture; client connectivity including Direct Market Access; communication via electronic media; pooling, allocation, and aggregation of a single order across two or more investors/funds; dealing systems; charges, fees and expenses

3.1 Order Placing

3.1.1 Parties to an Order

The parties to an order consist of:

- **Investors and buy-side firms** – investors include pension funds, insurance companies, fund management groups, charities and trusts (professional investors), as well as private individuals.

Most professional investors have delegated their investment decisions to fund managers or buy-side firms. Before the buy-side firm places an order on behalf of its customer, it needs to ensure that the order is compatible with the customer's investment objectives. This is known as **pre-trade compliance**. For example, the buy-side firm needs to ensure that the order matches the investor's time horizons, risk appetite and ethical or other considerations that the investor has made the firm aware of.

- **Sell-side firms** – buy-side firms and private individuals place orders with banks and stock exchange member firms (sell-side firms), and the sell-side firms, in turn, fill those orders.

3.1.2 Contents of an Order

An order contains a number of features such as:

- Buy or sell – a specific quantity of a specific financial instrument, such as an equity, bond, currency or derivative, as well as a number of instructions relating to the price of that instrument, such as:
  - **at best** or **at market** – meaning buy or sell at the best available price the member firm can obtain at the time;
  - **limit** – where a price is specified, meaning:
    - if selling, do not sell for a price lower than the limit price;
    - if buying, do not pay more than the limit price.
  - **stop loss** – sell if and when the market price falls to this level.
- Time-related features:
  - **good till cancelled** or **open order** – there is no time limit on this order.
  - **expiry date** – if the order cannot be filled by this date then it should be treated as cancelled.
  - **fill or kill** – if the order is, say, to buy 10,000 shares of ABC plc, then either complete the order in full or reject it if the member firm can only obtain, say, 5,000 shares.

3.1.3 Client Connectivity

Orders may be placed by the buy-side (and, therefore, received at the sell-side) by a number of methods, including by:

- telephone and/or fax;
- entering the order details into a secure web page provided by the sell-side firm;
- sending the sell-side firm a SWIFT message. SWIFT is covered more fully in Chapter 6, Section 5;
- entering the order details directly into the sell-side firm's order management system. Typically, this would be facilitated by using a third party 'hub and spoke' order-routing service. Providers of such services include:
  - Omgeo, through its Trade Suite Product;
  - Thomson Reuters, through its Autex and other products;
  - Bloomberg, through its POMS and TOMS systems;
  - many other package products and systems developed in-house by fund managers.

Many of these systems, in turn, make use of the FIX protocol, a messaging standard developed specifically for the real-time electronic exchange of securities transactions. FIX is a public-domain specification owned and maintained by FIX protocol Ltd. FIX is covered more fully in Chapter 6.

Also see Section 4.3 for information on automated order-routing (Direct Market Access).

3.2   Filling the Order

3.2.1   Agency Orders and Principal Orders

The sell-side firm has to decide whether to fill this order as agent or as principal. It has to make its decision according to the MiFID rules explained in Chapter 2.

If it is filling the order as agent, then it will forward the order to an investment exchange and charge the investor a **commission**.

If it is filling it as **principal**, then it will not forward the order to an exchange, but it will (assuming the order is to buy) sell the investor the required quantity of the instrument from its own 'book' or position, ie, it will sell the investor stock that is owned by the sell-side firm. The opposite is true if the order is to sell: the sell-side firm will buy the stock from the investor and add it to its own position or book. In the case of principal orders, the sell-side firm's revenue consists of the **difference between the buying price and the selling price**, instead of a commission.

Whether the sell-side firms act as agent or principal when they fill customers' orders varies according to the type of financial instrument that is being traded. Here is a brief summary of the most usual market practices:

- **Bonds** – usually, the sell-side firm acts as principal. Traditionally, the sell-side firm that received the order would contact several market makers (other sell-side firms that specialise in making a market in the given bond) by telephone to find the best price available to its client. In recent years, a number of internet-based trading systems have set up that provide a more formal market for these instruments.
- **Futures and options** – the sell-side firm always acts as agent. Futures and options are always traded on investment exchanges and each individual futures or options contract is unique to one exchange. Therefore, client orders are always submitted to an order queue such as the LIFFE UTP system.
- **Foreign exchange** – usually, the sell-side firm acts as principal. Traditionally, this has been a telephone market where the firm that received the order would phone other banks to establish the best rate. In recent years a number of FX web portals have been developed. Thomson Reuters also offers an automated dealing service, Thomson Reuters Dealing Direct.
- **OTC derivatives such as swaps** – usually, the sell-side firm acts as principal. Traditionally, this has been a telephone market where the firm that received the order would phone other banks to establish the best rate. In recent years a number of FX web portals have been developed.
- **Equities** – the sell-side firm may act as agent or principal. Its activities are governed by the regulatory rules and also by individual client agreements.

No matter whether the sell-side firm is acting as agent or principal, it has to fulfil obligations to its customer in terms of best execution (see Section 3.2.2) and Treating Customers Fairly (see Section 3.2.3).

3.2.2   Best Execution

Investment firms have a duty under the MiFID rules to provide their clients with **best execution**. Best execution rules have existed for many years, but their scope changed as a result of the implementation of MiFID in November 2007.

The FCA Conduct of Business Rule 11.2.1 defines best execution as follows: *'A firm must take all reasonable steps to obtain, when executing orders, the best possible result for its clients taking into account the execution factors.'*

The execution factors are then defined as: *'Price, costs, speed, likelihood of execution and settlement, size, nature or any other consideration relevant to the execution of an order.'*

MiFID Requirements

As stated in Chapter 2, the MiFID regulations (Article 21) require firms that execute orders on behalf of clients to:

1. establish an execution policy, which must contain information on the venues used to execute client orders – those venues must allow it to obtain consistently the best possible result for execution for their clients;
2. disclose the policy to clients and obtain their consent to that policy;
3. monitor the effectiveness of arrangements in order to identify and correct any deficiencies and review the appropriateness of the venues in its execution policy at least yearly; and
4. upon client request, be ready to demonstrate that the client's order has been executed in line with their execution policy.

These MiFID requirements have been implemented by the FCA within Conduct of Business Rules (COBS) 11.2.14 to 11.2.18 inclusive.

The practical implication of these rules is as follows:

1. Firms must always execute orders from the same types of customers (retail, professional, market counterparty, etc) for the same type of instrument (equities, bonds, futures, etc) in the same way, according to a predefined policy that the firm considers should provide the customer with best execution.
2. Firms must tell the customer what the policy is, and obtain their consent to it.
3. Firms must check that the policy they have defined is usually achieving best execution. If they find that in certain circumstances it is not, then they must amend it. They must carry out these monitoring and (if necessary) amendment processes at least once each year.

If the client requests it, the firm must provide the client with evidence that a particular order has been executed in line with its defined policy.

Practical Implications

Broadly speaking, best execution places an obligation on the sell-side firm to get the lowest available price for its customer when the customer is buying, and the highest available price when the customer is selling.

If a financial instrument is quoted on only one investment exchange, and that exchange trades it on an order-driven system, then this obligation is usually fulfilled simply by placing an order on the order queue. The exchange's own systems will then match it with an opposite order appropriately.

There are situations, however, where the sell-side firm needs to take more care and use more skill in handling the order. For example:

1. **When the order is very large** – if the order is to buy or sell a very large amount of stock, then simply placing the entire order on the order queue in one operation will have the effect of moving the price adversely. In such a situation the sell-side firm has two alternatives.
    a. It could split the order up into smaller parcels and feed it on to the order book over a few days. This may, however, delay execution.
    b. It could (if the order was to sell) purchase the stock from the investor as a principal transaction, and dispose of the stock that it now owns over a few days. If it does this, it needs to be able to prove that the price it charged the investor was not lower than the prevailing order book price at the time. If the order was to buy, then it could sell the stock to the investor as a principal transaction, and purchase the stock that it is now obliged to deliver over a few days. If it does this it needs to be able to prove that the price paid by the investor was not higher than the prevailing order book price at the time.

3. **When the instrument is quoted on more than one exchange** – the shares of large multinational companies are often quoted on many stock exchanges. The main market for Sony Corporation shares, for example, is the Tokyo Stock Exchange (where Sony shares are priced in JPY), but Sony shares are also quoted on the LSE (both in JPY and GBP), the New York Stock Exchange (in USD) and on Deutsche Börse (in EUR). In such a case, a sell-side firm that has access to all of these exchanges should research the prevailing price levels on all of them to establish the most favourable price for the client. However, the two parties have also to take into account some other factors when deciding which exchange to route the order to.
    a. Tokyo is the main market where most of the trades take place. There might be less liquidity in the other markets, meaning that:
        –   the less liquid markets do not usually offer the best prices, and
        –   the order might take longer to fill on one of the less liquid markets.
    b. On the other hand, say the investor is located in the US, and has requested execution today. By the start of the working day in the US, the Tokyo market has already closed and therefore execution today is not possible. The NYSE will be open, however; the European exchanges may also still be open.
    c. The customer might want to pay for Sony shares in JPY. Because Deutsche Börse prices Sony shares in EUR and the NYSE prices them in USD, there would be additional foreign exchange transaction costs and risk in trading in New York or Frankfurt.
    d. It is possible that the sell-side firm that receives the order is not, itself, a member of the exchange that is offering the best price and the most liquid market. For example, not all London-based firms are members of the Tokyo Stock Exchange. If this is the case, then a London firm might have to use another broker in Tokyo to place the order on its behalf. This would involve two lots of brokers' commission, which could invalidate the price advantage if it was very slight to begin with.

3.2.3 Treating Customers Fairly

The above examples show that there can be a practical conflict between **best execution** and **execution at the best price**. The final rule that the sell-side firm needs to take into account is **Treating Customers Fairly**. This rule exists because of the possibilities of conflict of interest between the sell-side firm and the investor.

For example, a sell-side firm may wish to invest its own capital in purchasing Sony shares. At the same time, the firm has a client that wishes to sell a large quantity of Sony shares. If a large sell order hits the market before the buy orders, it could have the effect of moving the price in the sell-side firm's favour. The firm has to manage its order execution process paying special attention to two of the FCA's Principles for Businesses that were first examined in Chapter 2:

- **Principle 6** (customers' interests) requires a firm to pay due regard to the interests of its customers and to treat them fairly.
- **Principle 8** (conflicts of interest) requires a firm to manage conflicts of interest fairly.

Note that the regulatory rules do not prescribe the method by which the sell-side firm manages conflicts of interest. How this, or any other, conflict of interest is managed is up to the firm concerned. However, the firm has to be able to demonstrate that it is managing this conflict in accordance with FCA Principles 6 and 8.

3.3 Pooling and Allocation

3.3.1 Order Flow Steps

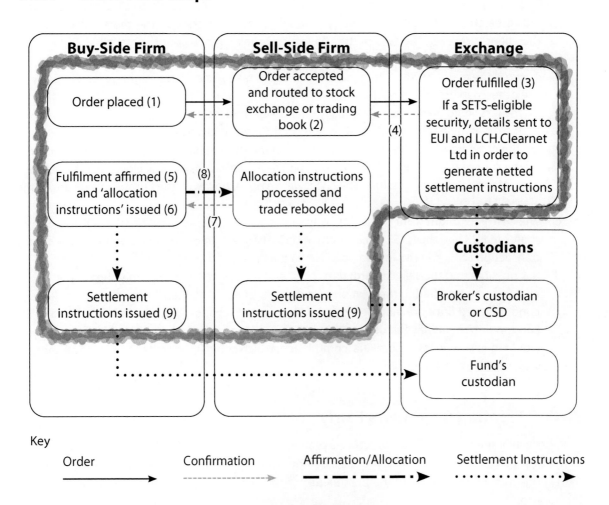

(The parts of this diagram that are covered in this chapter are circled.)

1. The **fund manager** sends the order to the sell-side firm.
2. The **sell-side firm** acknowledges it and makes a decision as to how to execute it, ie, whether to fill it by placing it with an investment exchange or MTF, which exchange to route it to if there is a choice of exchanges, or whether to fill it by buying and selling from its own book.
3. The **sell-side firm** then executes it, either as a single transaction or, if the order is for a large amount, by breaking it down into smaller amounts.
4. When the **sell-side firm** has completed the order, it sends a confirmation to the fund manager. The confirmation will include, *inter alia*, details of:
   - the name of the client for whom the order was executed;
   - the name of the stock and whether it was bought or sold;
   - the trade date of the purchase or sale;
   - the value date of the purchase or sale;
   - the price of the trade – if the order was split into more than one order on an order queue this will be the average price of all the executed orders;
   - the net amount to be paid or received by the investor, including any fees and charges and, for a bond sale, any amount of accrued interest on the deal;
   - whether the firm acted as agent or principal; and
   - if it acted as agent, the name of the exchange that the deal was executed on.
5. The **fund manager** then checks the confirmation received from the sell-side firm. If it disagrees with the details, it takes the matter up with the sell-side firm, otherwise it is said to **affirm** the confirmation.
6. At the same time that the **fund manager** affirms, it also advises the sell-side firm of the **allocation details** of this order. The fund manager itself has placed this order on behalf of its own clients (or funds) – there may be just one of them or there may be many. At this stage the fund manager notifies the sell-side firm of the details of who its clients are and how many shares are to be allocated to each client.
7. The **sell-side firm** then splits the **parent** trade into a number of **child** trades, one for each fund, and re-confirms the allocations to the fund manager. The confirmation repeats the information in the original confirmation of the 'parent' trade (point 4 above).
8. The **fund manager** then re-affirms each of the individual fund transactions.
9. Both the fund manager and the sell-side firm then issue **settlement instructions** to their custodians.

All of these communications may be automated in the same way that the original order was automated, ie, the confirmations, affirmations and allocations may be transmitted by any of the following methods:

- by telephone or fax;
- by entering the information into a secure web page provided by the sell-side firm;
- by exchanging SWIFT messages;
- by entering the affirmation and allocation details directly into the sell-side firm's order management system. Typically, this would be facilitated by using a third party 'hub and spoke' order routing service, which in turn probably involves exchanging FIX protocol messages.

The following diagram shows how this is achieved using the **Omgeo Central Trade Manager** service provided by Thomson Reuters and DTCC:

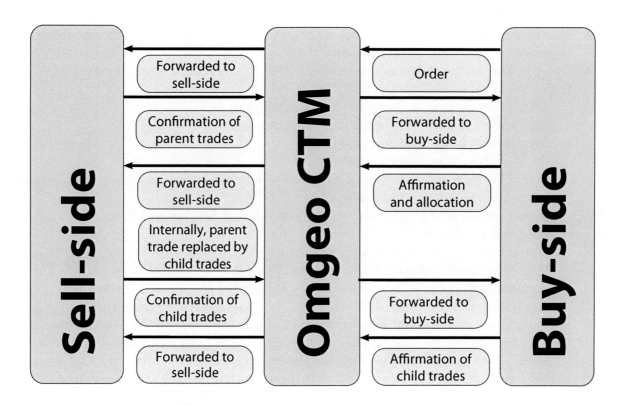

One of the key components at the heart of most STP solutions in the financial markets is the ability to exchange trade information with counterparties electronically. This basic need has driven the development of a number of **Electronic Trade Confirmation (ETC)** initiatives over the years. One of the most successful of these has been the Omgeo Central Trade Manager system, developed, maintained and operated by Thomson Reuters, now known as **Omgeo**. With several thousand installed users worldwide, Omgeo Central Trade Manager is at present the *de facto* standard for trade communication between broker and institution, making it a common element of integration and STP projects in the equity broking and fund management communities.

3.3.2   Order Flow Examples

The following are examples of three executed orders. Each example shows:

1. the trade computations;
2. the data flows between the buy-side and sell-side firms, and where applicable the exchange;
3. the decisions that the sell-side firm took to ensure best execution.

Example – Simple Agency Trade

1. On 20 February 2012 XYZ Fund Managers plc submits an order to ABC Investment Bank plc to sell 10,000 shares in HBOS plc 'at best'. This order is on behalf of XYZ's customer, the QRS Pension Fund.
2. The main market for HBOS shares is the LSE; and on a typical LSE trading day the daily turnover in HBOS shares is over five million shares. ABC, therefore, decides that placing this order on the SETS queue will ensure best execution, and that there is no danger of a single order of this size affecting the SETS price.
3. SETS matches the order to sell at a price of £11.69 per share. ABC charges XYZ 0.75% commission on this deal. The amount that XYZ's investor will receive on value date 23 February 2012 is, therefore:

Principal Amount		
£11.69 x 10,000 shares		£116,900.00
Less ABC's commission	0.75% of principal amount	−£876.75
Net proceeds payable to investor		£116,023.25

4. The steps involved between XYZ and ABC are as follows – all events take place on 20 February:
   a. XYZ submits the order;
   b. ABC places it on the SETS queue where it is matched and ABC is informed;
   c. ABC sends a confirmation to XYZ confirming that it has sold 10,000 HBOS plc on the London Stock Exchange at £11.69 per share, and giving details of the commission due and net proceeds payable to the investor on 23 February 2012;
   d. XYZ affirms this trade, and gives allocation details to ABC disclosing the identity of the investor – the QRS Pension Fund;
   e. ABC re-books the trade in the name of QRS Pension Fund, and re-confirms to XYZ;
   f. XYZ re-affirms the child trade.

Example – More Complex Agency Trade

DEF Investment Managers invests in the Asia-Pacific markets on behalf of a number of clients. On 20 February 2012 it submits an order to ABC Investment Bank plc to purchase one million shares in Sony Corporation at a maximum price of JPY6,725 per share: good till cancelled.

ABC Investment Bank is a member of all the world's major stock exchanges, including the Tokyo market. It investigates the prices available on the Tokyo exchange, LSE, NYSE and Deutsche Börse, and decides that only Tokyo has enough liquidity to handle an order of this size, taking best execution into account.

ABC finds that the turnover on Sony shares on the Tokyo exchange the previous day was 3,205,700 shares. It therefore divides the order into ten parcels of 100,000 shares each, and feeds them on to the Tokyo exchange's order queue over two days.

The trades are matched on the TSE's order queue as follows:

Trade date of match	Value date	Qty of shares	Share price in JPY	Principal amount in JPY
20 February	23 February	100,000	6,250	625,000,000
20 February	23 February	100,000	6,500	650,000,000
20 February	23 February	100,000	6,600	660,000,000
20 February	23 February	100,000	6,400	640,000,000
20 February	23 February	100,000	6,500	650,000,000
Total fulfilment – trade date 20 February		**500,000**	**(average) 6,450**	**3,225,000,000**
21 February	24 February	100,000	6,725	672,500,000
21 February	24 February	100,000	6,720	672.000,000
21 February	24 February	100,000	6,600	660,000,000
21 February	24 February	100,000	6,650	665,000,000
21 February	24 February	100,000	6,725	672,500,000
Total fulfilment – trade date 20 February		**500,000**	**(average) 6,684**	**3,342,000,000**

The steps involved between DEF and ABC are, therefore, as follows:

a. 20 February – DEF submits the order.
b. 20 February – at various times throughout the day, ABC places five lots of 100,000 on the TSE queue, each of which is matched and ABC is informed.
c. 20 February – ABC sends a confirmation to DEF confirming that it has bought 500,000 Sony Corp on the Tokyo Stock Exchange at JPY6,450 per share, and giving details of the commission due and net proceeds payable by the investor on 23 February 2012.
d. 20 February – DEF affirms this trade, and gives allocation details to ABC disclosing the identity of five investors – each of whom will receive and pay for 100,000 shares.
e. 20 February – ABC re-books the trade in the names of the five investors and re-confirms to DEF.
f. 20 February – DEF re-affirms the five child trades.
g. 21 February – ABC continues to 'work the order' at various times throughout the day, ABC places an additional five lots of 100,000 on the TSE queue, each of which is matched and ABC is informed.
h. 21 February – ABC sends a confirmation to DEF confirming that it has bought 500,000 Sony Corp on the Tokyo Stock Exchange at JPY6,684 per share, and giving details of the commission due and net proceeds payable by the investor on 24 February 2012.
i. 21 February – DEF affirms this trade, and gives allocation details to ABC disclosing the identity of five investors – each of whom will receive and pay for 100,000 shares.
j. 21 February – ABC re-books the trade in the names of the five investors, and re-confirms to DEF.
k. 21 February – DEF re-affirms the five child trades of today.

Example – Principal Trade

Orders to buy and sell corporate bonds are usually handled by the receiver as principal trades. On 20 February, XYZ Fund Managers places an order with ABC Investment Bank to buy $1,000,000 nominal (face value) of Ford Motor Co 4% bond maturing 23 August 2015. ABC determines that the best price available is from Megabank plc. As there are no other relevant execution factors in this case, best execution is achieved as a result of best price. Megabank makes a market in this bond, and is prepared to offer it to ABC at a price of 98% of face value. ABC accepts this offer and in turn sells it on to XYZ at 98.0625% of face value.

ABC issues confirmations to both Megabank and XYZ. The salient details of both confirmations are as follows:

ABC's confirmation to Megabank:

> Trade date: 20 February 2012
>
> Value date: 23 February 2012

We confirm our PURCHASE from you of:

USD1,000,000 Ford Motor Co 4% 23-8-2015 @ 98%	980,000.00
182 days' accrued interest	20,222.22
Total amount	1,000,222.22

ABC's confirmation to XYZ:

> Trade date: 20 February 2012
>
> Value date: 23 February 2012

We confirm our SALE to you of:

USD1,000,000 Ford Motor Co 4% 23-8-2015 @ 98.0625%	980,625.00
182 days' accrued interest	20,222.22
Total amount	1,000,847.22

ABC does not charge XYZ any commission on the deal. Its reward is the difference between the buying price of 98% and the selling price of 98.0625%: USD625.00.

3.4 Dealing Systems

3.4.1 Introduction

Both the buy-side firm and the sell-side firm need to use dealing systems to manage the processes of placing/taking orders, fulfilling them and dealing with the trade agreement, ie, the processes of confirmation, affirmation and allocation.

Dealing systems are 'mission-critical systems' where high availability and the ability to handle occasional surges in volume without degraded response times and/or other forms of system instability are essential requirements. If a dealing system is not available at times when markets are under pressure, then opportunities to deal may be lost, and the sell-side firm in particular may very well be unable to fulfil its obligations for best execution.

The usual **settlement cycle** (the difference between trade date and value date) in the **equity markets** is **three days**. Sometimes equity deals are carried out with special value dates that involve shorter periods. In some **government bond markets**, trade date and value date are often the **same day or only one working day later**. Therefore, the process of communication between the buy-side and sell-side firms needs to be highly automated. The dealing system is an essential part of both firms' STP strategy.

The functionality required of a dealing system by a buy-side firm is slightly different from that required of a sell-side firm. The buy-side firm is the customer, and the sell-side firm is the supplier.

Brokers compete on service levels. For simple agency trades many brokers can deliver the best price, so the level of service that they offer in terms of speed and efficiency of notification of execution, and their ability to facilitate STP for their customers, is an important differentiator. This means that sell-side firms need to provide whatever forms of connectivity their customers require. As not all customers' requirements are the same, this means that they must offer a wide variety of connections, and this increases the complexity of the configuration.

3.4.2 Buy-Side Dealing Systems

The actual functions required of a dealing system by any one fund manager will depend on the size of the firm and the range of investments and markets it trades in. The main capabilities of a typical dealing system for firms of this type usually include:

1. **STP compliance** – the system design should observe the principles of STP that were dealt with in Chapter 1.
2. **MiFID compliance** – users need to be able to provide the system with details of execution policies for different combinations of instrument types and client types (see Section 3.2), and the system then needs to use these policies to route orders to the appropriate execution venue.
3. **Support for investment decision-taking** – including portfolio modelling and 'what-if' scenario analysis: comparing portfolios to a model, generating proposed trades and examining their impact on portfolios and cash balances. This may involve the ability to integrate in-house data with external data supplied by Thomson Reuters, Bloomberg and others. Buy-side firms that deal with the private investor, in particular, need systems with facilities that can assess the impact of a particular potential trade on the client's income tax and capital gains tax liability.
4. **Support for all security types that the firm invests in** – this may include equities, bonds, futures, options and other derivatives, foreign exchange and money market instruments.
5. **Multi-currency capabilities** – the ability to track currencies at the system, portfolio and securities level, and to settle trades and report in any currency. Full European Monetary Union (EMU) support is required, plus automatic currency conversions when a fund that is denominated in one currency is settling trades in another currency.

6. **Customer reporting** – one of the ways that fund managers compete with one another when they are attracting business from large investing institutions is in the quality and flexibility of the reports that they can provide for these institutions. Many systems offer the ability to store, extract, calculate and present information in any way that clients or prospective clients need. Reports may be delivered on paper or via a client intranet, and firms usually require the ability to create their own report formats with TrueType fonts, define customised data fields, and specify unique calculations for reporting or analysis. Many firms will use dedicated report-writing applications to produce the reports themselves, but these applications have to extract the raw data from the dealing system. It is therefore important to be able to access the dealing system database using SQL (structured query language, see Chapter 8, Section 1.2.4) and web technologies.

7. **Performance measurement** – fund managers and their customers need to know how the fund has performed compared to benchmarks, and compared to prior periods. Most fund management systems will offer a comprehensive performance measurement suite with such features as daily performance, customised segmentation by portfolio, currency versus market performance and individual security level performance reports.

8. **Income and capital gains tax computation facilities** – firms that deal with the private investor in particular need facilities that can perform these calculations for clients.

9. **Broker connectivity and STP facilities** – fund manager dealing systems need to be able to issue orders to sell-side firms, receive automated confirmations from the sell-side and respond to confirmations with automated affirmations and allocations. If the buy-side firm is considering buying these facilities off-the-shelf from software and 'store and forward' network vendors (see Chapter 6, Section 5.3.3), then there are a large number to choose from. For larger firms, automated connectivity between their dealing systems and the dealing systems of the sell-side firms that they deal with may be established in any of the following ways:

   a. by sending a SWIFT message to the firms concerned;
   b. by sending a FIX protocol message to the firms concerned; often this will be sent to a central trade order management system such as OASYS – refer to the diagram at the end of Section 3.3.1.

3. **Support for algorithmic trading** – both by the firm on its own account, and also by its clients. Enabling clients to trade using these techniques may also imply providing them with direct market access. These terms are explained in Section 4.

4. **The ability to receive real-time market data feeds**.

3.4.3　Sell-Side Dealing Systems

Again, the actual functions required of a dealing system by any one sell-side firm will depend on the size of the firm and the range of investments and markets it trades in. The main functions of a typical dealing system for firms that deal in equities and bonds usually include:

1. **STP compliance** – the system design should observe the principles of STP that were dealt with in Chapter 1.
2. **MiFID compliance** – users need to be able to provide the system with details of execution policies for different combinations of instrument types and client types (see Section 3.2), and the system then needs to use these policies to route orders to the appropriate execution venue.
3. **Support for all security types that the firm invests in** – this may include equities, bonds, futures, options and other derivatives, foreign exchange and money market instruments.
4. **Multi-currency capabilities** – the ability to track currencies at the system, portfolio, and security level, and to settle trades and report in any currency. Full EMU support is required, plus automatic currency conversions when a fund that is denominated in one currency is settling trades in another currency.
5. **Connectivity to exchanges** – the system needs to supply connectivity to the order-driven and quote-driven trading systems of all the exchanges of which the firm is a member.

6. **Connectivity with buy-side clients** – the system needs to offer customers many forms of connectivity to manage their order flow and deal with the various stages of trade agreement. This may mean offering a very large number of options – as many options as the customer base requires. The system needs to be able to communicate with customers using the FIX and SWIFT message protocols; it also needs to communicate with customers using order management networks such as Omgeo Central Trade Manager and Autex. Some large clients may demand communication via email (including Excel or other attachments) web browser and secure FTP file transfer.

7. **Commission and charges calculation** – the system needs to be able to calculate commissions and other charges. As you will see from Section 3.5, there are many commission calculation methods, so the system requires considerable flexibility in this area. Once the commission has been calculated, firms need to be able to extract management information from the dealing system about their commission income, so that they can see who are their most/least profitable clients, exchanges, instrument types etc.

8. **Support for the trading book and ability to mark-to-market** (see Section 5.2.1) – for firms that trade as principal, the system needs to be able to keep a record of the firm's position in each instrument and the historic prices of each transaction in each instrument, and to be able to calculate both the realised and unrealised profit and loss on each instrument. This activity is covered in more detail in Section 5.2.

9. **Support for algorithmic trading** – if the firm's investment strategy employs this process. Algorithmic trading is the placing of buy or sell orders of a defined quantity into a quantitative model that automatically generates the timing of orders and the size of orders based on goals specified by the parameters and constraints of the algorithm. See Section 4.

3.5   Charges, Fees and Expenses

The investor has to pay commission and possibly other charges for each trade.

3.5.1   Commission and Commission Calculation Methods

The common methods of calculating commissions are as follows:

- **Flat fee** – this method is used by many 'execution-only' stockbrokers that serve the private investor. For each trade there will be a fee of £x, no matter how large or small the value of the trade.
- **Percentage** – this method is used for many equity transactions involving professional investors. The fee is x% of the value of the trade.
- **Basis points** – this method is used in some bond and OTC derivative transactions. A basis point (bp) is a unit that is equal to 1/100th of 1%; in this context commission is expressed as x basis points per one million nominal of face value (of the underlying instrument in the case of a derivative). For example, if the client is buying or selling $1,000,000 nominal of a corporate bond, and the commission is expressed as 'five basis points per million', then the commission that applied to the trade would be 0.05% of the face value bought or sold, ie, $500.00.
- **Per unit** – this method is widely used for futures and options contracts. The exchange concerned specifies, for each contract, how many units of the underlying instrument are referenced to 'one lot' of the derivative. The commission is, therefore, expressed as '£x per lot'.
- **Sliding scale** – a sliding scale may be applied to commissions that are based on percentages or basis points. The percentage reduces according to the size of the individual order. For example:
  ○ *commission = 1% on individual orders with value below £50,000;*
  ○ *commission = 0.85% on individual orders with value between £50,001 and £100,000;*
  ○ *commission = 0.75% on individual orders with value between £100,001 and £150,000.*
  Note that the size of the order, not the execution, determines the scale.

- **Reducing scale** – again, the commission rate reduces for clients that place large amounts of business with the firm. However, using this method, the cumulative value of the orders that the client has placed over a period of time is added together, and the commission is calculated according to the commission rate that applies to the total value of orders executed during the period, which is then multiplied by the cumulative value of those orders.

3.5.2 Commission Sharing

Under certain circumstances, commission may be charged by more than one broker. There are two reasons why this may be the case:

1. **Cross border trading** – in the case where a fund manager gives an order to a broker in one country and that broker decides that 'best execution' requires the order to be handled by an exchange in another country, if that broker is not a member of the overseas exchange it might appoint a local broker to act on its behalf. In such a case, both brokers would charge commission.
2. **Split services** – research and execution – the services that the sell-side supplies to the buy-side can be divided into investment research (advising buy-side firms which sectors and individual securities to invest in/divest from); and execution (getting the best price for the investor). There are some sell-side 'research boutiques' that are able to provide the research services but which may not have the market presence to get best prices. In such a case the buy-side firm may act on a research recommendation by one firm but place the order with another firm, instructing them to share the commission according to an agreed formula.

3.5.3 Other Fees and Expenses

Depending on which country the trade was executed in, and what type of financial instrument is being traded, there may be other charges or taxes. In the UK equity markets, the following apply:

Stamp Duty Reserve Tax

SDRT is a tax payable by buyers (but not sellers) of most equity shares. The current rate is 0.5%. It is payable by any individual or corporation that is purchasing:

- shares in a company that is incorporated in the UK;
- shares in a foreign company that maintains a share register in the UK;
- options to buy shares as defined above;
- rights arising from shares as defined above, such as the rights under a rights issue.

Stamp Duty

Stamp duty is a tax that is paid by the final investor, so trades between stock exchange member firms are exempt from stamp duty. The dealing system database, therefore, needs to contain information about:

- which individual instruments stamp duty applies to; and
- which individual trade types and counterparties it applies to.

In recent years, professional investors have successfully found many ways of gaining the benefits of investing in UK-listed equities without the need to pay stamp duty. They are able to do this by investing in derivative instruments that are themselves based on underlying equities. In particular, investment in the following asset classes enables investors to gain some of the benefits of investment in the underlying instrument without a change of ownership:

• Listed futures and options, both on individual equities and equity indexes, such as the FTSE 100 index.
• Contracts for difference (CFDs). A CFD is an agreement between two parties to exchange the difference between the opening (today) value and the closing (at a future date) value of a particular asset (normally a share). These are generally short-term contracts drawn up by both involved parties. The firm's exposure to default by its client is controlled by margin requirements and collateral deposits. A number of online stockbrokers offer CFD trading services both to professional investors and private individuals.

PTM Levy

A charge automatically imposed on investors, and collected by their brokers, when they sell or buy shares with an aggregate value in excess of £10,000. The charge is £1, and the money raised goes to the Panel of Takeovers and Mergers (PTM). The Panel writes and enforces the rules by which takeovers of companies listed on the LSE are conducted.

4. Algorithmic Trading

Learning Objective

4.3   Understand the purpose and consequences of algorithmic trading

4.1   Definition

Algorithmic trading is the use of computer programs for entering orders where the computer algorithm decides on aspects of the order such as the timing, price, or quantity, or in many cases initiates the order without human intervention.

Algorithmic trading is widely used by fund managers to divide large trades into several smaller trades in order to manage market impact and risk. Sell-side traders, and some hedge funds, provide liquidity to the market, generating and executing orders automatically.

A special class of algorithmic trading is **high-frequency trading (HFT)**, in which computers make complex decisions to initiate orders based on information that has been received and processed electronically, before human traders would have had the time to process this information. This has resulted in a dramatic change of the market behaviour, particularly in the way liquidity is provided.

Algorithmic trading may be used in any investment strategy, including market making, inter-market spreading, arbitrage, or pure speculation.

4.2   The Growth of Algorithmic Trading

According to a survey published by Boston-based research firm Aite Group, about third of all EU and US stock trades in 2006 were driven by automatic programs, or algorithms. In 2009, HFT firms accounted for 73% of all US equity trading volume.

By 2011, about 60% of all orders at the London Stock Exchange were entered by algo traders. American and European markets generally have a higher proportion of algo trades than other markets, and current estimates for the USA exchanges range between 50% and 80% of total trading. Foreign exchange markets also have active algo trading (about 25% of orders in 2006). Futures and options markets are considered to be fairly easily integrated into algorithmic trading, with about 20% of options volume believed to be computer-generated in 2010.

4.3   Problems and Concerns

Algorithmic and high-frequency trades have been the subject of much public debate since the US Securities and Exchange Commission (SEC) and the Commodity Futures Trading Commission implicated them in the 6 May 2010 'Flash Crash'. At 2.45pm on that day, the Dow Jones Industrial Average plunged about 900 points – about 9% – only to recover those losses within minutes. It was the second-largest point swing, and the biggest one-day point decline, in the history of the DJIA. Some of the individual price movements during the few minutes of the flash crash were bizarre. Shares of some prominent companies like Procter & Gamble and Accenture were trading as low as a penny or as high as $100,000.

The joint report *'portrayed a market so fragmented and fragile that a single large trade could send stocks into a sudden spiral'*. It explained how a large mutual fund that sold an unusually large number (75,000 contracts, worth $4.1 billion) of E-Mini S&P 500 contracts (a stock market index future traded on the Chicago Mercantile Exchange) first of all exhausted available buyers. This was followed by high-frequency traders who started aggressively selling, accelerating the effect of the mutual fund's selling and contributing to the sharp price declines that day.

The regulators found that high-frequency traders exacerbated price declines as they sold aggressively to eliminate their long positions and as they withdrew from the markets in the face of uncertainty.

4.3.1   Proposed Remedies

NYSE officials announced that new trading curbs, also known as **circuit-breakers**, would be tested during 2010. These circuit-breakers would halt trading for five minutes on any S&P 500 stock that rises or falls more than 10% in a five-minute period.

In September 2011, the *Financial Times* reported that some European exchanges had been contacted by their regulators, who were concerned that those exchanges' fee structures offered 'inappropriate incentives' to high-volume traders. European regulator ESMA, which is responsible for MiFID II, has considered whether exchange fees should be harmonised across Europe to prevent these kinds of incentives, but as yet has not reached such a decision.

4.3.2 Recent developments

Following the publication of Michael Lewis' book *'Flash Boys: A Wall Street Revolt'* (March 2014), the Federal Bureau of Investigation (FBI) opened an investigation into US stock exchanges and other trading platforms to determine whether certain services they provide give high-speed traders an unfair advantage. In particular, the FBI is examining whether contracts between exchanges and HFT trading firms allows these firms to place computer servers inside (or very near to) exchanges and gain access to extra bandwidth to speed up their access to information, such as prices and volume, giving HFT clients an unfair timing advantage – often in milliseconds – which allows them to make rapid and often risk-free trades before the rest of the market can react.

4.4 How Sell-Side Firms Provide Algorithmic Trading to their Clients

The mechanism that is used is known as **Direct Market Access**, or **DMA**. DMA is defined as the automated process of routing a securities order directly to an execution venue, thereby avoiding intervention by a third party. Execution venues include exchanges, alternative trading systems and electronic communication networks. To simplify, DMA enables the buy-side firm or investor to place orders directly on to the order queues of investment exchanges, avoiding the need to submit the order to an exchange member firm in the traditional manner.

If an investor is using algorithmic trading technology, then the timing of the order to the second is critical. Conventional order flow techniques are simply too slow to have the desired result. In addition, DMA is a more anonymous way of trading – it allows hedge funds, in particular, to offload large quantities of stock without tipping off the market.

5. Trade Capture and Risk Management for Front Office Functions

Learning Objective

4.4 Understand the basic IT characteristics of risk mitigation for the following front office functions: risk management; transaction capture; best execution

5.1 Risk Management

Fund managers (acting on behalf of investors), investors themselves and sell-side firms all have dealings with counterparties and clients, and all investors and some sell-side firms hold positions in financial instruments. As such, they are exposed to various forms of risk:

* credit risk – also known as counterparty risk;
* market risk – also known as position risk;
* operational risk.

In Chapter 2, we learned that:

$$\text{Capital ratio} = \frac{\text{Capital requirement}}{\text{(Credit risk exposure + market risk exposure + operational risk exposure)}}$$

Operational risk was examined in Chapter 2 and will also be further discussed in Chapters 8 and 9. In this chapter we shall now look at the first two risk elements – credit risk and market risk – more deeply in the context of IT in the front office.

5.1.1 Credit Risk

Credit risk is the risk associated with one party not fulfilling its contractual obligations to another party at a specific future date. In practical terms, this is likely to mean that there is the possibility of one or more of the following events occurring on a future date:

- An investor client or a trading counterparty may not be in a position to pay for a security purchase by the client or deliver securities to fulfil its obligations in respect of an agreed sale by the client on value date.

  This particular risk is normally mitigated by the central securities depository arranging simultaneous delivery-versus-payment settlement of the trade – refer to Chapter 3, Section 3. In addition, trades between exchange members (but not their clients) that are executed through an order-driven market are novated by a central counterparty.

- The counterparty for a futures, options or other derivative contract is unable to meet its obligations to make payments or deliveries under the terms of that contract at a future date.

  For exchange-traded derivatives, this risk is always mitigated by the presence of the central counterparty. For OTC derivatives, there may be no central counterparty to the trades, so each party remains exposed to this risk. CCPs do now offer specialised services to novate OTC derivatives contracts, but not all potential parties will take advantage of these services.

- The issuer of a bond is unable to meet its obligations to pay interest or redemption proceeds on the due date.

  There are no securities industry facilities equivalent to delivery-versus-payment or novation by a CCP to mitigate such risk. If such an event occurs, then the holder of the bond or equity concerned remains exposed to this risk.

5.1.2 Market Risk

This is the risk that the value of the investments owned by the investor might decline. There are a number of reasons why this may occur, including:

1. a general fall in the prices of most classes of instrument caused by global economic or political uncertainty;
2. a fall in the prices of shares issued by companies in a particular industry, caused by a poor economic outlook for that particular industry, or a fall in the prices of shares listed in a particular country because of economic or political uncertainty in that country;
3. a rise in interest rates for a particular currency (or, indeed, all currencies). This would cause a fall in bond prices because, for fixed income securities, market risk is closely tied to interest rate risk – as interest rates rise, bond prices decline, and vice versa;
4. a fall in the exchange rate of a particular currency. This would cause a fall in the value of investments held in that currency when they were held by overseas investors who value in a different currency.

There are a number of risk mitigation techniques that are routinely taken by investment professionals to mitigate market risk:

- **Diversification**, simply defined as 'not putting all your eggs in one basket', means spreading the investment portfolio across a wide range of industries and countries. This protects against the possibility of losses due to poor performance in a particular sector or country.
- **Hedging** is the purchase or sale of a commodity, security or other financial instrument for the purpose of offsetting the profit or loss of another security or investment. Thus, any loss on the original investment will be hedged, or offset, by a corresponding profit from the hedging instrument. Usually derivative instruments are used to hedge the underlying instruments (also known as 'cash instruments' in this context). Some examples are:
  - an investor who is concerned about a fall in interest rates could sell a futures contract or buy a put option on the interest rates for that currency;
  - an investor who is concerned about a fall in the exchange rate for a particular currency could sell a futures contract or buy a put option on that currency's exchange rate;
  - an investor who is concerned about a fall in the levels of share prices for a particular market could sell a futures contract or buy a put option on a particular stock market index, eg, the FTSE 100 (UK) or DAX (Germany).

There is an IT implication to hedging. In order for the dealers to hedge, the dealing and settlement systems that they use must be capable of trading, valuing and settling a wide range of both underlying and derivative instruments. IT systems will also link the hedge against its position to monitor the risk position.

5.2 Measuring Market and Credit Risk

Systems employed by the investment professionals need to have the capabilities to measure market and credit risk. Two techniques are described in this section: mark-to-market and value-at-risk (VaR).

5.2.1 Mark-to-Market

Mark-to-market is an accounting procedure by which assets are 'marked', or recorded, at their current market value, which may be higher or lower than their purchase price or book value. As a result of a mark-to-market calculation, all investments are valued in the dealing system at their current market value, and all profits and losses that result from price rises or falls are recognised on the day that they happen.

Example

Event	Date	Amount bought or sold	Trade price	Trade value	Cumulative position	Cumulative cost	Average price	Realised P&L	Un-realised P&L
1. Purchase of 10,000 shares in Megacorp at £10 per share	22 Feb	10,000	10.00	100,000	10,000	100,000	10.00		
2. Purchase additional 10,000 shares in Megacorp at £9.50 per share	22 Feb	10,000	9.50	95,000	20,000	195,000	9.75		
3. Sale of 12,000 shares in Megacorp at £9.90 per share	22 Feb	–12,000	9.90	–118,800	8,000	78,000	9.75	1,800	
4. Mark the remaining position of 8,000 shares to market at the current bid price – £9.95 per share	22 Feb				8,000	79,600	9.95		1,600

The steps involved and the calculations made in the example are explained below:

On 22 February, ABC Investment Bank carries out three trades in Megacorp plc:

1. **It buys 10,000 shares at £10 each at 9.00am.**
2. **It buys an additional 10,000 shares at £9.50 each at 10.00am. At this point its position is 20,000 shares and its average price per share is £9.75.**
3. **It sells 12,000 shares at £9.90 per share at 11.00am. Its position is now 8,000 shares, and it has made realised profit of £1,800.00. This is calculated as:**

Realised P&L = number of shares sold x (sale price – average cost price)

At the close of business the bid price of Megacorp on the exchange is £9.95 per share and the offer price is £10.00 per share. Because ABC has a long position in Megacorp, it marks the position to market at the bid price. As a result, it calculates unrealised profit of £1,600.00. This is calculated as:

Unrealised P&L = position x (mark-to-market price – average price)

In addition, as a result of the mark-to-market calculation, it is now holding the position in its book at a new price – £9.95 per share, the current bid price.

If it were to sell some or all of its holding in Megacorp on 23 February then it would calculate the realised P&L for that day as:

Realised P&L = number of shares sold x (sale price – £9.95)

In other words, the close of business mark-to-market price on day one becomes the opening average price on day two.

This example has introduced a number of terms that need to be defined:

- **Average price** (or weighted average price) is the average price per unit of a position. If the position is long (ie, positive), then further purchases modify the average price, and sales create P&L but do not modify the average price. If the position is short (ie, negative), then further sales modify the average price, and purchases create P&L but do not modify the average price.
- **Bid price and offer price** – the bid price is the highest price that a prospective buyer is willing to pay for a specific security. The offer, also called the 'asking price', is the lowest price acceptable to a prospective seller of the same security. The highest bid and lowest offer are quoted on most major exchanges, and the difference between the two prices is called the 'spread'.
- **Realised P&L** – P&L that arises as a result of selling securities.
- **Unrealised P&L** – P&L that arises as a result of the mark-to-market process (or P&L that could be realised if the securities were sold).

The IT Implications of Mark-to-Market

Mark-to-market is a widely used technique and firms will need to be supplied with systems that have this capability. Note that the example used the **weighted average price** method of calculating P&L. This is probably the most widely used method of calculating P&L, but there are other methods in use, including:

- **FIFO (First-In First-Out)** – in this method of P&L calculation, the 12,000 shares that were sold at 11.00am are deemed to comprise the 10,000 bought at 9.00am and 2,000 of the 10,000 shares bought at 10.00am. This, of course, affects the calculation of realised P&L on the 11.00am deal.
- **LIFO (Last-In First-Out)** – in this method of P&L calculation, the 12,000 shares that were sold at 11.00am are deemed to comprise the 10,000 bought at 10.00am and 2,000 of the 10,000 shares bought at 9.00am. LIFO is very rarely used in its pure form.

Firms that handle investments on behalf of UK private individuals will need to take into account the investor's liability to pay capital gains tax (CGT), if and when investments are sold.

Current UK tax law requires that P&L for CGT purposes should be calculated using the following guidelines:

- If shares are bought and sold on the same day, use the cost of those shares.
- If shares are sold that have been bought in the 30 days before the sale, use the cost of those shares.
- For all other holdings, use the weighted average price method.

When the firm is trading interest-bearing instruments, such as bonds, it also needs, as part of the mark-to-market process, to accrue interest on these instruments. This aspect is discussed more fully in Chapter 6.

5.2.2 Value-at-Risk (VaR)

Value-at-Risk (VaR) is a measure of how the market value of an asset or of a portfolio of assets is likely to decrease over a certain time period (usually over one or ten days) under usual conditions. It is typically used by security houses or investment banks to measure the market risk of their asset portfolios (**market value-at-risk**), but is actually a very general concept that has broad application.

VaR is the maximum amount at risk to be lost from an investment (under 'normal' market conditions) over a given holding period, at a particular confidence level. As such, it is the converse of shortfall probability, in that it represents the amount to be lost with a given probability, rather than the probability of a given amount to be lost.

VaR has three parameters:

- The **time horizon** (period) to be analysed (ie, the length of time over which one plans to hold the assets in the portfolio – the **holding period**). The typical holding period is one day, although ten days are used, for example, to compute capital requirements under the European Capital Requirements Directive (CRD). For some problems, even a holding period of one year is appropriate.
- The **confidence level** at which the estimate is made. If a firm wishes to use VaR as part of the Advanced Measurement Approach to calculating its Basel II capital requirements (see Chapter 2), then this must be 99%. Other firms that only use VaR for internal measurements may set it as low as 95%.
- The unit of the currency which will be used to denominate the VaR.

Limitations of VaR

The bankruptcy of Lehman Brothers in 2008 and the more recent Greek financial crisis exposed some weaknesses in the VaR concept. In particular, 'VaR with a confidence factor of 99%' means that in 1% of cases (that would be two–three trading days in a year with daily VaR) the loss is expected to be greater than the VaR amount. VaR does not say anything about the size of losses within this 1% of trading days, and by no means does it say anything about the maximum possible loss.

At the present time some academics are working on successor algorithms, most notably CoVaR (meaning Contagion Value-at-Risk), which performs the VaR calculation and then asks how it changes if one particular entity such as Lehman's – or Greece – finds itself in distress.

The IT Implications of VaR

In Chapter 2 we learned that a VaR calculation is part of 'Pillar 1' of the Basel II Accord. Firms that have decided to use the Advanced Measurement Approach to calculating their capital requirements will need to use techniques such as VaR to do so, and will need to be supplied with IT systems that can perform this calculation. The firm may choose to build its own VaR calculation software; alternatively there are a very large number of packaged products and online services that will perform this calculation. Since the financial crisis of 2007, many firms have had to undergo rigorous stress tests at the request of regulators, and also make plans for events such as the break-up of the euro and the collapse of specific counterparties and securities issuers. This has led many firms to replace or enhance the software that they use for this aspect of risk management.

5.2.3   Risk – Conclusion

In designing, implementing and maintaining applications to control the various forms of risk, one of the bigger challenges is to provide these applications with fast, consistent, accurate and reliable data covering counterparties and positions. Some of these challenges are addressed in Chapters 5 and 7.

End of Chapter Questions

Think of an answer for each question and refer to the appropriate section for confirmation.

1. List the information that you would normally expect to see on an order to sell securities at a maximum price.
    Section 3.1.2

2. What are the four steps that an investment firm must take to ensure compliance with Article 21 of MiFID in the context of 'best execution'?
    Section 3.2.2

3. List the information that you would expect a sell-side firm to include in the trade confirmation that it sends to a fund manager.
    Section 3.3.1

4. What is the name of the process by which a fund manager advises a sell-side firm of the identities of the investors concerned with a particular order?
    Section 3.3.1

5. What is the difference between a 'sliding scale' of commissions and a 'reducing scale' of commissions?
    Section 3.5.1

6. What was the cause of the 'Flash Crash' of 2010?
    Section 4.3

7. What is the purpose of and what is the economic driver behind direct market access?
    Section 4.4

8. What is the name of the risk management technique that is designed to ensure that all investments are recorded in the dealing system at their current market value?
    Section 5.2.1

9. Why is it necessary for certain firms to be able to calculate value-at-risk in order to meet their regulatory requirements connected with Basel II?
    Section 5.2.2

10. What does a CoVaR calculation set out to do?
    Section 5.2.2

Chapter Five
The Role of IT in the Pre-Settlement Phase

This syllabus area will provide approximately 5 of the 50 examination questions

1. Reference Information

Learning Objective

5.1 Understand the IT alignment to pre-settlement phase key risk indicators, including: reference data; Standard Settlement Instructions; client and counterparty agreements

The accuracy of reference data, also known as **static data**, is a significant factor in achieving STP. Incorrect or incomplete reference information is a common cause of trade processing errors.

The reference data challenge for securities firms can be said to be to:

1. gather the required data from disparate sources;
2. store it securely;
3. update it when necessary; and
4. utilise it appropriately.

This section explores the most important items of reference data that need to be held for financial instruments, clients and counterparties: 'internal' entities – ie, reference data that is concerned with the structure of the firm itself – and 'external' entities such as countries, exchanges, clearing houses and custodians that have a role in the trade flow.

1.1 Reference Data Overview

The description below refers to the diagram that follows (overleaf). ABC Investment Bank plc has a number of dealing teams or **trading books**. The trading books buy and sell financial **instruments** that include bonds, currencies, futures and options, and equities. The instruments, in turn have parameters, including **price calculation methods** – for all instruments – and **interest rates** and **interest calculation methods** – for bonds and currencies. There are also standard **identifiers** used throughout the industry to uniquely identify instruments, as well as rules that apply to the markets in which the instruments are traded.

In turn, all instruments are **denominated in a currency**; that is to say that bonds, equities, futures and options are normally traded and settled in a particular currency. There is a **public holiday calendar** associated with each currency, and on the public holidays for that currency no trades can settle, and investment exchanges are usually closed.

The instruments are bought from or sold to **trading parties**. This term includes exchanges, counterparties and clients. Every one of these is resident in a particular country, as is ABC Investment Bank plc itself. All the trading parties, as well as ABC Investment Bank plc, have appointed **settlement agents** (this term includes central counterparties (CCPs), central securities depositories (CSDs) and custodians) to settle trades in particular markets within a country. Settlement agents are unable to settle trades on a day which is a public holiday for the currency of the trade concerned.

ABC Investment Bank also has **credit policies** and **credit limits** that restrict the total amount of exposure that the firm is prepared to tolerate for particular trading books, trading parties, clients and countries.

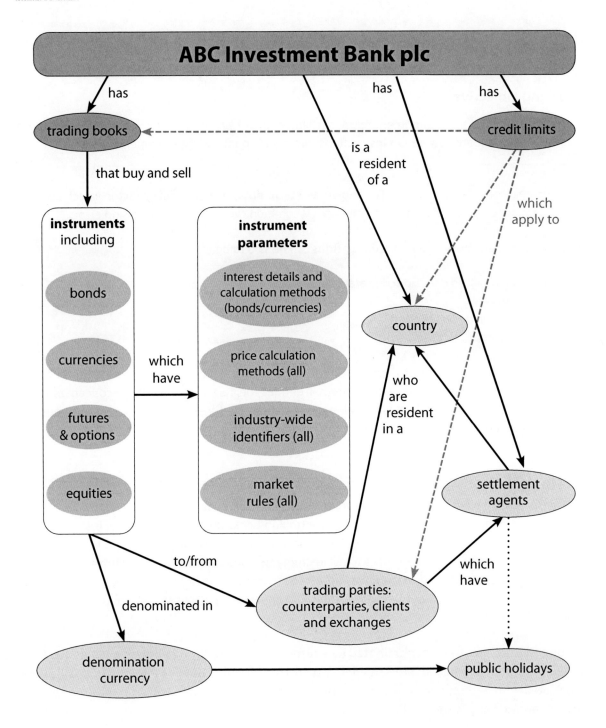

The following reference data elements also need to be maintained and are not shown on the diagram for the sake of simplicity:

1. **Standard settlement instructions (SSIs)** – both ABC Investment Bank and its trading parties have standard settlement instructions. SSIs could be different for each of ABC's customers. These control the selection of which settlement agent settles trades in particular instruments for the two parties concerned. SSIs are examined in Section 1.6.
2. **Commission rates** – when ABC is acting as agent it will charge customers commission. Commission rates will vary according to client and instrument class. Commission structures were examined in Chapter 4.

1.2   Reference Data and STP

Straight-through processing is the aim of all securities firms. Accurate reference data is essential for STP to ensure everything flows smoothly. Accurate reference data is needed, in particular to:

- calculate trade amounts, including principal amounts, interest, commissions, fees and taxes accurately; and
- enrich trades with accurate information about intended value dates, settlement agents and account codes at the settlement agents.

1.3   Duplication of Reference Data across Systems

One of the problems involved in managing the IT infrastructure of a large institution is that there may be a large number of individual business application systems in the configuration, all of which hold some of this large amount of reference data, and some of the information may be duplicated across the different systems. Where there is duplication of reference data, there is a danger that errors or inconsistencies may creep in – for example, the data about a particular instrument in one system might be slightly different from that in another system. The following diagram – which is explored more thoroughly in Chapter 7 – illustrates the problem. It is clear that, for example, every one of the systems in this configuration would need to hold details about all the currencies that the firm trades, so there is a danger that such data may become inconsistent between the systems.

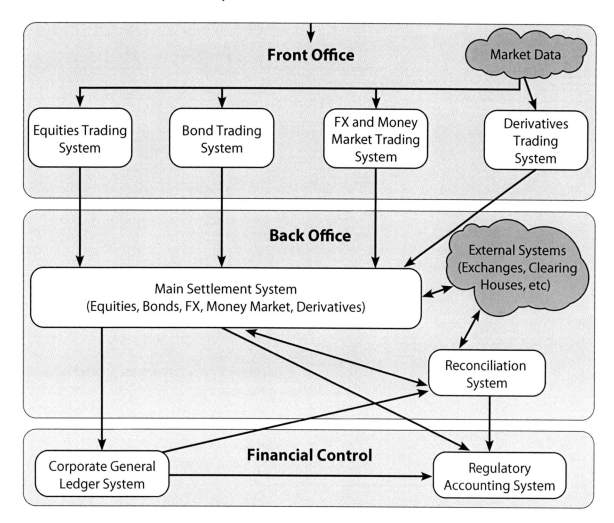

To overcome these issues, some firms have built separate **reference data repositories (RDRs)** that take in data from reliable sources, such as Bloomberg or Thomson Reuters, as well as manually updated data, and then feed this to all the other systems in the configuration; so the diagram now looks like this.

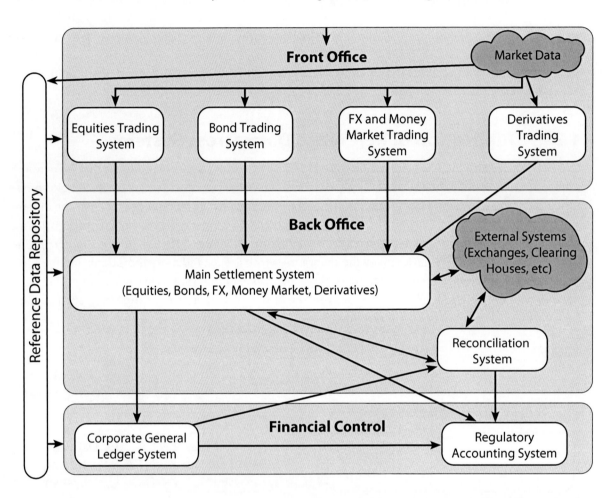

The advantages and disadvantages of using a reference data repository may be summarised as follows:

Reference Data Repositories	
Advantages	**Disadvantages**
Ensures consistency of reference data across all business applications.	May be costly to build or buy the system.
Some reference data elements may be fed from reliable external sources, eg, Bloomberg, Thomson Reuters, exchanges and clearing houses.	All other systems in the configuration will also need to be enhanced to utilise the RDR – this may be costly, and in some cases may be impractical; usually this is because the firm does not have the ability to amend the source code of a packaged application.
Data is maintained by a dedicated data management team that has expertise in this area.	May be costly to maintain the system itself and also the data in the system.

We shall now examine the most significant items of reference information that are held for each type of object in the diagram.

1.4   Instrument Reference Information

Reference data about financial instruments is publicly available and may be purchased from a large number of sources. The data that needs to be maintained includes the items discussed in Section 1.4.1 to Section 1.4.5 inclusive.

1.4.1   Trading Markets and Market Rules

All instruments can be said to be traded on a market. This may be a formal market, such as the LSE, or an informal market, such as 'the FX market' or 'the eurobond market'.

Market rules are used to determine, *inter alia*:

1. The **default settlement date** – for most securities markets this has been 'T+3', meaning that value date will be three working days after trade date, unless the trade parties agree otherwise. From October 2014 this will change to T+2 in most markets within the EEA. In the FX and money markets, value date is usually T+2.
2. What **fees and charges** apply – for example, stamp duty and PTM levy both apply to qualifying trades executed on the LSE even though the charges are not levied by the LSE itself.

Some instruments are only traded on one market; others, like the Sony shares that were examined in Chapter 4, are traded in many markets. Therefore, we also need to store:

3. The normal **trade currency** when this instrument is traded in this market.
4. The normal **settlement currency** when this instrument is traded in this market.

Each instrument that is added to the instrument master file needs to have a **market code**.

A **markets table** needs to be set up to provide information about the default settlement period, the usual settlement currency and the fees and charges that apply.

1.4.2 Unique Instrument Identifiers

For currencies, the unique instrument identifier is the three-alphabetic-character **ISO currency code**, eg, USD, GBP, EUR, etc.

For securities and listed derivatives, there are a number of coding schemes that attempt to uniquely identify an instrument. These coding schemes will identify instruments in messages transmitted to counterparties, clients, exchanges and settlement agents. These schemes include:

Name	Example	Description	Applies to Listed Futures and Options?
ISIN code	GB1234567890	A code that represents, for example, Sony Corporation ordinary shares. If the security is listed on more than one exchange, there is only one ISIN code. Most custodians and clearing houses identify securities by the ISIN code on messages.	Some coverage – not all the world's derivatives exchanges issue ISIN codes to the contracts that they list.
SEDOL code	12345F67	The coding system used by the LSE. However, SEDOL codes are allocated for all commonly traded securities, whether listed on the LSE or not. If a security is traded on exchanges in four countries, the security would have four SEDOL codes.	Some coverage.
CUSIP code	A1234R56	The coding system used by exchanges and clearing houses in the US and Canada.	North American markets only.
Ticker	IBM	A short security description used by stock exchange trading systems in the US and Canada. The UK equivalent is the **EPIC code**. Also used within the Bloomberg system.	Yes – Bloomberg allocates tickers to futures and options.
RIC code	IBM.N	The coding system used by Reuters.	Yes – Reuters allocates RIC codes to listed futures and options.

Note that the above table is not a complete list of all the possible coding schemes that can apply to securities and derivatives. There are a number of other schemes used by individual countries and exchanges.

In addition, the firm itself has to choose a unique identifier across its own systems. If a firm trades the same instrument across many markets, then an ISIN number may not be the most appropriate code to use as a unique identifier.

As an individual instrument may have several codes, flexible facilities need to exist to support this one (instrument) to many (code) relationship.

1.4.3   Price Calculation Methods

Normally we think of multiplying the quantity of an instrument by its price to get the trade's principal value. It is, however, a little more complex than that.

Some **shares** are traded in whole currency units, but some are traded in penny units. Hence 'buy 100 @ 98' may mean either 98.00 or 0.98 per share.

A **bond** price is a percentage of face value, hence 'buy 1,000 @ 98' means buy 1,000 @ 98% of 1,000.

Futures and options prices are more complex still: the price may refer to some element of the underlying instrument. For example, US Treasury bill futures are based on an underlying amount of $1,000,000 of a US government Treasury bill, which is a 90-day (one quarter of a year) instrument. As a result 'buy 100 @ 98' means: buy 100 lots of futures x 98 (the price) x 1,000,000 (face value)/4 (periods in the year)/100 (percentage price) =$2,450,000 (market exposure).

The following generic formula may be used in all of the above cases:

Principal amount = quantity traded x price x price multiplier/price divisor

Example

Instrument	Quantity	Price	Price Multiplier	Price Divisor	Principal Amount
Penny share	1,000	98	1	100	980
Pound share	1,000	98	1	100	98,000
Bond	1,000,000	98	1	100	980,000
T-bond future	10	98	1,000,000	400	2,450,000

Therefore the firm needs to store the necessary information to employ this formula, or an alternative formula that provides the same result, to extract the principal amount from a given quantity and price.

1.4.4   Interest Details and Accrued Interest Calculation Methods

See also Chapter 6, Section 4.1.1. In order to trade **bonds**, the firm needs to calculate interest. It therefore needs to store the following information:

1. The date from which interest becomes payable.
2. The date that the borrower will make the next interest payment.

From 1 and 2 we can derive the number of days in the current interest period.

3. The date when interest ceases to become payable – usually this is the maturity date of the bond.
4. The rate of interest that will be paid.

5. The interest calculation method. There are a number of commonly used methods, including:
    ○ **30/360** – there are deemed to be 360 days in a year, and all months are deemed to be 30 days long.
    ○ **Actual/360** – there are deemed to be 360 days in a year, and we follow the conventional calendar for determining the days in a month.
    ○ **Actual/365** – we follow the actual calendar. Although this rule is usually expressed as 'over 365'; if there are 366 days in a year then 366 is used as the divisor.
    ○ **Actual/Actual** – the conventional calendar is used for all calculations.

Most **bonds** (other than US Treasury bonds) that were issued before the advent of the euro on 1 January 1999 used 30/360 or actual/360. Virtually all bonds that were issued since EMU use actual/actual.

The formula for calculating interest using **actual/actual** is:

$$\text{Accrued interest} = t/s \times c/n$$

Where:
t = the actual number of calendar days from, and including, the last interest payment date to, and including, the value date.
s = the actual number of calendar days in the current interest period.
c = the annual rate of interest.
n = the number of interest payments per annum.

On the next coupon date, the buyer of a bond will receive the interest payment (also known as '**coupon payment**') for the whole of the interest period that ends at the next interest payment (coupon payment) date. However, since the buyer has not owned the bonds for the entire period, it has to pay the accrued interest for the period, for which it did not own the bonds to the seller. Systems, therefore, need to use the appropriate formula to calculate the interest payable from the last coupon date to the intended value date of the trade – this is the amount of interest that the buyer must pay the seller when the trade settles.

Example

The table below shows the calculations of accrued interest on a bond transaction for $1,000,000 face value of a bond paying a 5% coupon on 1 January and 1 July each year. The value date of the trade is 15 February. For the four different interest calculation methods, the results of the accrued interest calculation will be:

Calculation Method	No of days from last coupon (1 Jan) to value date (15 Feb)	Number of days in period (1 Jan to 30 June)	No of interest payments per year	Accrued interest in USD (for period 1 Jan to 15 Feb)
30/360	44	360	Not used	6,111.11
Actual/360	45	360	Not used	6,250.00
Actual/365	45	365	Not used	6,164.38
Actual/Actual	45	181	2	6,215.47

Note that **currencies**, as well as bonds, require accrued interest calculation methods so that interest may be calculated on money market loans and deposits, stock loans and repos.

The most common method of calculating interest on currencies in the wholesale markets is Actual/360. Nearly all currencies use this method; the exceptions are GBP and JPY which use Actual/365.

1.4.5   Other Information

Other information that needs to be stored for financial instruments includes:

- the name of the security;
- the date that it was issued;
- the date that it matures or expires (if any);
- the default trading book;
- the minimum size of a trade;
- the number of shares/units in issue; and
- the security issuer – as some issuers issue many securities, the firm may wish to apply a credit limit to the issuer as a whole.

1.5   Client/Counterparty Reference Information

1.5.1   Unique Identifiers for Trading Parties

The firm has to choose a unique identifier for use in its own systems. Which identifier it uses will vary according to its own individual needs. There are now three – but soon to be four – external identifiers that it needs to hold, one of which – the **BIC code** – is used for professional trade parties. Another –the **UK National Insurance Number** – is necessary if the firm offers tax-sheltered investments such as pensions and Individual Savings Accounts (ISAs) to UK private investors. The third is the **IBAN code**, which is increasingly being used to identify counterparties' bank and depot accounts in Europe. The fourth, and newest, trading party code is the **Legal Entity Identifier (LEI)**.

BIC Codes

The BIC code is used on messages between trading parties, exchanges and settlement agents. The BIC code is a standard format of **Bank Identifier Codes** approved by the International Organization for Standardization. It is the unique identification code of a particular bank. The **Society for Worldwide Interbank Financial Telecommunications (SWIFT)** handles the registration of these codes. For this reason, BIC codes are often called SWIFT addresses or codes. There are over 7,500 'live' codes (for partners actively connected to the SWIFT network) and an estimated 10,000 additional BIC codes which can be used for manual transactions.

The code is eight or eleven characters long, made up of:

- four characters – bank code;
- two characters – ISO 3166-1 alpha-2 country code;
- two characters – location code; and
- three characters – branch code, optional ('XXX' for primary office).

Where an eight-digit code is given, you may assume that it refers to the primary office.

For example, Deutsche Bank is an international bank; its head office is based in Frankfurt, Germany. Its BIC code for its head office is DEUTDEFF:

- DEUT identifies Deutsche Bank;
- DE is the country code for Germany; and
- FF is the code for Frankfurt.

Using an extended code of 11 digits (if the receiving bank has assigned branches or processing areas individual extended codes) allows the payment to be directed to a specific office. For example, DEUTDEFF500 would direct the payment to an office of Deutsche Bank in Bad Homburg.

IBAN Codes

Bank account numbers have traditionally been expressed in different forms in different countries, which has made the storage of depot and nostro account numbers in applications somewhat imprecise and complex.

As a result, in 2003 the European Union decided to adopt the **International Bank Account Number (IBAN) code** to overcome this problem. The IBAN was developed to facilitate payments within the European Union. The IBAN is not yet used as a standard in messaging, because the IBAN has not yet been widely adopted outside Europe. Adoption may take up to ten years, so it remains necessary to use the current ISO 9362 Bank Identifier Code system (BIC code) in conjunction with the Basic Bank Account Number (BBAN) or IBAN.

Currently all European non-CIS countries, as well as some African countries, and Turkey participate in the IBAN system, while, broadly speaking, the rest of the world (including the United States) remains outside of it.

The IBAN consists of a ISO 3166-1 alpha-2 country code, followed by two check digits (represented by kk in the examples below), and up to thirty alphanumeric characters for the domestic bank account number, called the BBAN (Basic Bank Account Number). It is up to each country's national banking community to decide on the length of the BBAN for accounts in that country, but its length must be fixed for any given country.

Example of a UK IBAN code

Format: GBkk BBBB SSSS SSCC CCCC CC

Example GB65 LOYD 3000 0000 1195 87

Where:
GB is the country code for the UK
65 is a check digit
LOYD is the abbreviation for Lloyds TSB Bank
3000 00 is the branch at Lloyds TSB where the account is held

00 1195 87 is the account number concerned at that branch

The IBAN must not contain spaces when stored electronically. When printed on paper, however, the norm is to express it in groups of four characters, the last group being of variable length.

The Legal Entity Identifier (LEI)

The **LEI for Financial Contracts** is a universal standard for identifying parties to financial contracts. It is a new standard, soon to be established by the US Treasury's Office of Financial Research, which was created by Dodd-Frank, and the standard is also backed by ESMA in Europe. The LEI is a key element in the broader effort to understand and monitor systemic risk across banks and capital markets.

Its creation is likely to have broad impact throughout the financial markets at a fundamental level. A solution for the identification of legal entities was proposed by the Depository Trust & Clearing Corporation (DTCC) and SWIFT, and consequently recommended by the umbrella Global Financial Markets Association (GFMA) trade association.

SWIFT will act as the registration authority, acting on behalf of International Organization for Standardization (ISO) to assign the ISO 17442 LEI standard. DTCC will act as the facilities manager which will receive, review and publish entity information.

LEIs will eventually become the standard way that organisations such as corporate bodies, partnerships, some charities and trusts are identified on regulatory trade reports and submissions to trade repositories (see Chapter 3, Section 3.6). One of the US regulators, the CFTC, is already demanding their use in regulatory trade reports.

There will be a central global register of LEIs that is expected to be managed by Avox, a subsidiary of the DTCC. The full specification of the LEI is still being worked on, but the code itself will be a 20-character alphanumeric code, and the other data that will be held by the LEI registrar will include at a minimum:

1. Name.
2. Address.
3. Country of incorporation.
4. Entity status.

Any trade could involve many LEIs, which will be encoded into the detailed transaction, such as: buyer, buyer's broker, seller, seller's broker, exchange where traded, clearing facility, company that issued the security being traded, etc. In addition, it is likely that any related 'infrastructure' firm involved in supporting that trade (deemed to be potentially systemically important) will also have its LEI encoded. The concept is to pin down legal entities for every transaction, and for every securities position.

Avox expects to have a web portal available to firms by July 2012 that will enable them to request LEIs for their trading counterparties, or enquire whether those parties already have an existing LEI.

Keeping track of relationships linked through LEIs will be exceptionally challenging, raising issues and questions such as:

- Each LEI itself needs to be kept absolutely up to date. This alone will be a daunting task.
- Additional data will be also be added to the register to link each LEI to its parent, subsidiaries and affiliate relationships.
- It will be the responsibility of each regulated firm to obtain LEIs for its unregulated clients as and when each regulator mandates the use of LEIs. This could be a daunting implementation task requiring extensive support from IT departments and change managers.

1.5.2 Other Party Information

For each trading party, the firm needs to keep a record of its Standard Settlement Instructions (SSIs) – these are examined in detail in Section 1.6.

Apart from SSI information, the firm needs to record at least the following about each counterparty and client:

- full name and address;
- any additional names and addresses to which trade confirmations should be sent;
- country of incorporation or residence;
- any credit limit granted to this party;
- the commission scale that applies to this party;
- type of party, eg, exchange, counterparty, professional investor, private investor.

Depending on which party type it is, the firm will need to hold additional information for regulatory purposes. Such additional information will include:

- for professional investors:
  - the date that they commenced dealing with this firm;
  - the date that a client agreement was sent to them;
  - the date that they signed and returned it;
  - which fund manager or financial adviser acts for them;
- for private investors, as for professional investors, plus in addition:
  - the relationship held with them, eg, execution-only broker, advisory broker, discretionary broker;
  - their appetite for risk, and how it was assessed;
  - connected account details, eg, there is an account for Mr John Smith and Mrs Jane Smith, as well as a joint account for Mr and Mrs John Smith – they are connected because they are husband and wife; they have a number of different accounts with the firm because they want to take advantage of tax shelters such as ISAs and pensions that apply to individuals – but the firm manages the money of the family as a whole.

This type of data is of course 'Know Your Customer' data that was examined in Chapter 2.

1.6 Standard Settlement Instructions (SSIs)

1.6.1 Overview

Standard Settlement Instructions are the main driver of the STP process from the point of trade agreement to final settlement. SSIs provide details of which **settlement agents** are going to be used to settle the trade by both the sell-side firm and the investors who use its services.

Both the cash-side and the stock-side of a securities trade will be settled – normally on a DvP basis – by the settlement agents chosen by the sell-side firm and the investor. Note that, where a fund manager is acting for a number of investors, it is the investors – not the fund manager – that choose their settlement agent. Settlement agents may be CSDs such as EUI, ICSDs such as Euroclear Bank in Belgium, or custodian banks.

In Chapter 4 we looked at the processes of confirmation, affirmation and allocation between sell-side and buy-side firms. Once these processes have been completed successfully, the next step is to send settlement instructions to the settlement agents, illustrated by the following diagram:

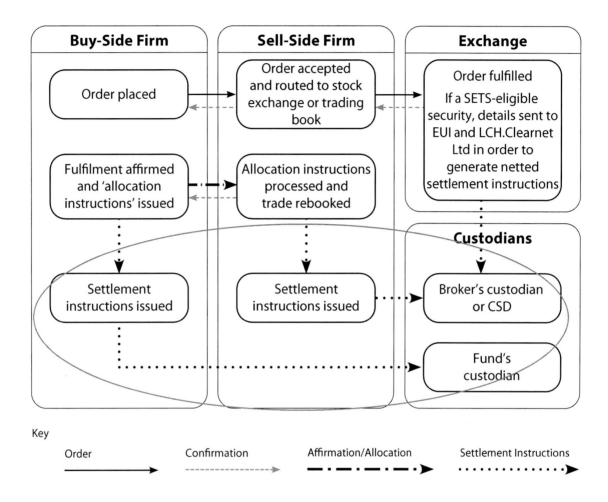

In order to generate instructions, both parties need to know who to send them to ('our' settlement agent) as well as details of the other party's ('their') settlement agent, and a firm needs to advise its agent of this information so that it can settle the trade. For this reason, the sell-side firm holds details of the SSIs of those investors with whom it deals regularly as reference data objects. SSIs are not usually added to or changed as a result of the confirmation/affirmation/allocation processes described in Chapter 4. Conversely, the fund manager (acting on behalf of the investor) holds the SSIs of those brokers it trades with regularly as part of its reference data.

1.6.2 Examples of SSI Data

The table overleaf shows the SSI-related data held by ABC Investment Bank for itself, and also by two of its investor clients for three major asset classes:

- UK-listed equities settled in GBP;
- corporate bonds traded in London and settled in EUR; and
- corporate bonds traded in London and settled in USD.

Trading Party	Asset Class	Settlement Currency	Stock Depot	Depot Account Code	Cash Nostro	Nostro Account Code	Instruction Method
Ourselves	LSE listed equities	GBP	EUI	123456	EUI	654321	EUI
Ourselves	OTC Bonds London Desk	EUR	Euroclear	911222	Euroclear	466-911222-EUR	Euclid
Ourselves	OTC Bonds London Desk	USD	Euroclear	911222	Euroclear	457-911222-GBP	Euclid
Megacorp Pension Fund	LSE listed equities	GBP	State Street London	256879	State Street London	108-256879-GBP	SWIFT
Megacorp Pension Fund	OTC Bonds London Desk	EUR	State Street London	256879	State Street London	107-256879-EUR	SWIFT
Megacorp Pension Fund	OTC Bonds London Desk	USD	State Street London	256879	State Street New York	168-256789-USD	SWIFT
Minicorp Pension Fund	LSE listed equities	GBP	Société Générale Paris	104867	Société Générale London	0-0876554332	SWIFT
Minicorp Pension Fund	OTC Bonds London Desk	EUR	Société Générale Paris	104867	Société Générale Paris	0-0876554332	SWIFT
Minicorp Pension Fund	OTC Bonds London Desk	USD	Société Générale Paris	104867	Société Générale New York	0-0876554332	SWIFT

The table introduces us to two new technical terms:

- **Depot** – the account with the settlement agent that is used to record transactions and balances in **security quantities** is often referred to as the 'depot account'.
- **Nostro** – the account with the settlement agent that is used to record transactions and balances in **money amounts** is often referred to as the 'nostro account'.

Key to the columns in the table:

- **Trading party** – identity of the party with which the firm is trading. The firm itself is also a trading party in this context.
- **Asset class** – identifies the type of asset concerned.
- **Settlement currency** – identifies the currency of settlement.
- **Stock depot** – identifies the settlement agent that will accept or make delivery of this type of asset on behalf of the trading party.
- **Depot account code** – identifies the relevant account number at the stock depot.
- **Cash nostro** – identifies the settlement agent that will accept or make payments for this type of asset on behalf of the trading party.
- **Nostro account code** – identifies the relevant account number of the cash nostro.
- **Instruction method** – the method that the trading party will use to send instructions to the settlement agent.

1.7   Other 'Internal' Reference Information

The firm also needs to set up a number of reference data elements that supply its business applications with information about the firm itself. These 'internal' data objects will include, but are not limited to:

- **Base currency** – a firm that invests in securities denominated in many currencies will wish to value them in the currency in which it produces its profit & loss (P&L) account. Usually, but not exclusively, this means that a firm that is incorporated in the UK will have a base currency of GBP; a firm incorporated in the US will choose USD, etc.
- **Commission rates and calculation methods** – these were covered in Chapter 4, Section 3.5.
- **Credit limits** – any credit limits the firm wishes to apply to its trading parties or individual trades, trading books and countries in which trading parties are incorporated or resident need to be set up as reference data objects. Some firms also set up limits that apply to individual issuers of securities, and stock market sectors such as pharmaceuticals, etc.

Trading Book/Dealing Desk Structure

Sell-side firms usually organise their dealing teams and trading books into an hierarchical 'book structure' that corresponds to profit and loss attribution by business area. A sample hierarchy might be:

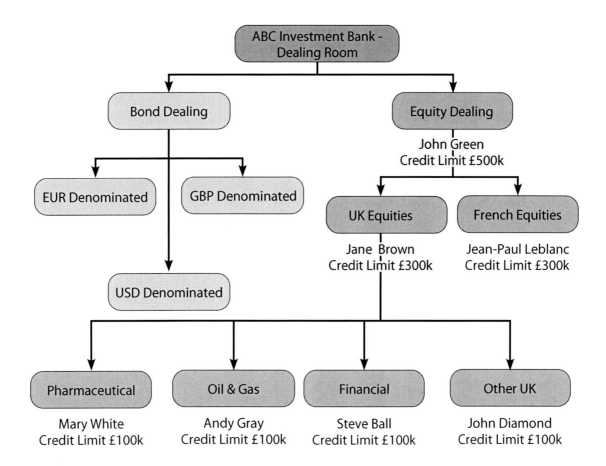

For each 'node' in the hierarchy, the reference data that is held needs to include:

- the identities of the manager of each team, and the authorised dealers in each team; and
- any credit limits that apply to the node concerned.

1.8   Other 'External' Reference Information

This is reference data that relates to entities that are not part of the firm, and are not themselves trading parties. It will include:

Country Information

The country in which the firm is incorporated, as well as those countries where the other parties involved in the trade life cycle are incorporated. This needs to be set up in a table so that:

a.   the firm is able to calculate its total risk exposure to any one country;
b.   the firm may apply limits by country;
c.   the firm may comply with any rules and regulations that, for example, prevent it from offering certain kinds of investments to residents of a particular country.

Countries are normally identified by a two-character ISO country code. For example, the code for the UK is GB; France is FR.

Bank Holidays and Working Days

A public holiday table needs to be set up so that dealing applications are able to validate and default value dates correctly. Trades cannot settle on a public holiday that applies to the countries concerned. Some countries – mainly in the Middle East – work on Saturdays or Sundays but not on Fridays. Firms that trade in such markets may need a 'working days' table in addition to a bank holidays table.

Other Parties Involved in the Trade Cycle

As well as setting up records for each of the firm's trading parties, it will need to set up records for settlement agents, so that SSIs can refer to them, and possibly securities issuers, so that credit limits may be applied to them.

1.9   Summary of Key Risk Indicators

Clearly, accurate and consistent reference data is essential to the settlement, accounting and risk management processes. The following types of problems may indicate that there are problems in maintaining and using reference data correctly:

1.   **A high level of failed trades and unmatched instructions**. Settlement instructions and failed trades are dealt with in detail in Section 2 of Chapter 6 but, if a firm has an unusually high level of fails and unmatched, then this could be because the reference data used to calculate trade proceeds and/or determine the correct settlement agents is not accurate.
2.   **A high number of queries about realised and unrealised profits, and interest income**. If reported trading P&L amounts (Section 5.2 of Chapter 4) and/or interest earnings (Section 4.1.1 of Chapter 6) are frequently queried or found to be erroneous, then this could be because the reference data used in trade calculations is inaccurate.

1.10 Client and Counterparty Agreements

1.10.1 Definitions

Clients are the customers of the sell-side firm. **Counterparties** (sometimes known as 'market counterparties') are, broadly speaking, other sell-side firms with whom the firm does business, as well as (in the bond markets) central banks and governments. Financial regulation is designed to give clients a higher level of protection than counterparties, as counterparties are treated as fellow professionals.

Client agreements are, therefore, agreements between a firm and its clients. **Counterparty agreements** are agreements between fellow professionals.

1.10.2 Counterparty Agreements

Firm A may sign several counterparty agreements with Firm B, each one covering different business activities or asset classes. In the interests of simplicity and standardisation, individual agreements usually make reference to some industry-wide standards and protocols.

For example:

- If Firms A and B wish to trade **swaps**, or other **OTC derivatives**, with each other then their counterparty agreement will be based on the **International Swaps and Derivatives Association (ISDA) Master Agreement**. This is a standardised counterparty agreement for the OTC derivatives industry that is sponsored by ISDA. This means it contains general terms and conditions but does not, by itself, include details of any specific derivatives transactions the parties may enter into. The ISDA Master Agreement is a pre-printed form which will not itself be amended (save for writing in the names of the parties on the front and signature pages). However, it also has a manually produced schedule in which the parties are required to select certain options; the parties may modify sections of the Master Agreement if desired.
- If Firms A and B wish to trade **bonds** with each other, then their counterparty agreement would normally refer to the statutes and by-laws of the **International Capital Market Association (ICMA)**.

1.10.3 Client Agreements

The UK regulator defines client agreements as *'terms of business which have been signed by the client or to which the client has consented in writing'*. It then further defines 'terms of business' as *'a statement in a durable medium of the terms and conditions on which a firm will carry on a regulated activity with or for a client or retail customer'*.

The essence of client agreements is, therefore, that:

1. they accurately describe what services a firm will supply to its clients;
2. they accurately describe how the firm will be remunerated (eg, commissions paid by the client, commissions paid to it by others, etc);
3. they accurately describe what information (contract notes, statements, etc) the firm will supply to its clients as evidence that the services have been performed; and
4. the client must agree to the terms of the agreement by signing it or indicating their consent on some other document that refers to it.

The agreement must exist on a **durable medium**. The UK regulator defines a durable medium as:

a. paper; or
b. any instrument which enables the recipient to store information addressed personally to them in a way accessible for future reference for a period of time adequate for the purposes of the information and which allows the unchanged reproduction of the information stored; this includes, in particular, CD-ROMs, DVDs and the hard drive of the recipient's computer on which the electronic mail is stored, but not internet websites unless they fulfil the criteria in this definition.

2. The Trade Agreement Process

Learning Objective

5.2 Understand the IT implications of the trade agreement process

In Chapter 4 we looked at the process of a sell-side firm and a buy-side firm going through three stages of trade agreement – confirmation, affirmation and allocation. This three-stage process is how sell-side firms communicate with their **professional investors** (ie, institutional clients) when **equities** are traded. However, not all deals involve professional investors or equities; the trade agreement process is different in such cases.

In summary:

- When the sell-side firm is dealing with a **buy-side firm**, the processes are confirmation, affirmation and allocation.
- When the sell-side firm is dealing with a **retail investor**, the normal process is for the sell-side firm to send the investor a trade confirmation, but the trade confirmation is not normally responded to by the retail client.
- When the sell-side firm is dealing with a **market counterparty**, there are two possible practices: mutual exchange of confirmations; or use of a matching engine. These will be examined below.

2.1 Mutual Exchange of Confirmations

'Mutual exchange of confirmations' means simply that Firm A sends Firm B a confirmation note that begins to the effect: *'We confirm our purchase from you of…'*, while Firm B sends Firm A a confirmation note that begins to the effect: *'We confirm our sale to you of...'*

It is up to both parties to read the confirmation from the other party and check that their trade details agree with its trade details. If they agree, there is no need for any further communication between the parties; if they don't agree, then one party takes the matter up with the other party.

This method of trade agreement is used extensively in matching confirmations for foreign exchange and money market trades, as well as trades in OTC derivatives, such as swaps.

Until the late 1980s, using this method of trade agreement usually meant sending the confirmation by post, telex or fax, and employing people at both firms to read the messages and manually check them. From about 1990 onwards it became the practice to send these confirmations in the form of **SWIFT messages**, and to use software applications to compare the incoming and outgoing messages with each other. Using a dedicated matching application, confirmations that match are automatically flagged as such, while confirmations that are missing, apparently sent in error or disagree are forwarded to a queue of unmatched items to be dealt with as **exceptions**.

2.2 Matching Engines

Learning Objective

5.3   Understand the role of matching engines

2.2.1 The Traditional Role of Matching Engines

Matching engines provide a further level of automation of the trade agreement process. They have been provided by investment exchanges and clearing houses for many years to automate the process of confirmation matching between member firms.

The principles behind the traditional matching engines provided by exchanges and clearing houses are as follows:

- Both parties input their trade details to the matching engine database in real time, as soon as possible after the trade has been struck. This is usually achieved by building a real-time interface from the firm's relevant business application to the matching engine.
- The matching engine then compares the two trade reports, and provides them to both parties in real time.

An example of such matching engines is TRAX – Xtrakter Limited, a Euroclear subsidiary which compares the settlement instructions supplied by each party to the trade as part of the settlement process. Such systems then advise their members of any trades that cannot be matched. Most matching engines also facilitate trade reporting to regulators.

2.2.2 Newer Developments in the Use of Matching Engines

Traditional matching engines did not connect exchange member firms with non-member firms, nor did they support the confirmation/affirmation/allocation model, and nor did they store SSIs.

In 2002, Omgeo LLC launched the **Central Trade Manager**™, a central matching engine that involves the buy-side community and also supports block trades and allocations. This enables fund managers, brokers/dealers and custodian banks to share accurate SSIs automatically worldwide. The functions of CTM are shown in the following diagram, which is reproduced by permission of Omgeo LLC:

Example of a Buy Order using Omgeo Global Products - Both Cross Border and Offshore

2.3 The IT Implications of Trade Agreement – Summary of IT Requirements

This is a summary of the information that has been provided in Sections 2.1 and 2.2 of this chapter for each type of firm:

Sell-Side Firms

1. Need the technology to send confirmations for all asset classes that they trade in.
2. If they are involved in institutional equity sales, they will need the technology to support the confirmation/affirmation/allocation process. Institutional customers may require that they provide the facilities to communicate with them via central matching engines such as Omgeo.
3. If they are members of an investment exchange, they will need the technology to communicate with whatever matching engine is provided by those exchanges.
4. If they are active in the foreign exchange and money markets, they will need the technology to automatically match confirmations that are received on the 'mutual exchange' model of trade agreement.
5. The technology should be able to track the state of play of confirmations and trap any errors.

Buy-Side Firms

1. Need the technology to match confirmations for all asset classes that they trade in.
2. Need the technology to send affirmations and allocations to the sell-side.
3. The technology should be able to track the state of play of confirmations and trap any errors.

3. Reporting to Regulators

Learning Objective

5.4   Understand the IT requirements for reporting to regulators: wholesale vs retail

3.1 Reportable Transactions

Most trades that are executed by sell-side firms (as well as some that are executed by buy-side firms) need to be reported to the UK regulator. The current rules state that such transaction reports should be made *'as quickly as possible and by not later than the close of the working day following the day upon which that transaction took place'*. The UK regulator uses the information contained in trade reports to monitor for market abuse and insider dealing.

The actual regulations concerning which firms need to make trade reports in which instruments are quite complex but, in summary, any trade that involves a bond or an equity, or a derivative where the underlying instrument is a bond or equity, is reportable.

3.2 Contents of a Transaction Report

The UK regulator's rules for the minimum contents of a transaction report are set out in Annex 1 to Rule SUP 17.

3.3 How to Report a Transaction to the Regulators

All the central matching engines offer regulatory trade reporting as a by-product of the matching service – as trades are submitted to the matching engine they are forwarded to the regulators concerned. The UK regulator recognises these systems as **Approved Reporting Mechanisms**, and publishes an up-to-date list of approved reporting mechanisms on its website.

3.4 The IT Implications of Regulatory Transaction Reporting

The interfaces that a firm needs to use a central matching engine are the same as those that it needs to comply with its regulatory reporting requirements, so no additional software needs to be developed. However, suppliers of permitted reporting systems take this role very seriously. Although the regulator only specifies that transaction reports should be made *'as quickly as possible'*, Approved Reporting Mechanisms require that all trade reports are received within 30 minutes of execution time; if the firm fails to meet this deadline it will be fined on a sliding scale – the later the trade report, the bigger the fine.

Therefore, high availability of the applications that interface with the reporting systems is a key requirement.

4.   Reporting to Customers

Learning Objective

5.5   Understand the IT requirements for reporting to customers: wholesale vs retail

4.1   Legal and Regulatory Requirements

Precisely what information needs to be supplied to customers, at what frequency and by which media, will be governed by the client agreement or counterparty agreement (see Section 1.10). These agreements will take into account the requirements of regulators and tax authorities.

Firms that serve the retail investor have more regulatory demands on them than firms that deal with wholesale or professional investors.

The relevant UK regulations are contained in Conduct of Business (COBS) Rules 16.3.1 through to 16.3.9, and the main provisions of these rules are as follows.

Rule 16.3.1 (together with COBS 16 Annex 2R) mandates the minimum contents of a periodic statement of account for a retail customer. These are as follows:

Periodic information (all cases):

1.   The name of the firm.
2.   The name or other designation of the retail client's account.
3.   A statement of the contents and the valuation of the portfolio, including details of:
     a.   each designated investment held, its market value or fair value if market value is unavailable;
     b.   the cash balance at the beginning and at the end of the reporting period; and
     c.   the performance of the portfolio during the reporting period.
4.   The total amount of fees and charges incurred during the reporting period, itemising at least total management fees and total costs associated with execution, and including, where relevant, a statement that a more detailed breakdown will be provided on request.
5.   A comparison of performance during the period covered by the statement with the investment performance benchmark (if any) agreed between the firm and the client.
6.   The total amount of dividends, interest and other payments received during the reporting period in relation to the client's portfolio.
7.   Information about other corporate actions giving rights in relation to designated investments held in the portfolio.

Rule 16.3.2 deals with the frequency of statements for retail customers. The rule mandates that:

•   Statements must be sent to retail clients at least once every six months, but the client is entitled to insist on statements being sent every three months.
•   Firms must inform retail clients that they have this right.

It grants an exception when there are no transactions to report for the period – there is no need to send a six-monthly or three-monthly statement if this is the case, but the firm must still send an annual statement.

Rule 16.3.3 mandates the contents of a trade confirmation message to a retail client.

There is a further obligation on firms that hold client assets, and that is to provide **tax vouchers** to the holders. The tax voucher is evidence of the fact that the income has been paid, and shows whether or not any income tax was withheld from the payment.

4.2   Commercial Requirements for Customer Reporting

While these rules mandate minimum standards, professional investors and high net worth individual customers will often demand certain reporting standards which the firm must adhere to in order to remain competitive. Typically, these might include the following types of report:

- **List of and valuation of the holdings at the statement date** – customers may demand that this report:
    - ○ Compares the performance of the fund to a **benchmark**. For example, a fund that is entirely invested in UK equities might have its performance compared to the performance of the FTSE 100 index, while a fund that is wholly invested in German equities might have its performance compared to the performance of the DAX index. In the case of funds that are invested in many sectors, there will be the need to compare performance to many indices. This places an obligation on the IT department to provide both the interfaces required to source such information from the index providers, and the software that can make the comparisons.
    - ○ **Makes an attempt at 'performance attribution'** – performance attribution analysis attempts to explain why a portfolio had a certain return. It does so by breaking down the performance and attributing the results based on the decisions made by the fund manager on asset allocation, sector choice and security selection. There are a number of generally accepted mathematical formulae for this analysis and, if it is a requirement, then the IT department will need to provide software that can use these formulae.
- **Capital cash statement** – showing the amount of cash in the customer's account at statement date, plus movements in and out.
- **Income statement** – showing all dividends, coupons, bank account interest and other income for the period covered by the statement.
- **Corporate actions statements** – showing the effect of any corporate actions on the portfolio during the period.
- **Capital gains tax reports and tax vouchers** (because these are private clients, tax becomes an issue in capturing transaction data in the right tax period).

End of Chapter Questions

Think of an answer for each question and refer to the appropriate section for confirmation.

1. List the advantages and disadvantages of building and maintaining a reference data repository.
    Section 1.3

2. What information about a security may be determined from the market in which it is traded?
    Section 1.4.1

3. Which instrument coding system allocates a unique identifier to each combination of security and the country in which it is traded?
    Section 1.4.2

4. List the reference data items that need to be held for a bond in order to calculate interest on bonds.
    Section 1.4.4

5. What is the name of the unique identifier that is used by SWIFT to identify banks and other trading parties?
    Section 1.5.1

6. What is the difference between a depot and a nostro account?
    Section 1.6.2

7. What is the UK regulator's definition of a client agreement?
    Section 1.10.3

8. For which asset classes can the trade agreement process be described as 'mutual exchange of confirmations'?
    Section 2.1

9. List the IT requirements for the trade agreement process for a sell-side firm.
    Section 2.3

10. Why does the UK regulator require firms to report trades in real time?
    Section 3.1

Chapter Six
The Role of IT in the Settlement and Post-Settlement Phases

This syllabus area will provide approximately 5 of the 50 examination questions

1.   The IT Requirements of Transaction Instructions

Learning Objective

6.1   Understand the IT support requirements of transaction instructions

1.1   Introduction

In Chapter 5 we looked at the role of SSIs. Once all the trade agreement processes are completed, the firm's settlement system needs to send **settlement instruction messages** to its settlement agents.

A settlement instruction is, as its name suggests, an instruction sent by a trading party to a settlement agent, instructing it to make or accept delivery of securities (usually) in exchange for receipt or payment of funds.

If the process of delivery of the securities is to be inextricably linked to the receipt of funds it is said to be a **delivery-versus-payment (DvP)** instruction. If payment and delivery are not inextricably linked, then it is said to be **free of payment (FoP)**. DvP is the norm in the securities markets, as sending instructions FoP creates credit risk. For this reason, most firms have very strict rules as to in what circumstances an FoP instruction may be issued.

This means that many application systems that automatically generate settlement instructions are usually designed to require a second level of authorisation before an FoP instruction can be sent out.

1.2 Contents of Settlement Instructions

Field Name	Explanation of Contents	Example Data
From:	Identity of the firm sending the instruction (note 1).	ABC Investment Bank
To:	Identity of the settlement agent receiving the instruction (note 1).	Euroclear Brussels
Value date	Earliest date on which the instruction should be carried out.	5 March 2012
Deliver/receive	Whether securities are to be delivered or received.	Deliver
Settlement basis	Whether delivery-versus-payment or free of payment.	Versus payment
Quantity of securities	The number of shares (equity) or face value of bonds to be delivered.	1,000,000
Security reference	The ID of the security being delivered or received (note 2).	DEF plc 5% bond maturing 28 January 2015
Settlement currency	The currency of the cash to be paid or received.	EUR
Net settlement value	The amount of cash to be paid or received.	985,000.00
Our depot account	The firm's stock account number with the settlement agent.	123456789
Our cash account	The firm's cash account number with the settlement agent.	987654321
Counterparty depot details	Full details of the counterparty's stock settlement account, including account code (note 3).	Société Générale Paris, account no.104867, in favour of Minicorp Pension Fund
Counterparty nostro details	Full details of the counterparty's cash settlement account, including account code (note 3).	Société Générale Paris, acct no.0-0876554332, in favour of Minicorp Pension Fund
Our reference	Our reference for the instruction. We would expect the settlement agent to quote this on all subsequent communications with us about this instruction.	aa-111222333-1
Transmission date time	The date and time that the settlement instruction was sent.	01/03/2012 10:33:00

Notes to Table

1. The identity of the sender and receiver are usually represented by a BIC code – see Chapter 5.
2. The identity of the security is usually represented by an ISIN code, SEDOL code, CUSIP code or some other standard identifier. The most widely used code in Europe is ISIN – see Chapter 5.
3. The identity of both the other party and its settlement agent are usually represented either by BIC codes or CSD/ICSD participant codes.

1.3 Transmission of Settlement Instructions

Settlement instructions are usually transmitted in one of the following three ways:

- In the form of **SWIFT messages** – refer to Section 5 for more information about the SWIFT network and SWIFT standards.
- Using a **proprietary standard message** developed by the settlement agent, and transmitted using an interface or portal designed by that settlement agent. Most commercial custodians, as well as the CSDs and ICSDs, supply systems to their customers that provide for secure communication. Traditionally these were PC systems that required physical installation at the customer site but, increasingly, these systems are web-based applications.
- By **email, fax and telex** – these traditional means of communication are being used less and less, as they do not lend themselves so readily to the STP concept as the other methods do.

In a high-volume, STP-based environment, the firm's settlement system usually generates settlement instructions automatically, and communicates directly with the firm's chosen method of transmission.

1.4 Information Supplied by Settlement Agents between Receipt of Instruction and Actual Settlement Event

Between the time that the settlement agent receives the instruction and the date that the trade actually settles, settlement agents usually communicate the status of trades that are pending settlement to the firm. The format of such status messages will be similar to the following:

Field Name	Explanation of Contents	Example Data
From	Identity of the settlement agent sending the status message.	Euroclear Brussels
To	Identity of the firm receiving the status message.	ABC Investment Bank
Our trade reference	Euroclear's unique reference for the instruction.	Kkee4455tt
Your trade reference	The reference that ABC quoted on the original settlement instruction.	aa-111222333-1
Date and time of the message	The date and time that the message was sent.	02/03/2012 09:00:00
Brief details of the instruction	Action, security, security quantity, cash currency, cash amount.	DvP 1,000,000 DEF plc 5% bond maturing 28 January 2015 to Société Générale in favour of Minicorp for €985,000.00
Status code	A code to represent the status of the instruction.	See below

Status codes: Each settlement agent will issue its customers with a list of status codes and their meanings. The codes in the table below are purely illustrative.

Code	Meaning	Action to be taken by firm
UNM0	Unmatched – you have sent an instruction but your counterparty hasn't. Trade isn't due to settle until T+1 or later.	Take up with trade party.
UNM1	Urgent unmatched – as above, but trade is due for settlement tomorrow or earlier.	Take up with trade party – as a matter of urgency.
CUNM	A trade party has alleged a trade against you; but you have not sent any instruction.	Investigate internally/take up with trade party.
USEC	Trade is matched, but you don't have any stock to deliver.	Ascertain why you have no stock. Try to borrow if necessary.
CSEC	Trade is matched, but counterparty has no stock to deliver.	Take up with trade party.
COLL	Trade is matched, but you don't have sufficient credit in your account with the settlement agent to pay for the stock.	Investigate why. If the cash is held in a different bank account, transfer it, or else negotiate a line of credit.
OTH	Other reason why this instruction might not take effect – usually this means that the other party has insufficient cash or collateral in his account to pay for the stock.	Take up with trade party.
OK	The instruction is OK for future settlement.	No action is needed.

Most CSDs and ICSDs make this information available to participants in real time; it is up to business applications in the firm's configuration to access it. Some commercial custodians make it available in real time, but some send it in the form of a SWIFT message once each day, at the end of the day.

The status of a trade may change many times between the time that the instruction was received by the agent and the date and time that it actually settles. For example, the status history of this trade might be as follows:

Sequence	Date/time	Event	Status now
1	1 Mar 2012 10:33:00	ABC sends the instruction. XYZ has not yet sent its instruction.	UNM0
2	1 Mar 2012 12:14:00	XYZ sends its instruction, but ABC does not yet have the stock to deliver.	USEC
3	2 Mar 2012 07:00:00	As a result of the successful settlement of another instruction, ABC now has stock to deliver.	OK
4	2 Mar 2012 08:00:00	As a result of a processing error, ABC incorrectly cancels this instruction.	CUNM
5	2 Mar 2012 11:00:00	ABC corrects the error that resulted in (4).	OK

1.5 Information Supplied by Settlement Agents when the Trade Actually Settles

1.5.1 The Process of Settling the Trade – Settling within Tolerance

The settlement agent will settle the trade provided that:

1. value date has been reached;
2. the seller has the stock to deliver;
3. the buyer has the cash or credit to pay for it; and
4. the seller's instructions match the buyer's instructions.

In determining whether instructions match, the settlement agent usually has the ability to 'settle within tolerance'. That is to say that, if the instructions match in every respect apart from a minor difference in the cash consideration, then the agent will settle the trade using the cash figure supplied by the seller. What is considered to be a 'minor difference' varies from market to market; in the case of trades settling at Euroclear Bank, for example, the threshold is set at the equivalent of USD25.00.

1.5.2 Information Provided by the Agent when the Trade Settles

The settlement agent will provide the following information when the trade settles:

Field Name	Explanation of Contents	Example Data
From	Identity of the settlement agent sending the status message.	Euroclear Brussels
To	Identity of the firm receiving the status message.	ABC Investment Bank
Our trade reference	Euroclear's unique reference for the instruction.	Kkee4455tt
Your trade reference	The reference that ABC quoted on the original settlement instruction.	aa-111222333-1
Date and time of the message	The date and time that the message was sent.	02/03/2012 09:00:00
Deliver or receive	Whether stock has been delivered or received.	Deliver
Security reference	The ID of the security being delivered or received.	ICI plc 5% bond maturing 28 January 2015
Stock amount	Amount of stock actually delivered or received.	1,000,000
Settlement currency	The currency of the cash that was received or paid.	EUR
Settlement amount	The amount of cash that was received or paid.	985,000.00

1.6 The Significance of Instruction Reference Numbers

1.6.1 The Role of Instruction Reference Numbers in the STP Process

When ABC sent the instruction, it provided its unique reference number (aa-111222333-1). Euroclear quoted this number on all the messages it sent back to ABC about the trade. The existence of this unique number facilitates STP, and also facilitates the update of the trade record in ABC's systems with the latest status of the instruction.

1.6.2 Instruction Reference Numbers and Trade Reference Numbers – Are They the Same Thing?

Some settlement systems quote the trade reference to the custodian. There are a number of reasons why this may not be the best idea, including the following:

1. Some trade types, by definition, will generate two or more instructions. For example, a stock loan might generate the following:
   a. an initial DvP instruction to settle the start leg;
   b. one or more (cash only) margin payments or refunds of margin payments as price movements create the need to increase or reduce collateral;
   c. one or more (cash only) interim payments of fees if the loan crosses several month ends;
   d. a final DvP instruction to close the transaction, returning the stock and the cash collateral.
2. Sometimes it may not be possible to settle the whole transaction in one operation. The parties may agree to accept partial delivery in return for partial payment.
3. The effect of settlement netting – several trades may be consolidated into a single settlement.
4. If errors are made in trade processing, then sometimes settlement instructions need to be cancelled and re-issued. Therefore, a single trade has gone through multiple trade versions, each one creating changed settlement instructions.

For these reasons, it is generally considered 'best practice', when designing a settlement system, to have a many (trades) to many (instructions) relationship between trades and settlement instructions.

2. Stock Lending, Stock Borrowing and Repo Transactions

Learning Objective

6.2 Understand the purposes of stock lending and repos, their IT implications and the importance of segregation

2.1 Introduction

As well as being bought and sold, securities may be lent and borrowed, and also used as collateral for firms that need to borrow cash. There are two broad categories of transactions of this type – stock loans and repos. The word 'repo' is short for **sale and re-purchase agreement**.

The term '**stock lending**' is usually used to describe a transaction where:

1. The motivation of the **borrower** (of stock) is to acquire a specific quantity of a given stock to meet a commitment to deliver, ie, they have sold some stock without owning it.
2. The motivation of the **lender** (of stock) is to provide the securities the borrower requires, and to attract collateral to protect itself against default; they usually charge a fee or interest.

A **repo transaction**, by contrast, is one where:

1. The motivation of the **lender** (of stock) is to borrow cash at a better rate of interest than it would if it borrowed on an unsecured basis.
2. The motivation of the **borrower** (of stock) is to lend cash on a secured basis.

In other words, the business purpose of a stock loan is to enable one party to lend securities to another, and the business purpose of a repo is to allow one party to use securities as collateral for its cash borrowing.

In processing terms the two transaction types share the following characteristics:

- They both use collateral to reduce the lender's credit risk.
- They both employ the concepts of nominal ownership and beneficial ownership that preserve the lender's rights to any income or other benefits provided by ownership of the security being lent.

2.1.1 The Essence of the Stock Lending/Borrowing Transaction

The following diagram explains the stock lending transaction:

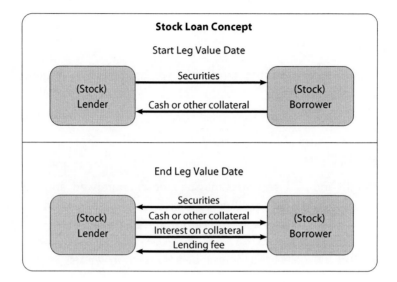

The transaction has a start leg and an end leg.

- On the value date of the **start leg**, the lender delivers securities to the borrower in exchange for collateral. The purpose of the cash collateral is to provide the lender with security in case the borrower does not return the securities that were borrowed.
- On the value date of the **end leg**, the securities are returned to the borrower and the collateral is returned to the lender. At the same time, the lender is paid a lending fee, and the borrower is paid interest on the collateral.

2.1.2 The Essence of the Repo Transaction

The repo also involves an exchange of cash for securities in both legs of the transaction, but this time the lender of cash is using the securities as collateral in case the borrower is unable to return the cash at the end of the loan period. The mechanism of the exchange of cash and collateral is that Party B 'sells' the securities to Party A under an agreement where A can repurchase them at a later date.

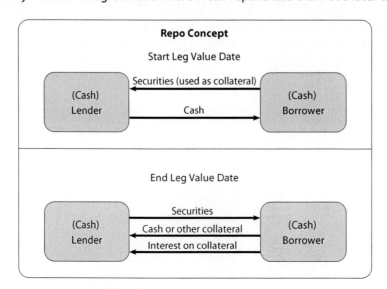

2.1.3   The Differences Between the Two Types of Transaction

Stock loans and repos are very similar transactions that are often confused with each other. In Chapter 3 we learned that repos – or sale and repurchase agreements – are 'transactions where Party A lends money to Party B, provided that Party B provides Party A with collateral in the form of government bonds'. The two transactions are, therefore, very similar – Party A delivers stock and receives cash on the value date of the opening leg, and on the value date of the closing leg the stock is returned against payment of the cash collateral plus interest. Like stock loans, repos change nominal ownership but not beneficial ownership, and also the same SLIs (see Section 2.3) are involved in providing intermediary services.

The differences between the two types of transaction are as follows:

- **Business purpose** – the business purpose of the repo transaction is to lower the interest expenses of the seller (of stock), who is also the borrower (of cash). The way that this works is as follows: ABC Investment Bank has a credit rating of A. As such, the lowest interest rate it could obtain as a commercial borrower is, say 5.5%. However, it has holdings of an AAA-rated government bond that it can offer as collateral. Because governments (usually) have higher credit ratings than banks, a lender will be prepared to offer ABC a loan at 5% providing that it provides government bonds as collateral. If ABC is unable to repay the loan, the lender will sell the government bonds.
- **Acceptable instruments** – a large number of individual equities and bonds are acceptable instruments for stock loans, but only a small number of Organisation for Economic Co-operation and Development (OECD) government bonds are acceptable in repo transactions.
- **No stock lending fee** – in a stock loan transaction, there is both interest to be paid by the lender of stock on the collateral, and also a fee to be paid by the stock borrower for the use of the stock. In the case of repos, only the collateral interest is payable.

Securities lending is a large activity, providing liquidity to bond and equity markets globally. Lending grew rapidly in the decade until 2007, although values are estimated to have declined somewhat since the financial crisis as investment banks and hedge funds reduce the size of their balance sheets. The International Securities Lending Association (www.isla.co.uk) estimates that securities on loan globally (bonds and equities) are around US$4–5 trillion.

2.1.4   Reasons Why Market Participants Carry Out These Transactions

There are a number of reasons why market participants may wish to lend or borrow securities.

Reasons for Borrowing Securities

- Market makers and other sell-side firms often run short positions; ie, they have sold more stock than they have bought. They will, therefore, borrow stock in order to settle their sales on the correct value date.
- Any buy-side or sell-side firm may have a situation where securities that it has bought cannot be delivered for some reason. If they have, in turn, sold the stock to another party, then they, of course, will be unable to deliver what they have not received. They therefore borrow stock to cover for delivery failures.
- Hedge funds often sell stock short because they expect the price of the security concerned to fall in the future, when they will buy it back at the lower price. They too will borrow stock in order to settle these short sales on the correct value date.

- Hedge funds also use stock lending as part of strategies to influence the management of the company concerned, particularly in matters relating to mergers and acquisitions. If a hedge fund borrows stock, then it can vote the borrowed stock at company meetings. This is explained in Section 2.2.1 of this chapter.

Reasons for Lending Securities

- Traditional fund managers do not sell short; they are sometimes referred to as 'long only' fund managers in this context. They are prepared to lend stock because of the fee they receive for doing so, ie, they have a large number of assets and this helps generate an extra income from fees.

Reasons for Using Repos as Distinct from Unsecured Lending and Borrowing

- Market makers, and other firms that deal as principal, have to finance their inventory of long positions. One of the ways that they can do this is to use these long positions in repo transactions as collateral for potential borrowers, and in return they receive cash, which they can use to fund their trading books. Because they have provided collateral, they will be charged a lower rate of interest than if they borrowed unsecured. This is because, in the event of the borrower being unable to meet its obligations, the lender of cash could seize the securities that were offered as collateral and sell them.

2.2 Other Factors Affecting Stock Lending Transactions

Stock loans are complex transactions. Some other factors that IT staff need to be aware of include the following.

2.2.1 Legal and Beneficial Ownership

Under UK law, the **borrower** of the securities becomes the **nominal owner** of them. The rights of the **lender** are protected, however, as it remains the **beneficial owner**.

What this means in practice is that the borrower receives all dividends, coupons and any other corporate action proceeds that are paid during the period of the loan. However, the borrower, in effect, holds the assets in trust for the lender, and has an obligation to repay any proceeds received of this kind to the lender.

It also means that the borrower acquires (and therefore the lender loses) the right to vote at company meetings, which is how hedge funds are able to use borrowed stock to influence the companies whose shares have been borrowed. If the lender wishes to vote, then they must recall the securities.

2.2.2 Non-Cash Collateral

In the simple examples in Sections 2.1.1 and 2.1.2, the borrower of stock supplied the lender with cash collateral. The lender is free to invest this collateral, and that, more than the lending fee, is where the lender gets the majority of its additional income as a result of the transaction. However, some lenders will accept government bonds or other types of security, or letters of credit, as an alternative form of collateral.

2.3   The Use of Specialised Lending Intermediaries (SLIs)

There are many securities firms that act as specialised intermediaries in the stock lending area. There are several reasons why their presence is required in order to create a liquid and efficient market.

A borrower could always borrow a relatively small number of shares for a short period from another fund manager (fund managers are the largest source of loans) if the borrower and the lender knew of each other's existence, but, for example, if the borrower wanted to borrow a very large quantity of shares for a long period – say seven months – and use government bonds as collateral, then it might run into some or all of these problems:

1. It cannot find a fund manager willing to lend such a large amount.
2. It cannot find a fund manager willing to lend for such a long period.
3. It cannot find a fund manager prepared to accept non-cash collateral.

In these circumstances, it can put the lending request to a **specialised lending intermediary (SLI)**, of which there are many. SLIs include the stock lending divisions of investment banks, as well as specialist niche firms. SLIs have a list of fund manager clients and will divide the large loan request into a number of smaller parcels, for shorter periods. If one of their clients needs its stock back after, say, one month, then they will reassign that part of the loan to another client.

SLIs also deal with the problem that a borrower doesn't want to provide cash collateral, but the lenders insist on it. The SLI takes the government bond and does a repo transaction with it that provides the SLI with the cash to provide to the lenders.

SLIs usually act as principal in transactions, making a small margin on collateral interest rates and stock lending fees.

2.3.1   Tri-Party Repo Services

Tri-Party Repo and Delivery-by-Value (DBV)

In Section 2.1.4 we learned that market makers need to fund their inventory and will lend stock in order to attract the cash collateral for this purpose. Their problem is determining which stock they can lend. They are obviously not in a position to lend stock that they need to deliver for their sales. **Settlement agents**, such as Euroclear, operate a special service for such firms. Internationally, this service is known as tri-party repo, but in the UK market it is called 'Delivery-by-Value' (DbV).

The way that DbV works is that the market maker and an SLI agree that the market maker needs to borrow, say, £10,000,000 to finance its trading book 'overnight' (ie, for one day). Both parties input a special DbV transaction that just quotes this amount, and the collateral (say, £10,500,000) that the SLI needs. That evening Euroclear finds securities to the value of £10.5 million in the market maker's account that are not needed for delivery to clients and transfers them, against payment, to the SLI's account. The following day Euroclear returns the securities to the market maker, and the cash to the SLI. The market maker then re-evaluates its funding requirements for the next day and the process is repeated.

Other Custodian Services

CSDs, ICSDs and custody banks also offer automatic borrowing and lending services to those participants that require them. If EUI sees that Member A is unable to deliver 500 shares of a particular stock to meet a sale commitment, it will find another participant (Member B) that can lend the stock to Member A. Member A will be charged a fee by EUI, the majority of which will be paid to the other party. When EUI can see that Member A no longer needs the borrowing, it will automatically be repaid to Member B. Members A and B are unaware of each other and, in the event of the default of Member A, then EUI has to find the stock to return to B. For this reason, members that wish to participate in automated borrowing services have to 'pledge' their holdings at the CSD to the CSD.

2.4   Segregation of Client Assets

The existence of the stock lending and repo markets is one of the reasons that all regulators, the UK regulator included, have strict rules on the segregation of client assets.

In practice, what this means is that firms that hold client securities have to keep them in separate accounts at the CSD or custodian. In the UK, these separate accounts are often known as **nominee accounts**. The use of nominee accounts makes it much easier to comply with the client reporting rules that were described in Section 4 of Chapter 5, and also makes it easier to ensure that client assets are not inadvertently used in collateral-based transactions.

The text of the UK regulator's rules on the subject of segregation, first set out in **Principle 10**, states: '*A firm must arrange adequate protection for clients' assets when it is responsible for them*.'

Client Assets Rule 6.4.1 expands this principle to state that:

1. A firm must not enter into arrangements for securities financing transactions in respect of safe custody assets held by it on behalf of a client or otherwise use such safe custody assets for its own account or the account of another client of the firm, unless:
    a. the client has given express prior consent to the use of the safe custody assets on specified terms; and
    b. the use of that client's safe custody assets is restricted to the specified terms to which the client consents.
2. A firm must not enter into arrangements for securities financing transactions in respect of safe custody assets held by it on behalf of a client in an omnibus account held by a third party, or otherwise use safe custody assets held in such an account for its own account or for the account of another client unless, in addition to the conditions set out in (1):
    a. each client whose safe custody assets are held together in an omnibus account has given express prior consent in accordance with (1)(a); or
    b. the firm has in place systems and controls which ensure that only safe custody assets belonging to clients who have given express prior consent in accordance with the requirements of (1)(a) are used.
3. For the purposes of obtaining the express prior consent of a retail client under this rule, the signature of the retail client or an equivalent alternative mechanism is required.

The effect of these rules is that **client assets may not be used in stock lending or repo transactions without the express written agreement of the client concerned**.

2.5   The IT Implications of Stock Loans and Repos

Firms that have a business requirement to be active participants in the stock lending and repo markets need to have business applications that are able to:

- manage collateral – that is to say that they have to be able to:
  - revalue securities to ensure that the collateral placed or received is adequate;
  - send messages to, and receive messages from, counterparties about collateral requirement changes;
- send the relevant instructions to settlement agents to settle the transactions;
- calculate collateral interest charges and stock lending fees using the calculations in Section 4.1.1;
- identify securities that are available to be used in stock lending and repo transactions (see example below); and
- ensure that the investment and custody records correctly reflect which holdings are out on loan; this will ensure that holdings on loan are not sold accidentally and that client reporting accurately reflects this.

Example

On 2 March ABC Investment Bank was asked by an SLI whether it was in a position to lend 750,000 Megabank shares from its account at EUI from 5 March for an indefinite period. The position in the dealer's book is that he is long one million shares, so apparently ABC could lend 750K. However, a closer look at the dealer's book on a settled trades basis reveals that:

Date	Description	Number of shares available
2 March	Position in dealer's book	1,000,000
2 March	Less: expected receipts from counterparties for purchases value 1 March that have not been received	−500,000
2 March	Current position at the depot	500,000
5 March	Add: deliveries due from counterparties for purchases with value 5 March	100,000
5 March	Less: deliveries due to counterparties for sales with value 5 March	−400,000
5 March	Expected position in the depot at 5 March	Between 100,000 and 700,000

If all the deliveries and receipts that were due on 1 March and 5 March are made on 5 March, then ABC could lend 700,000 shares – not the 750K that was requested. The worst position that ABC could find itself in is that none of its expected receipts actually occur, but it still has to deliver out 100K shares on 5 March. In that case it could only lend 100,000 shares.

The necessary IT infrastructure to carry out these activities is often to be found within the back office settlement system for equities and bonds. There are, however, a number of specialised stock lending and collateral management package systems on the market that interface with a firm's main settlement system to provide this type of functionality.

3. Cash Funding

3.1   Introduction

Once the instructions have been sent out, both parties have to ensure that they will have the cash available to pay for their purchases, and the stock available to deliver for their sales. Therefore, most settlement systems incorporate a cash flow projection module that shows them how much funding they need. Sometimes this module is referred to as a **maturity ladder**.

3.2   Example of a Maturity Ladder

3.2.1   Information Contained in the Maturity Ladder

The tables in this section show examples of a maturity ladder produced at the close of business on 5 March 2007 for ABC Investment Bank's USD bank account with Euroclear Brussels for the next three working days.

In the real world, the maturity ladder would show the expected cash movements for all the firm's bank accounts in all currencies (one page for each individual currency bank account) for the next five working days. The table shows only three days; the last two days have been omitted in this example in order to simplify it.

We can see the following information in the maturity ladder:

1. The closing balance of the US$ account at Euroclear for today (5 March) is US$2,000,000.00.
2. The report (in older settlement systems this will indeed be a printed report, but in more modern systems it will probably be a real-time online enquiry) then lists the numbers of trades and total net values of all the various trade types (security purchases, sales, stock lending transactions, FX transactions, etc) that are due to settle on 6 March. Included among these are one overdue security purchase with a value of US$1 million, and one overdue unsettled security sale with a value of US$1.5 million. These trades should have settled on or before 5 March, but for some reason have not settled.
3. If you add the value of all the transactions that should settle on or before 6 March to the 5 March cash balance, then we have a projected balance on this account for 6 March of US$3,650,000.
4. The process is then repeated for 7 March, when the projected balance of the account is now US$8,350,000, and 8 March when it becomes US$7,850,000.

3.2.2   What the Maturity Ladder Shows Us

The conclusions we can draw from looking at this maturity ladder are:

1. On 6 March, we have excess funds of US$3.65 million on this account.
2. On 7 March, we have a shortage of US$8.35 million on this account.
3. On 8 March we have a shortage of US$7.85 million on this account.

ABC Investment Bank plc - Maturity Ladder								
Nostro Name:		Euroclear Brussels		Currency: USD			Date	05 March 2007
Cash Balance on Account as at:		05/03/07	2,000,000.00	06/03/07	3,650,000.00		07/03/07	-8,350,000.00
Items Due For Settlement on:	nbr of txns	06/03/07		nbr of txns	07/03/07	nbr of txns	08/03/07	
Overdue security purchases	0		0.00	0	0	0		
Overdue security sales	1		500,000.00	0	0	0		
Security purchases	1		-1,000,000.00	6	-13,500,000.00	1		-1,250,000.00
Security sales	4		1,500,000.00	3	1,500,000.00	10		1,750,000.00
Stock lending open leg txns	2		750,000.00	0	0.00	0		0.00
Stock borrowing open leg txns	1		-250,000.00	0	0.00	0		0.00
Stock lending return leg txns	2		-400,000.00	0	0.00	0		0.00
Stock borrowing return leg leg txns	3		300,000.00	0	0.00	0		0.00
Repo open leg transactions	0		0.00	0	0	0		0.00
Repo closing leg transactions	0		0.00	0	0	0		0.00
Money market transactions	0		0.00	0	0.00	0		0.00
FX purchases	1		250,000.00	0	0.00	0		0.00
FX sales	0		0.00	0	0.00	0		0.00
Other cash movements	0		0.00	0	0.00	0		0.00
Cash Flow Projection For		06/03/07	3,650,000.00	07/03/07	-8,350,000.00		08/03/07	-7,850,000.00

3.2.3   Possible Actions the Firm Could Take to Fund the Account Correctly

Excess Funds on 6 March

For 6 March, the firm's treasurer could put US$3 million on overnight deposit for 6 March, to earn a higher rate of interest than Euroclear pays on a nostro account. If we assume that the firm could earn 4% overnight, then the following day (when the deposit matures) US$3,000.333.33 will be paid back into the account (interest being calculated as 3,000,000 x 4% x 1 day/360 days in a year).

Inadequate Funds on 7 and 8 March

The firm may be able to resolve this issue by any one of the following means:

1. Perhaps it has excess funds on another nostro that it could transfer into the account.
2. It could borrow US$8.5 million for two days on the money markets at, say, 5%.
3. If it has government bonds that it could use as collateral, it could borrow US$8.5 million indefinitely by using these bonds as collateral for a repo transaction, paying only 4% interest.

If it takes the third option – the repo – then the maturity ladder now looks like the illustration on the next page. The new transactions are highlighted. You will see that the treasurer has been able to keep the projected balances on this account at between US$0.15 million and US$0.65 million for the period, ensuring that the account is funded adequately for the period, and that any excess funds are swept into higher interest-bearing vehicles.

ABC Investment Bank plc - Maturity Ladder								
Nostro Name:		Euroclear Brussels			Currency: USD		Date	05 March 2007
Cash Balance on Account as at:		05/03/07	2,000,000.00	06/03/07	650,000.00		07/03/07	150,333.00
Items Due For Settlement on:	nbr of txns	06/03/07		nbr of txns	07/03/07	nbr of txns	08/03/07	
Overdue security purchases	0		0.00	0		0	0	
Overdue security sales	I		500,000.00	0		0	0	
Security purchases	I		-1,000,000.00	6	-13,500,000.00	I		-1,250,000.00
Security sales	4		1,500,000.00	3	1,500,000.00	10		1,750,000.00
Stock lending open leg txns	2		750,000.00	0	0.00	0		0.00
Stock borrowing open leg txns	I		-250,000.00	0	0.00	0		0.00
Stock lending return leg txns	2		-400,000.00	0	0.00	0		0.00
Stock borrowing return leg leg txns	3		300,000.00	0	0.00	0		0.00
Repo open leg transactions	0		0.00	I	8,500,000.00	0		0.00
Repo closing leg transactions	0		0.00	0	0	0		0.00
Money market transactions	I		-3,000,000.00	I	3,000,333.00	0		0.00
FX purchases	I		250,000.00	0	0.00	0		0.00
FX sales	0		0.00	0	0.00	0		0.00
Other cash movements	0		0.00	0	0.00	0		0.00
Cash Flow Projection For		06/03/07	650,000.00	07/03/07	150,333.00		08/03/07	650,333.00

4. The Function of IT within the Settlement Process

Learning Objective

6.4 Understand the function of IT within the settlement process: front office systems; back office systems; financial control systems

4.1 The Settlement System and its Place in the Configuration

Let us look again at the systems configuration diagram of a typical investment bank that we first saw in Chapter 2, Section 6:

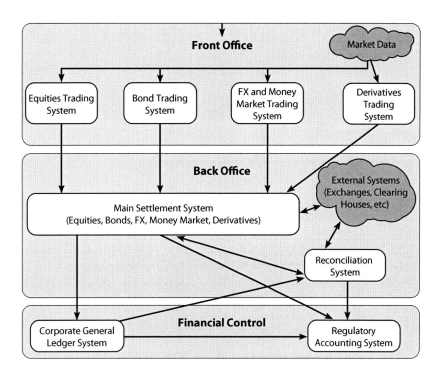

In most firms, the main settlement system fits into the configuration in the following way:

1. It holds much of the reference (static) data that was discussed in Chapter 5.
2. It takes in real-time trade feeds from the various front office systems and enriches them with reference data such as:
   - SSIs for trading parties and the firm itself;
   - rules and parameters used to calculate trade proceeds, trade interest, commissions, fees and expenses.
3. It then decides on the appropriate format and delivery method of settlement instruction messages and transmits those messages to settlement agents.
4. Between trade date and settlement date it receives status update messages from settlement agents, and updates its database with the latest trade statuses advised by the agents. It will then provide facilities for back office personnel to monitor potential settlement failures which may arise because of missing or incorrect SSIs, incorrect or missing settlement instructions sent out, shortages of stock to deliver, etc.
5. On settlement date, it receives messages from the settlement agents informing it which trades have either fully settled or partially settled, and updates its database with the outcome of these messages. It then provides the operations personnel with facilities to monitor and control actual settlement failures, ie, trades that have not settled by contractual value date.
6. It provides facilities for the firm to manage its funding by means of management reports, such as a maturity ladder.
7. The settlement system usually performs interest accruals – see below, Section 4.1.1.
8. It feeds data to the corporate general ledger system and the regulatory accounting system – these will be discussed in Chapter 7 – and the reconciliation system – this is discussed later in this chapter.
9. Depending on the configuration details at the individual firm, either the front office systems or the settlement system will handle regulatory trade reporting and central matching – these were dealt with in Chapter 5.
10. It will usually be the system that controls corporate actions, dividends and coupon processing, option expiry and exercise, etc.
11. It is usually this system that controls the mark-to-market activity that was discussed in Chapter 4, Section 5.2.1.

12. It may also supply data to a system or service designed to calculate VaR (Chapter 4, Section 5.2.2).

13. It will also supply the firm's management with a wide variety of management information, such as statistics about settlement failures, their reasons and cost. These may be needed by asset class, trading book, settlement agent, or any combination of these entities.

4.1.1   Interest Accruals

When a firm enters into any of the following types of transactions:

- purchase or sale of bonds;
- stock borrowing, lending and repos; or
- money market loans and deposits,

it needs to account for the interest that will be paid on the next coupon date of the bond or the termination date of the other types of contract. This process is known as **interest accrual**, and is part of the risk management process that was discussed in Chapter 4. See also Chapter 5, Section 1.4.4.

Definitions

Accrual is an accounting term. It is defined as a method of accounting in which each item is entered as it is earned or incurred, regardless of when actual payments are received or made.

Accrued interest is defined as the interest that has accumulated on a transaction since the last interest payment date or start date, up to but not including the current date.

Example – Accrued Interest Calculation

On trade date 5 March, value date 7 March, ABC Investment Bank borrowed £1,000,000 for 30 days at 5% interest, calculated on the actual/actual basis (see Chapter 5, Section 1.4.4). The maturity date is therefore 6 April. On 6 April, ABC will repay the principal amount of £1,000,000 + 30 days' interest:

Repayment amount = 1,000,000 +(1,000,000 x 30/365 x 5%) = £1,004,109.59

However, as part of the mark-to-market process, ABC needs to account for this interest expense on each day that it occurs, not all in one amount at the end of the loan period.

The settlement system is therefore required to process the interest accrual amounts shown in the table on the following page on each working day between 6 March and 6 April so that the interest cost is recorded in the general ledger on the day that it is incurred.

Please note the following:

1. It is the convention that no interest is payable or receivable on the start date of a transaction, but is payable at the end date.

2. The daily accrual convention is one day's interest on Mondays through to Thursdays, and three days' interest is to be accrued on Fridays, unless any or all of the days of the weekend following fall into the next month. If that is the case, the system should accrue to the month-end date – Saturday 31 March in this example. If there were a public holiday on the Monday following, then four days' interest would be accrued on the Friday, unless the Monday fell into the next calendar month.

3. If the firm has a financial month-end date of Saturday 31 March, then the firm would account for the total interest of £4,109.59 as:
   ◦ 24 days – £3,287.67 forming March expenses; and
   ◦ six days – £821.92 forming April expenses.

These matters are illustrated by the following table:

Day of week	Date	No. of working days	Accrual to date	Accrual for the day
Wednesday	07-Mar	0	0.00	0.00
Thursday	08-Mar	1	136.99	136.99
Friday	09-Mar	4	547.95	410.96
Monday	12-Mar	5	684.93	136.99
Tuesday	13-Mar	6	821.92	136.99
Wednesday	14-Mar	7	958.90	136.99
Thursday	15-Mar	8	1,095.89	136.99
Friday	16-Mar	11	1,506.85	410.96
Monday	19-Mar	12	1,643.84	136.99
Tuesday	20-Mar	13	1,780.82	136.99
Wednesday	21-Mar	14	1,917.81	136.99
Thursday	22-Mar	15	2,054.79	136.99
Friday	23-Mar	18	2,465.75	410.96
Monday	26-Mar	19	2,602.74	136.99
Tuesday	27-Mar	20	2,739.73	136.99
Wednesday	28-Mar	21	2,876.71	136.99
Thursday	29-Mar	22	3,013.70	136.99
Friday	30-Mar	24	3,287.67	273.97
Monday	02-Apr	26	3,561.64	273.97
Tuesday	03-Apr	27	3,698.63	136.99
Wednesday	04-Apr	28	3,835.62	136.99
Thursday	05-Apr	29	3,972.60	136.99
Friday	06-Apr	30	4,109.59	136.99

5. Messaging Standards

Learning Objective

6.5   Know the function of the following standards: SWIFT; FIX; FpML; XBRL

5.1   Introduction

Up until the 1970s, securities firms, institutional investors and other market players generally communicated with their settlement agents by letter, fax or telex, and many deals were re-keyed into several separate systems manually. Because of the scope and scale of the financial markets and the complexity of newer financial instruments and trade types, and because the size of trades grew rapidly from about 1975 onwards, this method of working became untenable, and market players of all types began to look for more automation. They began to move towards what we now call straight-through processing (STP). The first step in this direction was the founding of SWIFT.

5.2   An Introduction to SWIFT

The **Society for Worldwide Interbank Financial Telecommunication (SWIFT)** was founded in 1973, with the mission of creating a shared worldwide data processing and communications link, together with a common language for international financial transactions. This was an ambitious project that had the backing of 239 banks in 15 countries.

The next few years were spent defining message standards and building a secure store and forward telecommunications network. The first SWIFT message was sent in 1977.

Originally, SWIFT services were available only to firms that were regulated as banks, and the message standards related only to foreign exchange, money markets and interbank transfers. The first securities-related message standards were introduced in 1987, and membership was not offered to investment firms and fund managers until 1992.

Today there are SWIFT member firms in over 200 countries, exchanging over four billion messages annually, four times the volume exchanged in 1999.

We are concerned with two aspects of the SWIFT services in this workbook; the **secure store and forward communications network**, and the **SWIFT message standards**.

5.3   SWIFT Connectivity

SWIFT connectivity is based on the presence of:

- a secure IP-based network;
- SWIFTNet Link software that provides security and ensures interoperability between users;
- the store and forward principle.

5.3.1 The Secure IP-Based Network

This is a highly secure telecommunications network that, since 2005, has been based on the IP protocol, which in turn is the set of communications protocols that implement the protocol stack on which the internet runs. It is sometimes called the **TCP/IP protocol suite**, after the two most important protocols in it: the **Transmission Control Protocol (TCP)** and the **Internet Protocol (IP)**, which were also the first two defined.

SWIFT member firms usually access the network by means of a resilient permanent connection consisting of a leased line with another leased line as back-up. For each access port speed, SWIFT has calculated a throughput value in terms of **Transactions per Second (TPS)**. These throughput calculations are based on an expected **Committed Data Rate (CDR)** that is 70% of the nominal quoted bandwidth.

SWIFT publishes a list of **network partners**; these are telecoms utilities that offer access to the SWIFT network. The list includes household names such as AT&T and BT.

Member firms may also **outsource** SWIFT connectivity to a third party. Three forms of outsourcing are recognised by SWIFT:

a. Firms may connect via another customer; this is called a **shared connection**.
b. Firms may outsource the day-to-day operation of their connection to a third-party, called a **service bureau**.
c. In addition to the technical connectivity, firms may turn to a **member/concentrator** that provides additional business services such as taking care of SWIFT administration and invoicing on their behalf.

5.3.2 SWIFTNet Link

SWIFTNet Link is a suite of software products that ensures technical interoperability between users by providing the functionality required to communicate over these services. It is licensed both to SWIFT member firms directly, and also to software vendors who are able to embed it in their own products. When SWIFT supplies it directly, it is embedded in a packaged software application called **SWIFTAlliance™**.

Both Windows and UNIX platforms are supported by SWIFTNet Link. SWIFTAlliance and the third party products that compete with it are often referred to as **SWIFT Gateways**.

SWIFTNet Link incorporates a set of XML-based **Application Programming Interfaces (APIs)** which provide:

*   customer application to access SWIFTNet services;
*   local application to communicate with a remote application;
*   local and remote applications to establish end-to-end integrity, authentication and confidentiality;
*   local and remote applications to retrieve the current date and time from SWIFT's 'trusted time' service;
*   local and remote applications to support features such as load balancing, which are specifically designed for high-availability and high-throughput environments; and
*   local and remote applications to communicate securely using **SWIFTNet PKI**.

SWIFTNet PKI

SWIFTNet PKI provides the security layer that is essential in the SWIFT environment. When a firm agrees with another firm that they will send and/or receive SWIFT messages with one another, the first thing that they do is to exchange **authenticator keys**, using the SWIFT network for this purpose. Authenticator keys encrypt the outgoing message, and ensure that only the recipient that it was intended for is able to decrypt it.

SWIFTNet PKI uses **digital certificates** to provide the highest levels of authentication of institutions, end-users and servers. Digital certificates convey the trust between institutions and SWIFT as the trusted third party. SWIFTNet PKI is additional to the network security provided on the protocol and the connection level.

Key-exchange ensures:

- **Authenticity** – correspondents are guaranteed the identity of the originator of any instruction, statement, query or response. By verifying the signature, the receiver of a message can confirm that the sender specified in the header of the message owned the private key used for signing the message.
- **Integrity** – correspondents are guaranteed that the data they receive exactly matches the original as produced by the sender. By verifying the signature the receiver of a message can confirm that the message content has not been changed during transmission.
- **Non-repudiation** – correspondents are able to prove that the claimed originator has effectively signed the message, as it can be proved that the originator is the sole owner of the unique signing key needed to produce the digital signature.
- **Confidentiality** – the message-level encryption guarantees that only the intended recipient can read and interpret the data as it can be proved that the originator is the sole owner of the unique decryption key.
- **Access control** – the access for an individual to their private key, stored in a smart card, is controlled through a private password.

5.3.3   The Store and Forward Principle

SWIFT connectivity is based on the store and forward principle. This is a communications technique in which messages are sent to an intermediate station where they are kept and sent at a later time to the final destination or to another intermediate station. Reasons for using this method include the following:

- Origin and destination stations may not be available for communications at the same time. This, in turn, could be because of:
  - time zone differences between the sender and the recipient;
  - the sender's country and the recipient's country have different working days and/or public holidays;
  - the recipient's systems are not working due to hardware or software failure, or 'disasters' such as earthquake, civil unrest, etc.
- One or more circuits may not have enough capacity for peak traffic and there is a need to give priority to certain messages, without losing the others.

5.3.4 Interaction of the Firm's Systems with the SWIFT Network

The following diagram shows the interaction between the sending firm's systems, the SWIFT network and the receiving firm's systems. The assumptions are that the sending firm is based in London and is generating settlement instructions to be sent to a settlement agent in Tokyo. Tokyo is, of course, in a different time zone and uses a different public holiday calendar from London.

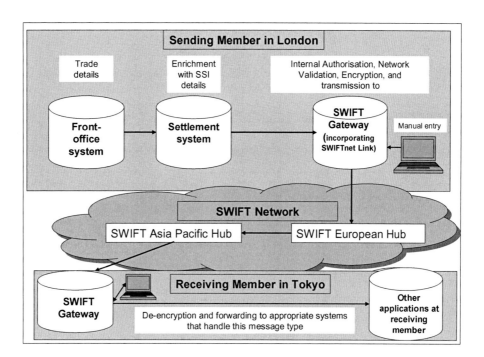

At the Sending Firm

1. Trades are captured in the relevant front office system and forwarded to the firm's settlement system.
2. The settlement system enriches the trade with SSI details, and any other relevant reference data, and formats a settlement instruction message. This, in turn, is forwarded to the firm's SWIFT Gateway application, where:
    a. The Gateway product validates the trade according to SWIFT's network validation rules, which deal with field specifications (eg, whether alpha or numeric content is required, whether fields are mandatory or optional etc). If a message fails validation then it is sent to a repair queue.
    b. The Gateway product provides facilities for manual authorisation of this instruction before it is sent out. In Section 1.1 of this chapter we learned that the firm may require more levels of authorisation for FoP instructions than it does for DvP instructions. The firm is able to set up business rules in the Gateway product to control these policies.
    c. The Gateway product allows direct input through a user interface (shown in the diagram). This allows users to set up business rules in the Gateway product, manually authorise transactions and repair transactions when necessary.
    d. Once the message has been validated and authorised, it is then encrypted and sent to SWIFT. The message will, in fact, be received at one of SWIFT's European hubs (there is more than one of these for business resilience reasons), but this fact is transparent to the sender.

At SWIFT

1. The message is received at the European hub, and time-stamped with the date and time of receipt.
2. It is then network-validated. If network validation is successful, SWIFT sends an **ACK** (meaning acknowledged) message back to the sender confirming that it is able to process the message. If the message fails network validation, then SWIFT sends a **NACK** (not acknowledged) message back to the sender. This process is known as the **ACK/NACK** protocol.
3. Once 'ACK'd, SWIFT identifies that this message is destined for a firm in Tokyo, so it forwards it to one of its Asia Pacific hubs in real time.
4. The Asia Pacific hub then verifies whether the Tokyo firm is online to SWIFT. If it is, it forwards it to the member; if the member is not online, it stores the message until it detects that the member has come online.

At the Receiving Firm

1. The message is received at this member firm's Gateway system and decrypted.
2. The Gateway system then uses business rules that have been set up in this system to tell it what to do with the message. For example, if it is a settlement instruction message sent by one of the firm's custody clients, it may need to be forwarded to one business application; if it is an FX trade confirmation, sent by a counterparty, it may need to be forwarded to another business application.
3. There will be some messages where the identity of the destination system will not be clear to the Gateway system. This may be due to the quality of the data in the incoming message, lack of clarity and coverage in the business rules entered into the Gateway system, or for some other reason. For this reason Gateway systems provide a human interface that incorporates the ability to display messages held in a repair queue and manually dispose of them, as well as the ability to input the business rules in the first place.

5.4   SWIFT Message Standards

The second function of SWIFT is to devise agreed standards for the content, sequence and validation rules for the messages that are used by its members. It does this by a process of consultation with its member firms, and the various trade associations that they belong to. Once SWIFT has confirmed a standard, this standard is then adopted by the International Organization for Standardization (ISO). ISO is a United Nations-sponsored organisation that sets international standards that can be used in any type of business and are accepted around the world as proof that a business can provide assured quality. ISO has appointed SWIFT as the 'registration authority' of standards for financial services messages.

5.4.1   Introduction to FIN Messages (Also Known as MT Messages)

The range of SWIFT messages that were developed before 2000 are known as FIN messages. They are represented as tagged data and cover a wide range of financial transactions.

Each FIN message is assigned a message identifier code, such as MT300, which is a foreign exchange trade confirmation message. For this reason, FIN messages are often referred to as MT messages.

There are 176 different business-related MT messages (as well as some system management messages), and there are two ISO standards that govern the content of these messages. The scope of the MT message series is summarised by the following table:

Series	No. of individual messages in series	Purpose of the series	Examples	Relevant ISO standard
MT100	11	Customer payments and cheques	MT111 – Request to stop payment of a cheque	ISO 7775
MT200	10	Financial institution transfers	MT202 – General financial institution transfer	ISO 7775
MT300	20	Foreign exchange, money markets and derivatives	MT300 – Foreign exchange confirmation MT360 – interest rate swap confirmation	ISO 7775
MT400	11	Collections and cash letters	MT400 – Advice of payment	ISO 7775
MT500	57	Securities markets	MT502 – Order to buy or sell MT514 – Trade allocation instruction MT543 – Instruction to deliver against payment MT547 – Confirmation that DvP instruction has settled	ISO 15022
MT600	13	Precious metals	MT600 – Trade confirmation	ISO 7775
MT700	22	Documentary credits and guarantees	M700 – Issue of a documentary credit	ISO 7775
MT800	11	Traveller's cheques	MT810 – Traveller's cheque refund request	ISO 7775
MT900	21	Cash management and customer status	MT950 – Statement message	ISO 7775

The messages that will commonly be used by securities firms will be found in the MT100, 200, 300 and 900 series (for managing firms' cash activities) and the MT500 series (for managing firms' securities business).

5.4.2   Underlying ISO Standards for MT Messages

The ISO standard that governs all the series, except for the MT500 series, is **ISO 7775**. This standard was developed during the 1980s and applied to all the messages that were developed up to 1997, including the then current MT500 series securities messages.

In the late 1990s SWIFT and its members realised that the original ISO 7775 messages were too restrictive, did not reflect the full complexity of modern trading instruments, and were still too ambiguous to ensure that full STP could be achieved.

Thus was born the **ISO 15022** standard, based on a data dictionary approach. Initially (in 1997) ISO 15022 was applied to the securities message category as this represented the fastest-growing usage of the SWIFT network. Old message types were replaced and many new ones introduced. ISO 15022 trade initiation and confirmation messages were introduced in 1997, and settlement and reconciliation in 1998. There was no standards release in 1999 due to Y2K distractions, and the old MT500 series ISO 7775 standard message types were removed from the network in 2002.

5.4.3 Example of a FIN Message

The next picture is an example of a FIN message. It is an MT950, which is a statement of a bank account sent by the account operator to the account holder, which could be a securities firm. This is how the message would look if it were opened in an application such as Microsoft Notepad. Note that SWIFT Gateway applications contain software that will display and print FIN messages in a more user-friendly form.

```
{1:F01WELAGB2XAXXX4802160443}{2:O9500131981202NWBKGB2LCXXX024039002898
1202023 IN}{4:
:20:6000010089597099
:25:60000 10000895970
:28C:01499/001
:60F:C050701GBP360335,86
:61:050704D39745,03NCHK018348
:61:050704D240,NCHK018349
:61:050704D4095,03NCHK018435
:61:050704D54,NCHK018447
:61:050704D114,47NCHK018452
:61:050704D472,50NCHK018464
:61:050704D550,03NCHK018470
:61:050704D402,96NCHK018472
:61:050704D110,60NCHK018478
:61:050704D117,50NCHK018518
:61:050704D7815,26NCHK018522
:61:050704D1464,50NCHK018524
:61:050704D94,NCHK018532
:61:050704D2222,51NCHK018537
:61:050704D239,85NCHK018541
:61:050704D2812,11NCHK018544
:61:050704D104,58NCHK018549
:61:050704D78,NCHK018566
:61:050704D5634,07NCHK018574
:61:050704D2402,86NCHK018590
:61:050704D641,84NCHK018592
:61:050704D60,NCHK018611
:61:050704D281,29NCHK018615
:61:050704D472,50NCHK018618
:61:050704D50042,26NCHK018643
:61:050704D325,NSTOCLER MED UL PRM
:61:050704D1198,75NSTOSKANDIA PREMIUM
:61:050704D15751,41NSTOL B WEST
:61:050704D1225,NSTOCARR SHEPPARDS P
:61:050704D4488,81NSTOUNUM LIMITED
:62M:C050704GBP217079,14
-}{5:{CHK:4ADDAB891385}{DWS7661 MESSAGE NOT TO BE AUTHENTICATED}}
```

The Header Line

The message begins with a header line, (ie, the first line in the picture):

```
{1:F01WELAGB2XAXXX4802160443}{2:O9500131981202NWBKGB2LCXXX024039002898
1202023 IN}{4:
```

Within the header line we can now see:

- the BIC code of the receiver – WELAGB2X;
- the fact that this is an MT950 – 2:O950; and
- the BIC code of the sender – NWBKGB2L.

Header lines are standard for all MT messages, if this message was not an MT950 but an MT535 – statement of securities holdings – then the string 2:O950 would change to 2:O535.

The header line is then followed by a number of lines of tagged data:

MT950 Detailed Tags

:25:600001000895970 – Tag 25 tells you that this is the statement for account number 600001000895970 that this firm holds with NatWest – the owner of BIC code NWBKGB2L.

:28C:01499/001 – Tag 28C tells you that this is page one of statement number 1499 for this account.

:60F:C050701GBP360335,86 – Tag 60F tells you the opening balance for this account on this page of this statement. The firm has a credit balance (C) of GBP360,335.86, which was brought forward from the closing balance on July 1 2005.

:61:050704D39745,03NCHK018348 – Tag 61 is repeated many times. There is one instance for each entry that has been posted to this account on statement number 1499. This particular entry tells us that on 4 July 2007 the account was Debited (D) with GBP39,745.03. If it had been credited then 'D' would be replaced by 'C'. The description of the entry is 'NCHK018348; this means that cheque number 018348 is being debited to the account. Note that the tag 61 entry does not include the ISO currency code; this is implied from Tag 60F.

:62M:C050704GBP217079,14 – Tag 62M shows the closing balance of Page 1 of statement number 1499. It is a credit balance (C) for the date of 4 July 2005 of GBP217,079.14.
If you were to add up the values of Tag 60F and all the individual values of the Tag 61 items it would come to this amount.

Any FIN message may be interpreted in a similar way to this one. SWIFT distributes the **SWIFT Standards Guide** to all its members; this provides the rules for interpretation of an incoming message and the population of an outgoing message, as well as the network validation rules that apply to the message type.

5.5 New SWIFT Initiatives in the 21st Century

5.5.1 XML and ISO 20022

The tagged data structure of the MT message series has served the investment community well for many years, but many aspects of it are now somewhat dated. One of the main drivers for change is the growth of the use of **Extensible Markup Language**, better known as **XML**, throughout industry and commerce.

XML is a flexible way to create common information formats and share both the format and the data on the internet, intranets, and elsewhere. XML is a formal recommendation from the World Wide Web Consortium (W3C) similar to the language of today's web pages, the **Hypertext Markup Language (HTML)**.

With the evolution of XML technology in the late 1990s work began on what was called ISO 15022 2nd Edition (also known as **SWIFTML**). This evolved into the first early implementations of ISO 20022 using an enhanced approach to standards based on business entity interaction behavioural models and XML schema-based message data models for the transactional messages supporting these models.

SWIFT's first implementation of XML and the new standard was in a series of messages designed for players in the mutual funds industry in 2003. This was followed by a new real-time cash management offering in 2006. The ISO 20022 standard has further evolved to incorporate lessons from the first implementations of ISO 20022 funds messages, and to converge with other standards such as **FpML, FIX, TWIST, ACCORD** and successful examples of market-specific best practice such as SMPG (Securities Market Practice Group) rules.

In 2004 a significant increase in scope was agreed for ISO 20022, expanding from securities and related financial instruments to the broader scope of all financial services. All SWIFT messages developed since 2004 have been based on ISO 20022. These messages are known as '**MX**' messages and are in XML form. ISO 20022 uses a data dictionary (see Chapter 3, Section 2.6.1) for all messages. So far the new MX messages have only been used for new products, but eventually MX messages will replace the MT message series. It is anticipated that there will be a period of 'dual operation' of both the MT and MX message series lasting several years.

5.5.2   Closed User Groups

SWIFT membership was originally available only to banks, so at that time the service could be used only to communicate between banks, not between banks and their customers. Securities firms and investment funds were admitted as members in 1992, but there was no method by which a SWIFT member firm could use the SWIFT network to communicate with its (mainly corporate and government department in this context) clients that didn't themselves qualify for membership. The rules were changed in 2002; it is now possible for banks and their corporate customers to communicate using SWIFT in two ways:

1. **The Standardised Corporate Environment (SCORE)** – SCORE is based on a closed user group, administered by SWIFT, where corporates can interact with financial institutions. To be eligible for SCORE, corporates must be listed on a regulated stock exchange of a country which is a member of the **Financial Action Task Force (FATF)**. Subsidiaries can also join SCORE if they are majority-owned by an eligible company (ie, listed in one of the FATF countries), duly incorporated, in good financial standing and subject to regular audits by an independent audit firm in accordance with internationally recognised accounting standards.
2. **Member-Administered Closed User Groups (MA-CUG)** – companies not eligible for the SCORE model can join SWIFT by registering in a closed user group set-up and being managed by their financial institution (ie, the financial institution decides which customers can participate). Within the MA-CUG, a corporate can communicate only with its bank, which decides which kinds of messages and files (payments, treasury, reporting and securities) can be exchanged. If a corporate wishes to communicate with several banks it can register in multiple MA-CUGs, resulting in similar multi-banking capabilities as SCORE. Participants that use SCORE may only send and receive messages that conform to SWIFT standards and are therefore capable of being network validated. Participants in an MA-CUG may send and receive any data they care to, but SWIFT will not, and cannot, network-validate the messages.

5.5.3 SWIFTNet FileAct

This is SWIFT's interactive communications service that is utilised for the sending of files between parties and, in effect, will supersede the existing FIN service, for example, providing support for the transmission of mass payments or reporting information. Although it is file-based, the initiator of the file transfer will always send a request first, and wait for the response across the IP network before sending the file and waiting for the subsequent acknowledgement. In this way, it can be shown to be an interactive service.

5.5.4 SWIFTNet InterAct

This is SWIFT's interactive communications service that is based on the exchange of request and response messages between two parties. The exchange of messages can be either synchronous or asynchronous. Effectively, this means that it can be used either for direct application-to-application transactional messaging, as is the case of CLS Bank which is based on this service; or it can be utilised in a 'push' architecture to provide real-time status and other information. This will also form the basis of the successor to the FIN service.

5.6 Financial Interface eXchange (FIX) Protocol

The Financial Interface eXchange (FIX) protocol was initiated in 1992 by a group of institutions and brokers interested in streamlining their trading processes. It is an open message standard, controlled by no single entity, that can be structured to match the business requirements of each firm. At the time that the FIX protocol was founded, institutions and brokers that were not banks had only recently become eligible to join SWIFT, and the founding firms were not satisfied with the ISO 7775 securities messages that were then available on the SWIFT network.

FIX does not impose a single type of carrier (eg, it will work with leased lines, private networks, internet, etc), nor a single security protocol. It is, however, important to note that FIX is not a network in itself and that communication is made directly between each broker/institution pair by prior bilateral agreement. Thus a fund management institution may have 50 or 60 connections to brokers worldwide, some via the internet, others via direct dial or leased connections, and still others connected via private networks such as Omgeo or Autex.

In summary, each broker/institution connection can be thought of as a two-way conversational link taking place between applications at each end. These applications are often referred to as **FIX engines** and can operate either as stand-alone or fully integrated solutions.

The structure of the organisation is based around a series of committees comprised of interested parties within the broking and institutional communities. These committees are focused on business, technical and regional issues, with working groups examining the impact of new technology, such as XML, and potential expansion of the protocol to cover other users, such as exchanges and Electronic Crossing Networks (ECN).

The protocol is defined at two levels: session and application. The session level is concerned with the delivery of data, while the application level defines business-related data content. Broadly, business messages cover the communication between brokers and institutions of the following information:

- indications of interest;
- orders and order acknowledgment;
- fills;
- account allocations;
- news, email, program trading lists; and
- administrative messages.

The protocol has been deliberately designed to support both domestic and cross-border trading in a varied spread of instrument and security types, such as:

- equities;
- bonds;
- depositary receipts;
- derivatives;
- futures; and
- foreign exchange-trading.

Because the FIX standards are 'open source', they may be downloaded from the FIX protocol website (www.fixprotocol.org).

The current version of the FIX protocol is version 5.0, released in October 2006 and last amended in April 2009.

FIX Functionality Matrix												
Equities	FIX 4.4	FIX 5.0	**Futures & Options**	FIX 4.4	FIX 5.0	**Fixed Income**	FIX 4.4	FIX 5.0	**Foreign Exchange**	FIX 4.4	FIX 5.0
	[Apr 2003]	[Oct 2006]		[Apr 2003]	[Oct 2006]		[Apr 2003]	[Oct 200		[Apr 2003]	[Oct 2006]
Basic Order flow			Basic Order flow			Basic Order flow			Basic Order Flow (spots and forwards)		
IOIs and Advertisements			Multi-leg Order flow			Multi-leg Order flow (Repos, swaps/switches/rolls)			Basic Order Flow (swaps)		
Quotes			IOIs and Advertisements			IOIs (offerings)			Quotes (spots, outright forwards, FX swaps)		
Market Data			Quotes			Quotes			Market Data (executable streaming prices)		
Allocations			Market Data			Allocations			Allocations		
Confirms / Affirms			Allocations			Confirms / Affirms			Confirms / Affirms		
Trade Reporting			Confirms / Affirms			Trade Reporting			Trade Reporting		
Program Trading			Trade Reporting			Collateral Management					
Algorithmic Trading			Security and Position Reporting								
			Collateral Management								
Legend			No Support			Some Support			Good Support		

5.7 FᴘML – Financial Products Markup Language

FpML (Financial products Markup Language) is an XML message standard for the OTC derivatives industry. The FpML standard was first published by JP Morgan and PricewaterhouseCoopers on 9 June 1999 in a paper titled '*Introducing FpML: A New Standard for E-commerce*'. As a result, the FpML Standards Committee was founded.

All categories of privately negotiated derivatives will eventually be included within the standard. The standard is managed by the ISDA on behalf of a community of investment banks that make a market in OTC derivatives. The standard is freely licensed, so any firm that trades the instruments that it supports may use it in their own software.

The current version is Version 5, Service Pack 2, which was released in April 2009. The core scope includes the products of Foreign Exchange (FX) Swaps and Options, Interest Rate Swaps, Inflation Swaps, Asset Swaps, Swaptions, Credit Default Swaps, Credit Default Swap Indices, Credit Default Swap Baskets, Tranches on Credit Default Swap Indices, Equity Options, Equity Swaps, Total Return Swaps, and many others. The core processes include trading, valuation, confirmation, novations, increases, amendments, terminations, allocations, position reporting, cash flow matching, a formal definition of party roles, as well as trade notification between asset managers and custodians.

FpML is distinct from similar financial standards such as SWIFT because it provides no network or specification of a transport mechanism.

5.8 XBRL

XBRL is an abbreviation for Extensible Business Reporting Language. This is an XML message standard for exchanging information about corporate data such as balance sheets and profit and loss accounts between the company concerned and its auditors, regulators, customers, research analysts and other interested parties. XBRL standards are compatible with ISO 20022.

Historically the standard has been used only to transmit accounting data, but there are now moves to adopt it as a standard for the company concerned to announce corporate action data to the securities markets.

6. Post-Settlement Reconciliation Procedures

Learning Objective

6.6   Understand the function of IT within post-settlement reconciliation procedures, including: reconciliation requirements and record-keeping; ensuring cash and stock movements are recorded; journal movements; corporate actions (including dividends, bonus issues and rights issues)

6.1   Introduction

All firms need to reconcile data held in their business application systems to ensure its integrity. In this context, 'data' includes the following:

1.   Cash amounts connected with all types of transaction.
2.   Cash balances that arise from all types of transaction.
3.   Stock and derivative quantities connected with all types of transaction.
4.   Stock and derivative balances (positions) that arise from all types of transaction.

Data needs to be reconciled externally as well as internally. Owing to the size of the data to be reconciled, computer systems are needed for this task.

External reconciliation is the act of reconciling data, such as cash movements on nostro accounts and stock movements on depot accounts, with the settlement agents that operate those accounts on the firm's behalf.

Internal reconciliation is the act of reconciling data held in one of the firm's business applications (such as its settlement system) with data held on one or more of its other business application systems.

6.2   External Reconciliation

If the firm holds client assets, then it is a UK **regulatory requirement** to reconcile them. For example, if a private client broker holds stock belonging to its clients in a segregated account at EUI, it must reconcile the settled holdings that it reports to clients on the statements it sends them to the holdings reported by EUI to the firm.

6.2.1   Reconciliation of Clients' Securities

The rules about the reconciliation of clients' securities are covered by Section 6.5 of the Client Asset (CASS) Rules, which state:

CASS 6.5.4

Carrying out internal reconciliations of the safe custody assets held for each client with the safe custody assets held by the firm and third parties is an important step in the discharge of the firm's obligations.

A firm should perform such internal reconciliations:

a.   as often as is necessary; and
b.   as soon as reasonably practicable after the date to which the reconciliation relates;
c.   to ensure the accuracy of the firm's records and accounts.

Reconciliation methods which can be adopted for these purposes include the 'total count method', which requires that all safe custody assets be counted and reconciled as at the same date.

If a firm chooses to use an alternative reconciliation method (for example the 'rolling stock method') it needs to ensure that:

•   all of a particular safe custody asset are counted and reconciled as at the same date; and
•   all safe custody assets are counted and reconciled during a period of six months.

CASS 6.5.5

A firm that uses an alternative reconciliation method must first send a written confirmation to the UK regulator from the firm's auditor that the firm has in place systems and controls which are adequate to enable it to use the method effectively.

CASS 6.5.6

A firm must conduct, on a regular basis, reconciliations between its internal accounts and records and those of any third parties by whom those safe custody assets are held.

CASS 6.5.7

Where a firm deposits safe custody assets belonging to a client with a third party, in complying with the requirements of CASS 6.5.6, the firm should seek to ensure that the third party will deliver to the firm a statement as at a date or dates specified by the firm which details the description and amounts of all the safe custody assets credited to the account, and that this statement is delivered in adequate time to allow the firm to carry out the periodic reconciliations required in CASS 6.5.6.

CASS 6.5.8

A firm should perform the reconciliation required by CASS 6.5.6:

•   as regularly as is necessary; and
•   as soon as reasonably practicable after the date to which the reconciliation relates;
•   to ensure the accuracy of its internal accounts and records against those of third parties by whom safe custody assets are held.

CASS 6.5.9

Whenever possible, a firm should ensure that reconciliations are carried out by a person (for example an employee of the firm) who is independent of the production or maintenance of the records to be reconciled.

CASS 6.5.10

A firm must promptly correct any discrepancies which are revealed in the reconciliations envisaged by this section, and make good, or provide the equivalent of, any unreconciled shortfall for which there are reasonable grounds for concluding that the firm is responsible.

CASS 6.5.11

Items recorded or held within a suspense or error account fall within the scope of discrepancies.

CASS 6.5.12

A firm may, where justified, conclude that another person is responsible for an irreconcilable shortfall despite the existence of a dispute with that other person about the unreconciled item. In those circumstances, the firm is not required to make good the shortfall but is expected to take reasonable steps to resolve the position with the other person.

6.2.2   Reconciliation of Client Money

The rules about the reconciliation of client money are covered by Section 7.6 of the Client Money Rules. Rule 7.6.2 states that:

A firm must maintain its records and accounts in a way that ensures their accuracy, and in particular their correspondence to the client money held for clients.

And **Rule 7.6.6** explains the role that reconciliation plays in meeting these requirements:

Carrying out internal reconciliations of records and accounts of the entitlement of each client for whom the firm holds client money with the records and accounts of the client money the firm holds in client bank accounts and client transaction accounts should be one of the steps a firm takes to satisfy its obligations under CASS 7.6.2 R, and where relevant SYSC 4.1.1 R and SYSC 6.1.1 R.

A firm should perform such internal reconciliations:

a.   as often as is necessary; and
b.   as soon as reasonably practicable after the date to which the reconciliation relates;

to ensure the accuracy of the firm's records and accounts.

The standard method of internal client money reconciliation sets out a method of reconciliation of client money balances that the FSAFCA believes should be one of the steps that a firm takes when carrying out internal reconciliations of client money.

Rules 7.6.14 and **7.6.15** set out what the firm's obligations are if it finds a discrepancy in such reconciliation.

Rule 7.6.14 states:

'When any discrepancy arises as a result of the reconciliation between a firm's internal records and those of third parties that hold client money, the firm must identify the reason for the discrepancy and correct it as soon as possible, unless the discrepancy arises solely as a result of timing differences between the accounting systems of the party providing the statement or confirmation and that of the firm.'

And **Rule 7.6.15** states:

'While a firm is unable to resolve a difference arising from a reconciliation between a firm's internal records and those of third parties that hold client money, and one record or a set of records examined by the firm during its reconciliation indicates that there is a need to have a greater amount of client money or approved collateral than is in fact the case, the firm must assume, until the matter is finally resolved, that the record or set of records is accurate and pay its own money into a relevant account.'

6.2.3   Good Business Practice – Avoidance of Losses

Even if the FCA did not mandate rules about external reconciliation, it is an essential part of the control process and, unless it is done regularly and accurately, the firm is exposed to the risk of losses caused by:

- Fraudulent activity by its employees or others – this is the reason that the FCA recommends, that: *'Whenever possible, a firm should ensure that reconciliations are carried out by a person (for example, an employee of the firm) who is independent of the production or maintenance of the records to be reconciled'*.
- Losses due to processing errors made within the firm.
- Losses due to processing errors made outside the firm, for example, by settlement agents and trading parties.

Consider the following example of the losses that can arise as a result of processing errors.

Example

ABC Investment Bank's client John Smith purchased 1,000 shares in Maxicorp at £10 per share for settlement on 1 March. ABC is holding them in custody for him at EUI. For some reason the shares were never delivered to ABC's EUI account, but the EUI depot balance was updated in ABC's system as if they had been delivered. ABC is regularly sending John Smith statements that tell him ABC have the 1,000 shares, but it doesn't have them – they are still with the party who sold them.

The potential losses that could arise from this processing problem – unless it were detected and resolved in time – could include:

- • Dividend payments – on 1 April Maxicorp pays a dividend of £0.50 per share. John Smith, therefore, expects ABC to pay him £500.00. If the stock were in ABC's EUI account, then EUI would pay ABC and ABC would pay John Smith. Because ABC doesn't have the shares, ABC makes a loss of £500.00 when it pays Smith.
- • Corporate actions – on 1 May Megacorp offers to take over Maxicorp for £15 per share. Mr John Smith wishes to accept the offer. As ABC doesn't have the shares to sell, it will have to pay John Smith the proceeds, and will lose £15,000.

6.2.4   Other Issues Relating to Reconciliation

Journal Vouchers, Bank Charges and Interest

Banks and other settlement agents charge the firm fees for using its services, and interest on overdrawn balances, and they usually pay interest on credit balances on the nostro account. The first that the firm knows about these is when they appear on the bank statement; therefore these charges are identified by the reconciliation process. When such postings are identified, they need to be posted into the general ledger by means of a journal voucher.

6.2.5   How is External Reconciliation Usually Achieved?

Most large firms reconcile their settlement agents' bank statements on a daily basis. The settlement agents provide the necessary information in a number of ways, including SWIFT messages and information in other forms that may be supplied on their electronic banking systems. The relevant SWIFT messages are:

Message no.	Message Description	Usage
MT950	Statement Message	To reconcile nostro balances and transactions.
MT940	Customer Statement Message	To reconcile nostro balances and transactions.
MT535	Statement of Holdings	To reconcile the balances of each security at the depot.
MT536	Statement of Transactions	To reconcile the actual settlements of stock that have taken place at the depot.

Note that the firm may use either the MT950 or the MT940 to reconcile the bank account – they are two alternative messages that fulfil the same purpose; the difference is that there are additional 'narrative' tags on the MT940 that don't appear on the MT950.

The MT940, MT950 and MT536 messages will include the unique instruction reference number that was described in Section 1.4.2 of Chapter 5.

The relevant messages are usually downloaded into a dedicated reconciliation application, which is likely to be a package product, or it may be developed in-house. The IT department then needs to organise a feed of the equivalent data from its internal systems. The reconciliation application then compares the transactions and balances reported by the agent with those reported by the internal system, matches items which appear in both systems, and provides a user interface for the reconciliation team to investigate and resolve items that are missing from one or other system, duplicated in one or other system, or have discrepancies between the systems.

These applications allow the users to construct business rules that define what is or is not a 'good match'. These business rules need to take into account some of the factors that we identified in Section 1 of this chapter, namely:

1. The importance of the unique, common instruction reference number that was quoted on the original instruction, and which the agent should return to us on all messages about this instruction – the reconciliation application will try to find this in order to match items.
2. The fact that the agent has the authority to 'settle within tolerance'. This means that there may be a small difference between the cash proceeds expected to pay for a purchase, and the amount that the agent reports on the bank statement. This will need to be written-off by a journal voucher.
3. The fact that the feed from the settlement system needs to contain equivalent information to that which arrives from the settlement agent so that the two records can be compared, and relevant business rules for transaction matching can be applied.

6.3   Internal Reconciliation

6.3.1   Why Is Internal Reconciliation Required?

Example

If ABC Investment Bank buys (as principal) 1,000 shares in Shell at £10.00 each on 5 March for value date 8 March from XYZ Fund Managers for settlement at EUI UK, then the following records will be created on 5 March:

Trade Dated Position in Trader's Book	1,000 shares
Value Dated Position in Trader's Book	0 shares
Settled Position at EUI	0 shares
Cost of Trade Dated Position	£10,000.00
Cost of Value Dated Position	£0
Bank Account Balance	£0
P&L in Trader's Book	£0

If the trade then settles in full on 8 March as intended, and the position in Shell is marked-to-market at £10.50 per share, then the records that were created on 5 March would be updated as follows:

Trade Dated Position in Trader's Book	1,000 shares
Value Dated Position in Trader's Book	1,000 shares
Settled Position at EUI	1,000 shares
Cost of Trade Dated Position	£10,500.00
Cost of Value Dated Position	£10,500.00
Bank Account Balance	−£10,000.00
P&L in Trader's Book	£500.00

The reason why internal reconciliation is required is that, as the trade in the example flows through the trade cycle, records may need to be created and updated in multiple business systems.

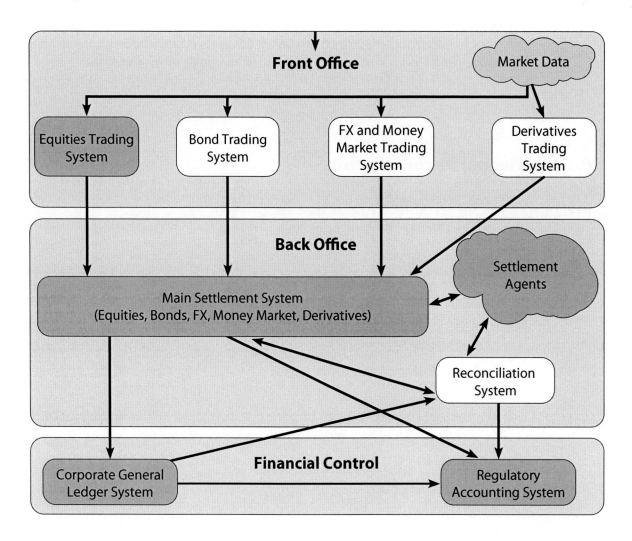

If the firm's configuration diagram were similar to the picture above, then all the systems that are shaded would need to be updated by this trade.

There are many reasons why these updates may not be made consistently in all the systems in the configuration (some of these reasons are explored in greater depth in Chapter 7); but the point is that the firm needs proactively to reconcile the data between systems in the configuration in order to identify and resolve problem trades and positions.

6.3.2 How is Internal Reconciliation Usually Achieved?

The same applications that support external reconciliation also support internal reconciliation. The main difference between the two types of reconciliation is that there are no external feeds involved. If, for example, it was required to reconcile the trade dated positions (and also the trades of the day) between the front office equity trading system and the main settlement system, then the IT department would need to develop:

- a feed from the front office system containing close-of-business trade dated positions;
- a feed from the main settlement system containing close-of-business trade dated positions;
- a feed from the front office system containing the trades of the day, and any trades of previous days that were cancelled or corrected today;
- a feed from the main settlement system containing the trades of the day, and any trades of previous days that were cancelled or corrected today.

The users would then need to create business rules in the reconciliation application that enable that system to compare the sets of records and highlight items that required attention. In order to do this, the feeds from the front office system and those from the settlement system need to have sufficient common data for the application to be able to apply the business rules.

End of Chapter Questions

Think of an answer for each question and refer to the appropriate section for confirmation.

1. List the circumstances under which a settlement agent will settle a trade.
    Section 1.5.1

2. What is the significance of an instruction reference number in the STP process?
    Section 1.6

3. What is the business purpose of a repo and how does it differ from the business purpose of a stock loan?
    Section 2.1

4. What is the business purpose of a maturity ladder?
    Section 3

5. List the usual business functions of a settlement system.
    Section 4.1

6. List the main components of SWIFTNet Link.
    Section 5.3.2

7. What five benefits are provided to SWIFT members through key exchange?
    Section 5.3.2

8. Which of the FIN message series conforms to ISO standard 15022?
    Section 5.4

9. What is the current version of the FIX protocol, when was it released and which ISO standard does it conform to?
    Section 5.6

10. Which SWIFT FIN messages are used to reconcile stock balances and positions with custodians?
    Section 6.2.5

Chapter Seven
The Impact of IT on Financial Control

This syllabus area will provide approximately 5 of the 50 examination questions

1. The Role of the Financial Control Department (FCD)

Learning Objective

7.1   Know the role of the financial control function

The core function of the financial control department (FCD) of a securities industry firm is to manage the financial resources of the business. Within the FCD there are likely to be the following sub-departments or sections specialising in different activities:

- **Management accounting**, also known as **product control** – this section produces the profit and loss (P&L) accounts and balance sheets for individual business units, and works closely with the managers of those business units to ensure that the income and expenditure of the units is correctly recorded, and that any financial risks are measured and appropriately contained.
- **Statutory reporting** – this section produces the firm's balance sheet and P&L account, which is then subject to both internal and external audit.
- **Regulatory reporting** – this section produces the financial and statistical returns demanded by the firm's regulator.
- **Tax management** – this section will be concerned with organising the firm's activities so that its tax liabilities are (legally) minimised.
- **Financial operations** – makes payments to suppliers, payments of expenses to staff members, etc.

2. The IT impact of the Financial Control Function

Learning Objective

7.2   Understand the relationship between the front office, settlement systems and the financial control function

---

2.1 Financial Control Department (FCD) Systems

Financial control is one of the departments that the IT department supports. The FCD will have its own dedicated IT applications which include:

- A **corporate general ledger system** (see Section 3 for more information about the general ledger). This system will record all the assets, liabilities, income and expenditure of the firm, and is likely to include specialist modules which:
  - enable the FCD to compare this year's P&L to the previous year's P&L, and to budgeted P&L.

- assist the FCD in allocating expenses across departments. For example:
  - If the firm occupies a single building and 25% of the space in that building is occupied by the settlements department, then the settlements department needs to be charged with 25% of the rent, electricity, gas, water and property taxes.
  - The cost of the IT department itself needs to be re-charged to those business units that benefit from it. The FCD may need to use a number of bases for making this re-charge. If, for example, there are five developers all working on an application used only by the settlements department, then the direct costs of these employees might be recharged directly to settlements. But other individuals in the IT department manage help desks, networks, desktop installations, etc, from which all business units benefit; the cost of these individuals may be re-charged according to headcount, so, if settlements employs 35% of all the firm's staff, it would be re-charged 35% of all these 'general' IT costs.
  - manage the firm's purchase ledger.
- A **regulatory accounting system** – this system will be used to calculate the financial and statistical information that the firm needs to send to its regulator.

However, most of the individual amounts that are posted to the general ledger are likely to be computed by other systems used by other business units. 'Computed' in this context means the following:

- the calculation of the money amount concerned; and also
- the decision as to which account in the general ledger the calculated amount is to be posted.

The IT department also supports the systems that perform these computations, and any problems encountered by these other systems may have an impact on the quality or the timeliness of the figures posted to the general ledger.

Section 2.2 shows a typical systems configuration diagram for a mid-sized investment bank operating from a single location and describes the accounting calculations made by each of the systems in the configuration. Note that this is a simplified diagram; the actual configuration diagram for most investment banks is usually much more complicated than this one, but it will generally follow this pattern.

2.2 Systems Configuration – A Typical Investment Bank

The bank trades equities, bonds, foreign exchange, loans and deposits and derivative instruments such as futures, options and swaps. It uses the following systems to process its transactions and manage the positions that arise as a result of these transactions.

2.2.1 Front Office Systems

This bank has four trading systems, each one specialising in processing orders placed by customers in different asset classes. Each of the four systems is linked to sources of market data that enable the dealer to 'see the market' – in other words, to be able to see the current levels of market prices, interest rates and exchange rates, economic and political news stories that may affect these rates and prices, and corporate announcements, such as company results, and also merger and acquisition activity that may affect the share price of just one company.

Some of this data will also be fed into the individual front office systems, where it will be used in either automated or manual trading decision support. Suppliers of market data include Thomson Reuters, Bloomberg and the major stock exchanges.

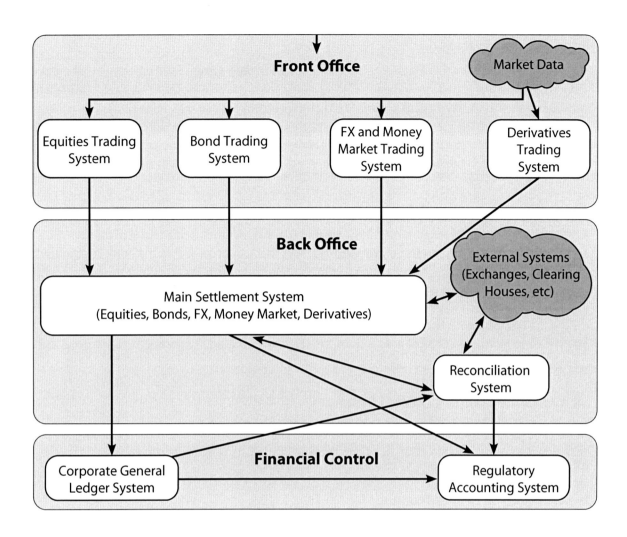

Equities Trading System

The equities trading system processes orders and transactions in individual equities, most of which are traded on one or more stock exchanges.

When trades are executed, details of the trade are then forwarded – usually electronically and in real time – to the main settlement system.

System Impact on Financial Control:

1. The equities trading system may be responsible for calculating **commissions** to be paid by clients for performing this service, as well as **fees** levied by stock exchanges and regulatory bodies that need to be passed on to the client.
2. **Trade processing error**s – if errors are made in trade processing, then incorrect trade details will be forwarded to the settlements system, and then to the general ledger. Trade processing errors may be of two kinds – human error and technical error.
   - Common **human errors** include buying a given stock instead of selling it, or buying the wrong stock – instead of buying the stock that the customer ordered, the dealer buys a stock with a similar name.
   - **Technical errors** include problems with the interface between this system and the settlement system that might cause trades to be forwarded later than required, not at all, more than once, or with incorrect details.

Bond Trading System

The bond trading system fills a similar role to the equities trading system for a different instrument class – bonds. Bonds are issued by companies, local authorities, national governments and 'supranational institutions' such as the World Bank and the EU. They may be bought and sold in the same way that equities are bought and sold. They also pay interest to the person or organisation that has purchased them.

Again, when trades are executed, they are forwarded – usually electronically and in real time – to the main settlement system.

System Impact on Financial Control:
1. This system is usually responsible for calculating the **interest** that is due to the holder.
2. The same types of **human trade processing errors** that can occur within the equity trading system also apply to this system, with additional complications due to the fact that bonds bear interest. This leads to the possibility of 'reference data errors', for example, the interest rate on a particular bond should be 5% but it has been set up in the system as 5.5%. This leads to incorrect data being sent to the main settlement system, which in turn feeds the same incorrect data to the general ledger.
3. The same kinds of **technical errors** that can occur with the equity trading system can also occur with this system.

FX and Money Market Trading System

This system processes orders and transactions in foreign exchange and money market loans and deposits. When the transactions are executed they are then forwarded – usually electronically and in real time – to the main settlement system.

System Impact on Financial Control:
1. This system is usually responsible for calculating **interest and trade proceeds**.
2. The same kinds of trade processing **human errors** that can occur in a bond or equity trading system also apply to this system.
3. The same kinds of **technical errors** that can occur with the equity trading system can also occur with this system.

Derivatives Trading System

This system processes transactions in relatively complex financial instruments, such as financial futures, traded options, interest rate swaps and currency swaps. By definition, these financial instruments are 'derived' from other instruments, such as equities, bonds and currencies. The instruments from which they are derived are known as 'underlying instruments'.

What derivatives have in common is that the calculations involved in fixing the price of a transaction are far from straightforward; this system will include modules that perform highly sophisticated financial analysis, including 'what-if' scenario analysis.

When trades are executed, the trade details are forwarded to the main settlement system – usually electronically and in real time.

The bank probably holds positions in individual derivative contracts as a result of customer order activity. These positions need to be revalued at the end of each business day in order that the bank can measure the market risk it is exposed to as a result of holding the position. Like the trade price calculation, the revaluation calculation is also complex.

System Impact on Financial Control:
Most of the money values that are posted to the general ledger for transactions and positions in derivative instruments are calculated by this system. The calculations are complex; their accuracy may also be affected by:

1. the accuracy of the market data sources available to this system;
2. the accuracy of the reference data for both the derived instrument and the underlying instrument that is held in this system;
3. human error;
4. technical error.

2.2.2 Back Office Systems

Main Settlement System

The functions of the main settlement system usually include:

1. Receiving real-time trade details from the front office systems and enriching those trade details with client-specific/instrument-specific settlement instructions.
2. Sending trade confirmations to clients and counterparties, and 'matching' confirmations received from counterparties with its own records of those trades.
3. Reporting trade details to regulators, in real time and within the maximum allowed period demanded by the regulators.
4. Sending settlement instructions to clearing houses, custodians and correspondent banks.
5. Receiving reports from clearing houses, custodians and correspondent banks about which trades have settled and which have not, and updating its records as a result of such reports.
6. Position management activity for bonds, equities and currencies. This involves making the following calculations:
   a. Positions in bonds and equities need to be revalued at the close of business each day as a result of changing market prices; the resulting gain or loss needs to be posted in the general ledger.
   b. For each day that the bank holds a position in a bond, it will earn one day's interest. This needs to be calculated, accrued, and posted in the general ledger system. Note that the settlement system does not usually perform these functions for positions in derivative instruments – position management for these instruments is usually performed by the front office system because of its specialised and complex nature.
7. Processing of changes to positions as a result of corporate actions, dividends, etc.
8. Forwarding details of trades, settlements and positions to the reconciliation system.
9. Forwarding details of all the activities listed in items 1–8 that affect the general ledger to the corporate general ledger system and the regulatory accounting system.

System Impact on Financial Control:
Because of the very wide range of functions that are performed by this system, its impact on the money values that are posted to the general ledger is very great.

This system usually forwards the results of its activities to the general ledger system at the end of processing the position management activity, at the end of the day.

The accuracy of what is reported may be affected by any or all of the following:

- Inaccurate reference data concerning client's standard settlement instructions – this would affect which general ledger account the amount receivable by or payable to the client was posted to.
- Inaccurate reference data concerning market prices, exchange rates and bond interest payment details – this would affect the accuracy of the position management entries.
- Corporate action processing problems.
- System limitations – the investment industry is one that continually innovates. One form of innovation is the invention of new types of equities, bonds and derivative contracts. Such innovation may involve new calculation methods and rules. If the settlements system is not enhanced to deal with these innovations, then the accuracy of its calculations may be impaired.
- Human errors in order or trade entry in the front office systems that have not been corrected – these may affect any general ledger posting.
- Problems in receiving data from the front office systems – these might cause the data that is being forwarded to the general ledger to be late, duplicated, incomplete or inaccurate.
- Problems on receiving data from the external agents such as clearing houses, custodians and correspondent banks – these might cause the data that is being forwarded to the general ledger to be late, duplicated, incomplete or inaccurate.
- Problems in the interface between this system and the corporate general ledger which might cause the data that is being forwarded to the general ledger to be late, duplicated, incomplete or inaccurate.

Reconciliation System

The reconciliation system takes in feeds about transactions, balances and positions from the main settlement systems and compares them to data received from the external agents (including payment banks, custodians, clearing houses and CSDs) so that the bank is able to prove that its records about transactions that have settled today, as well as the resulting position from such settlements, agrees with the records of the external agents concerned.

Many firms also use a specialist reconciliation system to check that the records held by the settlements system agree to those held by the various front office systems and the general ledger.

System Impact on Financial Control:
The purpose of this system is to prove that the data in the general ledger is consistent with the data held by the settlements system and by the external parties whom the firm has contracted to settle trades on its behalf. If reconciliations are not performed on a timely basis, then the firm can have no confidence that the figures reported in its general ledger are accurate.

2.2.3   Financial Control Systems

These were described in Section 2.1.

2.3   Conclusion

The IT impact of the financial control function is widespread. Not only does the IT department need to develop or purchase (and then maintain and enhance) dedicated systems for the finance department, but the accuracy of the data in these dedicated systems is affected by the performance and capabilities of virtually all the other application systems that the firm uses.

This has the following impacts on the IT department:

Development Impact
- In order for the general ledger to be updated on an accurate and timely basis, all systems in the configuration must be continually enhanced to deal with innovations in the structure of the products that are traded by the firm.
- Interfaces between systems need to be robust and automated – to avoid the problems of missing, duplicated, erroneous and/or late entries in the general ledger.

Support Impact
- Because of the complexity of the configuration, and the dispersed nature of activities within it, resolution of a support issue may be a complex process. If a user complains that an accounting entry is missing, duplicated or erroneous, then the cause of the problem may lie within the general ledger system itself, or any other system within the configuration.

3. The IT Requirements of General Ledger Accounts

Learning Objective

7.3   Know the purpose of the general ledger

3.1 Definition of the General Ledger

The general ledger, sometimes known as the nominal ledger, is the main accounting record of a business which uses the double-entry bookkeeping convention.

3.1.1 A Brief Introduction to the Double Entry Principle

Double-entry bookkeeping is a major study area in its own right, but this workbook provides a very simple introduction to the topic to enable students to follow the principles behind Sections 3 and 4.

The double-entry bookkeeping principle is based on the idea that each transaction is recorded in at least two ledger accounts. Each transaction results in at least one account being debited and at least one account being credited, with the total debits of the transaction being equal to the total credits. For example, if a new business is established by a shareholder putting in £1,000 in cash, then its general ledger will look like this:

Type of Asset (debit)	Value of Asset	Type of Liability (credit)	Value of Liabilities
Cash	£1,000	Shareholders' funds	£1,000
Total assets	£1,000	Total liabilities	£1,000

If the new business then purchases office equipment worth £500, then its general ledger will now look like this:

Type of Asset (debit)	Value of Asset	Type of Liability (credit)	Value of Liabilities
Cash	£500	Shareholders' funds	£1,000
Office equipment	£500		
Total assets	£1,000	Total liabilities	£1,000

The double-entry principle insists that, because the value of the office equipment has gone up by £500, then the value of something else – cash in this case – must have gone down by the same amount. The total assets and total liabilities of the business are unchanged at £1,000.

Use of the double-entry convention means that the accuracy of the accounts can be checked quickly – when all the accounts that have a debit balance are summed, they should equal the sum of all the accounts which have a credit balance. Without this facility there would be no quick means of checking accuracy.

The general ledger usually includes accounts for such items as current assets, fixed assets, liabilities, revenue and expense items, gains and losses. The general ledger is a summary of all of the transactions that occur in the company. It is built up by posting transactions to general ledger accounts as and when the business events occur.

There are seven basic categories in which all accounts are grouped. The following table shows the seven groups, together with some examples of each group in the finance industry:

General Ledger Account Category	Accounting Convention	Finance Industry Examples
Assets	Debit	Market value of securities purchased
		Interest receivable
		Money due from counterparties and clients
		Cash in the bank account
		Premises, furniture, fittings and equipment
Liabilities	Credit	Market value of securities sold
		Interest payable
		Money due to counterparties and clients
		Overdrawn bank accounts

General Ledger Account Category	Accounting Convention	Finance Industry Examples
Revenue	Credit	Net interest income, ie, interest received less interest paid
		Fees for client advice
Expenses	Debit	Salaries and other employee benefits
		Rent, property taxes, heat, light, power, etc
		All other expenses of running the business
Gains	Credit	Gains are profits (or increases in value) of an investment such as a stock or bond
		Gain is calculated by fair market value or the proceeds from the sale of the investment minus the sum of the purchase price and all costs associated with it
		If the investment is not converted into cash or another asset, the gain is then called an unrealised gain
Losses	Debit	The opposite of gains – losses arise when the investment is sold for less than the purchase price, or when the fair market value is less than the purchase price
Shareholders' equity	Debit	The net value of the business to its shareholders. Based on the accounting equation: **Assets – Liabilities = Shareholders' equity**

The balance sheet and the income statement are both derived from the general ledger, which is where posting to the accounts occurs.

Posting is the process of recording amounts as credits (right side) and as debits (left side) in the pages of the general ledger. The listing of the account names and the sum of the account balances is called a 'trial balance'. The purpose of the trial balance is, at a preliminary stage of the financial statement preparation process, to ensure the equality of the total debits and credits.

Because each bookkeeping entry debits one account and credits another in equal amounts, the double-entry bookkeeping system will ensure that the general ledger will always be in balance, thus maintaining the accounting equation:

Assets = Liabilities + Shareholders' Equity

The accounting equation is the mathematical structure of the balance sheet.

3.2   The Individual General Ledger Account

Learning Objective

7.4   Know the components of a general ledger account

The information that is held in an IT system about an individual general ledger account should include the following:

Reference Data Items

1. A unique alphanumeric code to identify the account.
2. The name of the account.
3. A code to represent the type of the account, ie, bank account, expense account, etc.
4. The identity of the currency in which postings are made for this account.

Balance Information Items

1. The opening balance of the account.
2. The date of the opening balance.
3. The closing balance of the account.
4. The date of the closing balance.

Transaction Information Items

1. The date that the transaction was carried out (business date).
2. The date that the transaction is expected to settle (value date).
3. The date that the transaction was entered into the general ledger system (entry date).
4. The money value of the transaction.
5. A description of the transaction.
6. A code to represent the type of the transaction (eg, securities purchase, FX sale, etc).
7. A 'configuration origin code' – this tells the user of the general ledger which of the many systems in the configuration produced the transaction; the presence of such a code is an invaluable aid to resolving support calls dealing with the types of problem referred to in Section 2.2.1 of this chapter.
8. A unique transaction reference number – ideally, this reference number will be used by all the systems (front office, back office and FCD) that have recorded this transaction.

3.2.1   A Typical General Ledger Category, its Accounts and its Sub-Accounts

Most finance industry general ledgers are structured along the lines of the following example. We are going to look at the general ledger structure for a particular type of account – equity positions.

Definitions

*   **Position** – the position that the firm holds in a particular equity is the net result of posting the money values of all the purchases of that equity, less the money values of any sales. When securities are bought for, say, £10 and sold for, say, £11, then the difference of £1 is a profit or gain. If the securities were purchased for £10 and sold for £9, then the difference of £1 is a loss.

- **Long positions, debit balances and assets** – if the quantity of shares purchased exceeds the quantity of shares sold, then the firm has a long position, which means that there is a debit balance in the general ledger, and the balance of the account concerned represents an asset to the business.
- **Short positions, credit balances and liabilities** – if the quantity of shares purchased is less than the quantity of shares sold, then the firm has a short position, which means that there is a credit balance in the general ledger, and the balance of the account concerned represents a liability to the business.

Example

General Ledger Accounts for Security Positions

ABC Investment Bank plc trades only in equities that are listed on either the London, New York or Deutsche Börse (ie, Frankfurt) stock exchanges. The securities that are traded on these exchanges may be priced in GBP, USD or EUR.

ABC, therefore, has three accounts in its general ledger, all of which have the account type of **security position** (SECPOS) accounts:

Account Type	Account Code	Account Description
SECPOS	POS-LSE	Securities listed on the London Stock Exchange
SECPOS	POS-NYSE	Securities listed on the New York Stock Exchange
SECPOS	POS-DBORSE	Securities listed on the Deutsche Börse

However, because ABC trades in three currencies, each one of the three accounts now has three sub-accounts – one for each currency, so the list of accounts now looks like this:

Account type	Unique Account Code	Account Description	Currency sub-account code
SECPOS	POS-LSE	Securities Listed on the London Stock Exchange	GBP
SECPOS	POS-LSE	Securities Listed on the London Stock Exchange	USD
SECPOS	POS-LSE	Securities Listed on the London Stock Exchange	EUR
SECPOS	POS-NYSE	Securities Listed on the New York Stock Exchange	GBP
SECPOS	POS-NYSE	Securities Listed on the New York Stock Exchange	USD
SECPOS	POS-NYSE	Securities Listed on the New York Stock Exchange	EUR
SECPOS	POS-DBORSE	Securities Listed on the Deutsche Börse	GBP
SECPOS	POS-DBORSE	Securities Listed on the Deutsche Börse	USD
SECPOS	POS-DBORSE	Securities Listed on the Deutsche Börse	EUR

Developing the example further, SONY Corporation shares are traded on all three of these exchanges, and ABC has traded this stock on all three of them. HBOS shares are traded only on the London exchange, where ABC has traded them.

In order to provide clarity and granularity within the general ledger, for each of the sub-account codes in the table above, the ledger now has sub-sub account codes for SONY and HBOS if appropriate. The security positions part of the ledger now begins to look like the table below – the account descriptions and any redundant rows have been removed to simplify the table:

Account type	Unique Account Code	Currency sub-account code	Instrument sub-sub account code	Closing Balance of the account	Date of Closing Balance
SECPOS	POS-LSE	GBP	SONY	100,012.50Dr	31 January 2007
SECPOS	POS-LSE	GBP	HBOS	175,000.00Cr	31 January 2007
SECPOS	POS-NYSE	USD	SONY	200,000.00Cr	31 January 2007
SECPOS	POS-DBORSE	EUR	SONY	150,000.00Dr	31 January 2007

The balances of POS-LSE/GBP/SONY and POS-DBORSE/EUR/SONY are debit balances because ABC has purchased more SONY shares on each of these accounts than it has sold. Conversely, the other two accounts have credit balances because ABC has sold more shares than it has bought.

The actual accounting entries that were passed across the POS-LSE/GBP/SONY in the month of January 2007 that resulted in the closing debit balance of £100,000.00 might be as shown in the sample general ledger report page below:

					ABC Investment Bank PLC General Ledger Postings and Balances Report			
Account Code:		POS-LSE	Currency	GBP	Instrument Account Code		**SONY**	
Business Date	**Value Date**	**Entry Date**	**Transaction Type**	**Origin Code**	**Transaction Description**	**Transaction Reference Number**	**Debit Amount**	**Credit Amount**
01/01/2007	01/01/2007	01/01/2007	BAL		Opening Balance of Account		0.00	
02/01/2007	05/01/2007	01/01/2007	PURCH	Equity	Purchased 20,000 shares at GBP11 per share	222222	220,000.00	
03/01/2007	07/01/2007	03/01/2007	SALE	Equity	Sold 10,000 shares at GBP11.30 per share	333333		113,000.00
03/01/2007	07/01/2007	03/01/2007	Trade P&L	Equity	Profit on trade 333333	333333	3,000.00	
29/01/2007	01/02/2007	29/01/2007	SALE	Equity	Sold 1,000 shares at 11.25	444444		11,250.00
29/01/2007	01/02/2007	29/01/2007	Trade P&L	Equity	Profit on trade 444444	444444	250.00	
31/01/2007	31/01/2007	31/01/2007	Revaluation	Setts	Revaluation of 9,000 shares - current market price GBP11.125	555555	1,125.00	
31/01/2007	31/01/2007	31/01/2007			Closing Balance of Account		100,125.00	

3.2.2 Selecting the Correct Account to Post an Entry To

Learning Objective

7.5 Know how account selection parameters are maintained

This is usually a function of the main settlement system, but this will not be the case for all securities firms. The process usually works along the lines of the following example, which is taken from the entry with transaction reference number 333333 in the sample general ledger page just illustrated. Let us look at this transaction in more detail:

On 3 January, ABC Investment Bank sold 10,000 shares in SONY Corporation to Client A at £11.30 per share, for value 7 January. The bank did not charge the client commission on this trade, so the amount payable by Client A is also £113,000 ie, 10,000 shares x £11.30.

As a result of this the following amounts (all in GBP) need to be posted to the general ledger:

Entry Number	Amount	Debit or Credit	Description	Account Type for Posting
1	113,000.00	Credit	The **principal amount** – ie, 10,000 shares x £11.30 per share	Security Position – (SECPOS)
2	3,000.00	Debit	The P&L (ie, profit and loss) on the trade	Security Position – (SECPOS)
3	3,000.00	Credit	The P&L on the trade	Security P&L (SECPL)
4	113,000.00	Debit	The **consideration** – ie, the amount to be paid by client A	Security Client (SECCLT)

For all of these entries, the firm needs to use a sub-account of the currency of the trade – GBP. It also needs to use a sub-sub-account for more detailed posting analysis. For entry numbers 1 to 3 the sub-sub account will be a code to represent whatever security is being traded. For entry number 4 the sub-sub account needs to represent whichever client the firm is trading with.

Most systems build the business rules for a decision of which account to post to by using an **explosion table** similar to the one illustrated in the following:

Account Selection Explosion Table								
Transaction Type	Operation	Amount Code	Dr or Cr	Account Type	Market Code	Account Code	Sub-Account	Sub-Sub-Account
Equity	Sell	Principal	Cr	SECPOS	LSE	POS-LSE	@currencyid	@securityid
Equity	Profit	PandL	Dr	SECPOS	LSE	POS-LSE	@currencyid	@securityid
Equity	Profit	PandL	Cr	SECPL	LSE	PL-LSE	@currencyid	@securityid
Equity	Sell	Consideration	Cr	SECCLT	(null)	SEC-CLT	@currencyid	@clientid

This table enables finance department users to specify – in each of the first six columns – different combinations of:

- **transaction type** – eg, equity, bond, foreign exchange, etc;
- **operation** – eg, buy, sell, lend, borrow, profit, loss, etc;
- **amount code** – a code to represent each of the relevant money amounts involved in the transaction;
- **account type** – eg, security position, security client, security P&L, etc;
- **market code** – a code to represent a particular market such as the LSE, NYSE, etc.

In the last three columns the user is able to specify (for each of the combinations entered in the first six columns):

- which distinct account code to use for each combination;
- the rule for deciding which sub-account to use: '@currencyid' means use the unique code that represents the currency being debited or credited on each posting event.
- the rule for deciding which sub-sub-account to use: '@securityid' means use the unique code that represents the security being traded on each posting event, and '@clientid' means use the unique code that represents the client from whom the securities were bought or sold.

In other words, these table column entries that begin with the '@' sign are 'indirect references' to system entities such as currencies, securities and clients. The firm may trade thousands of securities with hundreds of thousands of clients. The use of indirect references in an explosion table prevents the table becoming millions of rows long to cope with all the mathematical combinations involving clients, securities and currencies.

4.   The Stock Record

Learning Objective

7.6   Know the purpose of the stock record

4.1   Introduction and Purpose

Just as the general ledger allows firms to use the double-entry bookkeeping convention to record cash transactions and balances, the stock record allows firms to use the double-entry bookkeeping convention to record stock quantities and balances (including listed futures and options in this context) in the same way. The usual types of accounts affected by such postings are book, client and depot accounts.

The business principles and software application structures (double-entry bookkeeping, unique accounts and the use of account selection parameter tables and the underlying data used by these tables) that have been used to record money amounts may also be used to record stock quantities.

The stock record shows both the ownership of securities, and the location of the stock. It is often a component of the main settlement system, but may also be a stand-alone application with interfaces to the main settlement system. Some packaged stock record applications employ the terminology of 'long' and 'short' as alternatives to 'debit' and 'credit' respectively, others use the debit/credit terminology. When they use debit and credit terminology, different vendors do not use it consistently, as some applications are based in the premise that:

'A purchase of stock is a debit of money and a credit of stock.'

While the business logic of other applications is based on the premise that:

'A purchase of stock is a debit of money and also a debit of stock.'

To avoid ambiguity, this workbook will use the long/short terminology.

4.2 Example of Stock Record Postings

The following example transaction shows how the stock record balances change as a result of postings to the stock record on trade date, value date and actual settlement date.

On 3 January 2012, ABC Investment Bank's trading book number 1 purchased 20,000 shares in XYZ for Client A at £11.30 per share, for value 7 January 2012.

ABC's settlement agent is Euroclear. The trade does not settle, however, until 10 January 2012.

On trade date, the stock record balances are as follows:

ABC Investment Bank plc			
Stock record balances for 3 January 2012			
Instrument: XYZ Ordinary Shares			
Trade-Dated Balances			
Account Type	**Account ID**	**Sign**	**Quantity**
Book	Book 1	Long	20,000.00
Party	Client A	Short	20,000.00
Purchase and Sale Balance			0.00
Value-Dated Balances			
Account Type	**Account ID**	**Sign**	**Quantity**
Balance			0.00

This reflects the fact that Book 1 owns the shares and Client A owes them to the firm, but because value date has not been reached there is no value date balance.

On value date, 7 January 2012, the trade still has not settled, and the stock record balances now look like this:

ABC Investment Bank plc			
Stock record balances for 7 January 2012			
Instrument: XYZ Ordinary Shares			
Trade-Dated Balances			
Account Type	Account ID	Sign	Quantity
Book	Book 1	Long	20,000.00
Party	Client A	Short	20,000.00
Purchase and Sale Balance			0.00
Value-Dated Balances			
Account Type	Account ID	Sign	Quantity
Book	Book 1	Long	20,000.00
Party	Client A	Short	20,000.00
Balance			0.00

This reflects the fact that the trade has now reached value date and the shares are still owed to the firm by Client A. When the trade does settle, on 10 January, the stock record now looks like this:

ABC Investment Bank plc			
Stock record balances for 10 January 2012			
Instrument: XYZ Ordinary Shares			
Trade-Dated Balances			
Account Type	Account ID	Sign	Quantity
Book	Book 1	Long	20,000.00
Depot	Euroclear	Short	20,000.00
Purchase and Sale Balance			0.00
Value-Dated Balances			
Account Type	Account ID	Sign	Quantity
Book	Book 1	Long	20,000.00
Depot	Euroclear	Short	20,000.00
Balance			0.00

The stock record now reflects the fact that Client A no longer owes the firm the shares; instead, they are now held in its account at Euroclear.

The stock record may be used to identify, *inter alia*, the following:

1. trade-dated book positions in securities of all types that require to be marked-to-market;
2. value-dated book positions in bonds that need to have interest accruals calculated for them;
3. the actual settled position in the depot;
4. borrowing and lending opportunities.

End of Chapter Questions

Think of an answer for each question and refer to the appropriate section for confirmation.

1. List the five activities that are commonly performed by the Financial Control Department of a securities firm.
    Section 1

2. List the usual functions of a corporate general ledger system.
    Section 2.1
    -

3. Why do derivative contracts need to be revalued at the end of each business day?
    Section 2.2.1

4. What is the business reason for performing reconciliations between data held in the main settlement system and the corporate general ledger?
    Section 2.2.2

5. List the seven basic categories into which all general ledger accounts are grouped, together with whether each category is normally expected to be a debit balance or a credit balance.
    Section 3.1.1

6. How do we normally express the 'accounting equation'?
    Section 3.1.1

7. List the information that you would expect to see on a general ledger report page, divided into reference data items, balance information items and transaction information items.
    Section 3.2

8. Does holding a short position in a security create a debit balance or a credit balance in the general ledger?
    Section 3.2.1

9. Define an account selection explosion table – what is it that it allows finance department users to control?
    Section 3.2.2

10. On which date (trade, value or settlement) is the depot position updated in the stock record?
    Section 4.2

Chapter Eight
IT Management

This syllabus area will provide approximately 6 of the 50 examination questions

8

1. IT Infrastructure

This section deals with the IT architecture concepts of a typical investment firm.

1.1 Organisation Structure

Learning Objective

8.1 Know the typical roles and responsibilities within the IT department

Roles will vary between firms depending on the size of the firm concerned, and on factors such as whether the firm operates from a single location or multiple locations, whether it operates globally or in just a single country, and how many individual business units it has. However, the following roles are likely to be found in most organisations, although the reporting lines may vary significantly from the examples in this workbook.

Head of Information Technology (or Information Systems)

This individual is often known as the **Chief Information Officer**, or **CIO**. This is usually a board-level appointment. The CIO manages all the other staff of the division, and sets the company's IT strategy. All the following positions would usually report to the CIO.

Head of Production Support

This individual reports to the CIO and is usually responsible for the provision of all server and desktop facilities to all users and for the day-to-day running and support of the production (live) system.

The following positions normally report to this individual:

- **Database administrators or DBAs** – the role of the DBA is to:
  - develop and enforce database standards, guidelines, operational policies and procedures;
  - review physical structures;
  - review performance, maintenance and utilities associated with each structure;
  - review necessary storage media;
  - review SQL (Structured Query Language, see Section 1.2.4) performance and tuning;
  - review applications' access to the database structures;
  - review back-up and recovery strategies;
  - review, where required, the purge/archive criteria;
  - monitor database/subsystem performance issues;
  - review migration plans.
- **Help desk analysts** – the tasks involved in this position are discussed in more detail in Section 3.2.

Head of Development and Implementation

This individual reports to the CIO and is usually responsible for the commissioning of new applications. These applications may be developed internally, developed for the firm by others, or purchased as packages. The following individuals normally report to this position:

- **Business analysts** – responsible for discovering and documenting the business requirements.
- **Application designers/systems analysts** – responsible for designing the systems to meet the needs of the business as documented by the business analysts.
- **Programmers** – responsible for writing the application code as specified by the application designers.

Head of Testing

This individual reports to the CIO and is responsible for testing new software releases and implementing change control procedures. Change control procedures are described more fully in Section 5.4 of this chapter, and the testing process is described in Chapter 9.

Test analysts report to the head of testing.

Head of Change

This individual reports to the CIO and is responsible for managing major change programmes and individual projects. They often run matrix teams, pulling in staff from Development and Testing and the business lines. The processes that are used to govern these activities are described in more detail in Chapter 9, where the roles of the individuals reporting to this position will be examined in detail. These roles include:

- Programme managers.
- Project managers.

Head of Business Recovery

This individual reports to the CIO and is responsible for managing the company's business recovery plans, which are described in Section 4 of this chapter. Although this role is shown as part of the IT department in this workbook, it should be noted that in many firms this individual's reporting line may be to another board member.

Head of Information Security

This individual reports to the CIO and is responsible for the overall direction of all security functions associated with applications, voice and data communications and computing services within the firm The holder must be aware of the implications of the Data Protection Act in the UK, or equivalent other countries. They will also be the person who monitors compliance with Sarbanes-Oxley security requirements (see Chapter 2, Section 5.1) and other relevant legislation.

1.2 IT Infrastructure

Learning Objective

8.2   Know the typical building blocks of an IT infrastructure

8.3   Understand the roles and uses of relational databases, distributed systems and real-time messaging

The IT infrastructure of a typical financial services firm may be summarised by the following diagram.

Typical IT Architecture Concept

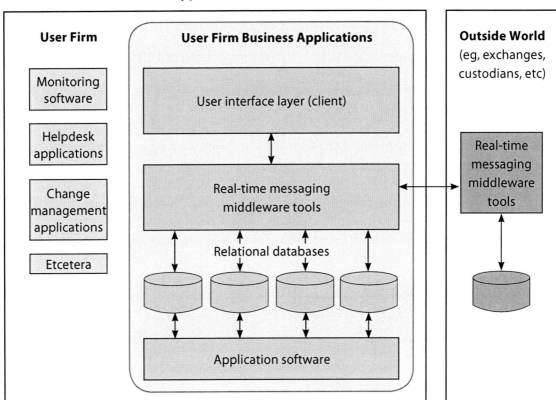

The user firm has a number of business applications (eg, settlement, dealing, financial accounting, etc). The majority of them are usually based on the architecture shown above.

1.2.1   Client

This is the component where users interact with the systems, eg, where users input data, view enquiries, etc. Very commonly it is a laptop or PC running just an internet browser (often called a 'thin client'), or a 'fat client', which is a PC on which an application other than a browser is installed. However, some systems (eg, Bloomberg) have dedicated terminals other than PCs, while older systems may still use 'green screens'.

There are also a large number of newer devices that are gaining popularity – for example iPhones, iPads, BlackBerries, mobile phones and interactive TV.

1.2.2 Application

This component holds the actual programs for processing. It is sometimes called the logic engine or business rules. It will hold the rules for the system, eg, it will validate a trade, create a customer, obtain a customer's details and so on.

1.2.3 Middleware/Real Time Messaging Layer

This component consists of software products that distribute and obtain real-time data to and from other parties. 'Other parties' could mean internal systems or external systems (such as banks, clearing houses, SWIFT and external emails).

1.2.4 Database

A database consists of an organised collection of data, eg, customer standing data, holding information, prices.

There are various models of databases (eg, the hierarchical model and the network model) – but the most common by far is the **relational database**.

A relational database contains a number of tables and relationships between them. A table normally represents a data item (eg, customers, holdings, transactions, etc). The relationships determine how the tables are linked together. For example, a dealing system will hold customers, holdings and trades. Therefore, three tables would be created – one each for customer, holding and trade. The relationships would be as follows: a trade must have a holding and a holding must have a customer. In effect, it will not be possible to a create a trade without a holding or a holding without a customer.

Each table is split into rows (or records). Each row represents a specific actual data item. For example, on the table, an individual row would be created for each actual customer.

Each row contains a number of columns (or fields). Each column represents an individual data item. For example, on the customer table, columns would exist for the customer name, address, post code, telephone number, etc. For the transaction table, columns will exist for trade date, settlement date, asset ID, value, nominal, commission and so on.

The standard method to interface with relational databases is using **SQL (Structured Query Language)**. There are SQL statements to obtain, insert, update and delete rows from tables – as well as creating, deleting and altering tables and columns.

However there are various software products that can be purchased that allow non-technical users to develop reports over a database (without the need to write complex SQL programs). The most common relational database products are ORACLE, IBM's DB2, Sybase, Microsoft's SQL-Server and the open-source product My SQL.

Examples of Using SQL

1. **Creating a customer**
    a. The user will enter the customer information into the 'Create Customer' screen within the 'Customer' component.

b.   The information entered will be passed to the 'Application' component.
c.   The 'Application' component will then check that all the data entered is correct and present – eg, a name has been entered, an address has been entered, etc.
d.   If anything is missing then the 'Application' component will pass an error back to the 'Customer' component which will display a suitable message for the user (eg, 'Customer name must be entered')
e.   If everything is valid, then the 'Application' component will pass data to the 'Database' component which will then insert a row into the relevant table(s).
f.   Also, the 'Application' component may also pass data to the 'Middleware' component which will send an email to the customer notifying them of their new details.

2.   **Entering and matching a trade**
a.   The user will enter the trade into the 'Enter Trade' screen within the 'Customer' component.
b.   The information entered will be passed to the 'Application' component – and this component will check the data entered is correct and present, eg, an asset has been entered, valid dates have been entered.
c.   If anything is missing, the 'Application' component will pass an error back to the 'Customer' component which will display a message for the user (eg, 'Invalid Asset ID').
d.   If everything is valid, then the 'Application' component will pass data to the 'Database' component to create an unmatched trade row on the 'Trade' table. It will also pass data to the 'Middleware' component which will pass details externally to the relevant matching service.
e.   Some time later, the matching service will pass details back on whether or not the trade has been matched to the 'Middleware' component. It will then pass details to the 'Application' component which will then pass them onto the 'Database' component which will update the relevant row on the 'Trade' table.

The 'Database' and 'Application' components are normally deployed on servers. A server machine is a high-performance host that is running one or more server programs and shares its resources.

Many mission-critical applications may be deployed as **distributed systems**. A distributed system is a configuration which contains a number of hardware elements that are connected by some transmission technology. Such systems consist of a number of executing programs which interact with each other via transmission lines. Many of the computers in a distributed system act as clients to servers.

There are many reasons for implementing a system in a distributed fashion:

1.   To ensure that processing power is as close to the users as possible.
2.   To ensure a high degree of robustness, for example via the use of data replication.
3.   To enable hardware to be easily added as the resource demands of the applications running on the distributed system start increasing.

There are many problems facing the designer of a distributed system, including predicting the performance of a particular design, keeping all the clocks in the system synchronised, and ensuring that, if a hardware element of the system malfunctions, users are, at best, only affected in a minimal way. Distributed systems have been in existence since the 1970s, but they were mainly closed systems confined to a physical location, such as a building. The rise of the internet has meant that many distributed systems are open to the world. This has given rise to a major problem: ensuring that such systems are secure. The best-known distributed system is the comparatively simple world wide web, which consists of a very large number of clients running browsers and a large number of web servers.

Data replication is the process of sharing information so as to ensure consistency between redundant resources, such as software or hardware components, to improve reliability, fault-tolerance, or accessibility. Data replication can be implemented either by storing the same data on multiple storage devices, or by executing the same computing task many times on different devices, in which case it is known as 'computation replication'.

In addition to the business applications themselves, firms will deploy systems such as help desk systems, change management systems and performance monitoring systems to monitor the health of the business applications. These tools are also usually based on relational database technology.

2. Measuring Performance and Managing Risk

Learning Objective

8.4   Understand the IT governance relating to: measuring IT performance; managing and monitoring risk; managing change; benefits realisation

This section deals with the techniques and processes that the IT department employs to manage the daily business activities of the investment firm. In managing day-to-day operations, the department seeks at all times to minimise operational risk. Let us first remind ourselves of the seven operational risk events that were identified by the Basel Committee (described in Chapter 2) and examine how poor IT practice can increase operational risk, while good practice can mitigate it:

1. **Internal fraud** – misappropriation of assets, tax evasion, intentional mismarking of positions and bribery. *These activities can be facilitated by practices that allow, inter alia, unauthorised access to applications and underlying data. They may be mitigated by the use of application password control and the deployment of systems that support the concept of segregation of duties.*
2. **External fraud** – theft of information, hacking damage, third-party theft and forgery. *As for (1) above, but in addition, these problems can be mitigated by the deployment of anti-virus software, anti-spyware, firewalls, etc.*
3. **Employment practices and workplace safety** – discrimination, workers, compensation, employee health and safety. *There are no specific IT-related issues to this event; it is a company-wide issue.*
4. **Clients, products, and business practice** – market manipulation, anti-trust, improper trade, product defects, fiduciary breaches and account churning. *'Product defects' in this context includes defects in the software and hardware that is used to process the firm's data. Good IT practice involves the use of standardised, reliable methodologies to discover and document business requirements, select software vendors and packages, build, test and deploy software and manage projects. It also involves the use of configuration management and change control procedures to ensure that the right software versions are deployed.*
5. **Damage to physical assets** – natural disasters, terrorism and vandalism. *See (6).*
6. **Business disruption and systems failures** – utility disruptions, software failures and hardware failures. *These risks may be mitigated by proper Business Recovery Plans, which are examined in Section 4. Software failures may also arise as a result of product defects (Basel II Event no.4).*
7. **Execution, delivery, and process management** – data entry errors, accounting errors, failed mandatory reporting and negligent loss of client assets. *These events, in turn, may be caused by product defects.*

Generally, the governance of the risk management of information technology can be divided into two categories within securities companies:

- maintaining 'business as usual' activity; and
- introducing business change.

The maintenance of **business as usual** activity is the responsibility of **Operations**. Operations in this context includes many business areas, including IT, settlements and finance. Therefore, Operations will keep track of a number of metrics and commitments with the business in order to continuously assess risk. In support of this structure, a number of IT owners may contribute to the underlying data that is being assessed and be asked to participate in regular status update calls throughout the business day.

For the introduction of **business change**, projects are often initiated at the request of the business and carried out in parallel to production activities. On a day-to-day basis, those supporting production are not often concerned about the progress of ongoing business change initiatives that are in the pipeline. However, if there is a critical issue with production and a business change is required immediately or during major deployment activities, the two differing governance structures of business as usual and business change work closely together. Typically, business change teams meet with a frequency sufficient to ensure that the delivery is on track, with a frequency that increases as the go-live date nears.

2.1 Maintaining 'Business as Usual' Activity

To manage the risk of maintaining adequate day-to-day systems within the IT function, operational procedures need to be put in place to manage, control and escalate risks and issues.

Some areas of risk management within the business as usual activity are as follows:

- Ensuring that business applications and the configurations that run them are stable, and are able to cope with normal business volumes.
- Recording deficiencies in the design or operation of systems that support the firm's activities and maintaining documentation of the workarounds to keep the process in control.
- Protecting the organisation from system security issues such as unauthorised access.
- Ensuring system development keeps pace with rapidly evolving user requirements.
- Ensuring that systems integrate effectively, minimising manual intervention and data integrity issues.

2.2 Introducing Business Change

By definition, the introduction of business change means that the way that business is done at a future date is going to change. Business change is usually delivered by a project or programme (a collection of related projects); the day that the business change occurs is known as the 'go live' date.

When a business change initiative is planned, it is necessary that there is an adequate governance structure to ensure that those impacted by the change have had an opportunity to communicate their assessment of the risks and impacts on their areas and customers.

Risks that need to be managed when delivering business change within the IT function include:

- aligning IT strategy with the business strategy;
- aligning the solution to the strategic business drivers;
- managing and monitoring risks of introducing the change on the business;
- providing visibility of risks and issues to responsible stakeholders;
- risk of over- (and under-) spend;
- risk of 'reinventing the wheel' – ie, implementing duplicate systems;
- delivery risk – ie, delivering late, or not delivering what is required;
- complexity risk – ie, the end solution becomes so complex that it increases cost and impacts delivery;
- scope expansion risk – ie, the scope grows and grows (also known as 'scope creep');
- managing external parties, eg, clients or suppliers.

The securities industry existed before information technology. It should be noted that the way that operational risk is managed within the information technology function is not different from how it is managed within operations, financial control, legal or compliance functions. Therefore, the CISI's *Operational Risk* workbook is a course that should be taken by those wishing to understand how risks are identified, measured, assessed, reported and mitigated.

2.3 'Change as Usual'?

Some people now argue that these traditional demarcations of 'business as usual' and 'change' are too simplistic. Because we live and work in such a rapidly changing world, firms ought to be managed to deal with constant change, or 'change as usual'. Proponents of this theory point out that, in this century, financial services firms have had to deal with a series of major changes that have been imposed from outside, one after the other, These have included Basel II and MiFID, and in the next few years will include Basel III and new EU and UK regulatory changes, as well as changes caused by new technologies, products and services and customer expectations. Given the scope of these never-ending series of changes, to talk of 'business as usual' is an oversimplification.

2.3.1 Benefits Realisation

Proponents of the 'change as usual' concept argue that an important step in the project life cycle which is often ignored is measuring whether or not a change programme or project has actually achieved the benefits that were intended.

This means that, for any new project:

- the intended benefits of that project must be documented and clearly understood at the outset, and agreed by senior management;
- they should be expressed in financial terms if possible, ie, the expected return on investment should be measurable or, better still, quantified;
- the identities of the business units that will enjoy these benefits must be known at the outset; and
- as part of the change plan, time and resources must be set aside to measure whether these intended benefits were or were not, in fact, achieved.

For more on Change Management, see Chapter 9.

3. The Management and Support of Applications

3.1 Data Security

Learning Objective

8.5   Know the common methods of securing data against hacking, phishing, scamming and spyware

---

3.1.1 Definitions of Terms

Hacking is the process of gaining unauthorised access to computer systems for the purpose of stealing and/or corrupting data.

Hacking is sometimes a highly technical and sophisticated process, but can be very low tech in nature. The journalists employed by the *News of the World* who hacked mobile phones, mainly guessed the PIN numbers of their victims – they did not need any advanced technology. Neither did Bradley Manning, the US soldier who was arrested in May 2010 on suspicion of having passed 250,000 diplomatic cables, and 500,000 army reports to the 'whistleblowing' website WikiLeaks. Manning was recently convicted for a large number of offences under the US Espionage Act and could face a sentence of up to 130 years in prison. According to the evidence in his trial, Manning simply burned the stolen files onto a CD using his office computer and walked out with the CD in his pocket.

The main criminal purposes of hacking are to facilitate identity fraud and cyber-espionage. Successful phishing expeditions, the installation of malware, the creation of Botnets and the instigation of DDoS attacks – these terms will be explained in this chapter – are therefore all forms of hacking.

There are various different types of hacking techniques and some of them are detailed below. It is important to note that some of them are very similar.

Identity fraud, which is more commonly known by the less accurate name of identity theft, is the process of stealing personal information, such as name and address details, kinship information, dates of birth, bank account and credit card details, passport information, driving licence information and computer system passwords, so that the criminal is able to pose as the person or organisation whose identity has been stolen.

The direct victim of this type of fraud may be the financial institution itself, and/or its customers. Some of the software applications that are involved in this type of crime will be described later in this section. It is important to realise that many of these tools also have legitimate uses, and this creates problems in identifying, immobilising and removing them.

The purpose of **cyber-espionage** is to steal valuable and often confidential information about products, services, patents, designs and other intellectual property. The UK Ministry of Defence has publicly stated that defence companies in particular face cyber-attacks almost daily, often from countries, seeking to steal sensitive information about new technology and weapons. Companies in other industries, such as financial institutions, might become targets if they have valuable intellectual property that gives them a competitive advantage.

Malware (short for **mal**icious soft**ware**) is software which is designed to gain surreptitious access to computer systems in order to disrupt normal operation or gather private information that may be used illegally.

Normal operation of a computer or network may be disrupted by **Hacking** or by a **Distributed Denial of Service (DDoS) Attack**.

Spyware is software that gathers information about a person or organisation without their knowledge, and may send such information to a third party. Most spyware is installed by using deceptive tactics (such as bundling itself with desirable software). When the user navigates to a webpage controlled by the spyware author, the page contains code which attacks the browser and forces the download and installation of spyware.

Spyware's presence is typically hidden from the user and can be very difficult to detect. Spyware can collect almost any type of data, including personal information such as Internet surfing habits, user logins and bank or credit account information. It can also interfere with user control of a computer by installing additional software or in changing computer settings, which can result in slow internet connection speeds, unauthorised changes in browser settings or changes to software settings.

Phishing is a very specific type of cybercrime designed to trick users into disclosing personal financial details. Cybercriminals will create a fake website that looks just like a bank's (or any other website where online financial transactions are conducted) website. They then try to trick users into visiting this site and typing in confidential data, such as login IDs, passwords or PINs. Typically, cybercriminals send out large numbers of emails containing a hyperlink to the fake site.

Scamming is a low-tech alternative to phishing and is usually carried out by phone. The caller simply invents a plausible story to persuade the recipient to disclose confidential information (such as bank details) that belongs to either the target itself or to customers of the target.

Viruses, Worms and Trojans

A **computer virus** is a software program that can copy itself and infect multiple files on an individual computer as well as spread from one computer to another. **Worms** are considered to be a subset of viruses. A worm is a computer program that replicates, but does not infect, other files. Instead, a worm installs itself once on a computer and then looks for a way to spread to other computers.

A **Trojan virus**, or **Trojan horse virus**, is a computer program that appears to be legitimate but actually results in unauthorised access to the victim's computer files. For a malicious program to accomplish its goals, it must be able to run without being detected, shut down, or deleted. Therefore, it is often disguised as something normal or desirable so that users may willingly install it without realising it. In broad terms, a Trojan horse is any program that invites the user to run it, concealing harmful or malicious code. The code may take effect immediately and can lead to many undesirable effects, such as deleting the user's files or installing further harmful software.

One of the most common ways that spyware is distributed is as a Trojan, bundled with a piece of desirable software that the user downloads from the Internet. When the user installs the software, the spyware is installed along with it. Spyware authors may include an end-user license agreement that states the behaviour of the spyware in loose terms which users may not read or understand.

Keylogging and Form Grabbing

Keystroke logging, often referred to as **keylogging**, is the action of recording (or logging) the keys struck on a keyboard, typically in a covert manner so that the person using the keyboard is unaware that their actions are being monitored. It has legitimate uses in studies of human-computer interaction and in software testing, where a set of keystrokes can be recorded in order that the exact keystrokes can be repeated in later tests. However, criminals often install keylogging applications as viruses or Trojans on computers in order to capture personal details.

Form grabbing is software that has the same purpose as illegal keystroke logging – it intercepts data submitted to web browsers, collects it before it passes over the internet and can pass it to criminals.

Botnets

A botnet is a network of computers controlled by cybercriminals using a Trojan or other malicious program. This diagram illustrates how a botnet is established:

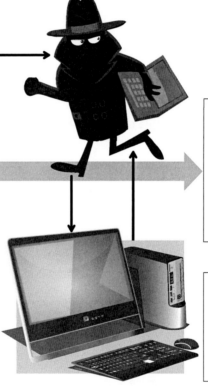

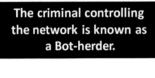
The criminal controlling the network is known as a Bot-herder.

Step 1
PC is infected by a Trojan after a user opens an email attachment, visits an infected website or plugs in an infected device.

Step 2
Infected PC finds the "command and control" server operated by the bot-herder who instructs it to infect other machines and gather information or do other damage.

Step 4
The network of affected PCs may now be used to steal data, hack into other machines, take part in DDoS attacks or commit other crimes.

Step 3
Malware connects to other computers and checks for vulnerabilities. If these are found, further machines are infected.

Distributed Denial of Service (DDoS) Attacks

A **denial-of-service attack (DoS attack)** or **distributed denial-of-service attack (DDoS attack)** is an attempt to make a machine or network resource unavailable to its intended users. It generally consists of efforts to temporarily or indefinitely interrupt or suspend services of a host connected to the internet, usually by bombarding that host with a very large number of requests to the extent that the server is unable to fulfil genuine user requests at all or only after unacceptable delays.

The victims of these attacks are usually sites or services hosted on high-profile web servers, such as banks, credit card payment gateways, large e-commerce companies and computer security databases. The motives for instigating DDoS attacks vary. Sometimes the motive is pure vandalism or sometimes the motive is political. In 2013 there were DDoS attacks against most of the retail banks in the Netherlands, and these have been linked to political protest against alleged tax evasion by these banks. In 2010 there were attacks on Amazon, PayPal and MasterCard made by a group called Anonymous. This group stated that it made these attacks in retaliation when these companies withdrew services from WikiLeaks as a result of the leaking of classified US government files by WikiLeaks. This type of politically motivated hacking has become known as 'Hacktivism'.

Revenge by disgruntled employees may also be a motive for some attacks, others are believed to be instigated by unscrupulous competitors, and criminals may use DDoS to prevent the target company informing affected customers that their security has been breached.

The attack itself may be instigated by a network of infected computers involved in a botnet, but is possible to launch an attack from a single computer – seventeen different methods of launching such attacks have been identified.

3.1.2   Prevention and Detection

The following steps are recommended:

1. Conduct an **impact analysis** of the systems you/your firm is using. Establish which of them are most likely to be attacked, and if they are attacked, what the likely consequences would be (eg, financial loss to the firm itself, financial loss to customers or others, reputational damage, regulator sanctions). Concentrate efforts on protecting those parts of the infrastructure where the likelihood of attack is high, and the consequences are most severe.
2. **Staff training**: Ensure that all staff are trained in basic security measures, such as keeping passwords private and regularly changing them, taking care of portable devices, recognising phishing and scamming, and taking care of customer information; and train technical staff in the use of anti-hacking software and hardware, such as vulnerability scanners and encryption software. Be aware of the 'insider threat'. The Bradley Manning case has shown that a disgruntled employee can steal vast quantities of sensitive data from what was supposed to be one of the securest environments in the world – the US Army.
3. **Personal devices and portable devices**: Increasingly, staff are demanding to be able to connect their own personal devices, such as smartphones and tablets, to corporate networks. When these devices are connected, employ software products that scan and check these devices for malware. Portable hardware is, of course, easy to lose or steal, so make sure that any sensitive data that is downloaded to such machines is encrypted.

4. Be open and approachable in any dealings with **online customers**. Use effective tools such as one-time password hardware to control access to networks by customers, and let them know how they can contact you if they have spotted a potential threat. Test all new releases of e-commerce software for security breaches. If you e-mail customers, always greet them by name. Phishers will not know your customer names unless they have already stolen your client data. If you are offering contactless payment systems, then try to encourage users to install anti-virus applications on their devices and to password-protect their smartphones.

5. Install **vulnerability scanners** to assess computers, networks and applications for weaknesses. A number of types of vulnerability scanners are available which are distinguished from one another by a focus on particular targets, such as ports, applications and databases. While functionality varies between the different types of scanners, they share a common, core purpose of identifying and recording the vulnerabilities identified in each target. These scanning programs should identify all entry points from the internet into the internal network of the company. Any attack to the network needs to start from these points. Identifying these entry points, however, is not at all an easy task. Some firms have used the services of 'ethical hackers' who have taken special network security training to perform this task successfully.

6. Identify where **firewalls** (systems that control the incoming and outgoing network traffic by analysing the data packets and determining whether they should be allowed through or not, based on a rule set) are needed, configure them correctly and keep them up-to-date. If a firewall is not configured properly, it can act like an open door for any intruder. Hence, it is vitally important to set the rules to allow traffic through the firewall that is important to the business.

7. **Encryption**: Identify what data needs to be encrypted and encrypt it. The problem is that a single enterprise might use several dozen different, and possibly incompatible, encryption tools, resulting in thousands of encryption keys – each of which must be securely stored, adequately protected and reliably retrievable. Encryption key management is the administration of tasks involved with protecting, storing, backing up and organising encryption keys. High-profile data losses and regulatory compliance requirements have spurred a dramatic increase in the use of encryption in the enterprise. There are now a number of encryption key management standards and products available to firms.

8. Keep **anti-virus software** up-to-date and periodically benchmark it against competing products. There are a number of websites that provide benchmarking services. In response to the emergence of **malware**, software vendors such as Norton, McAfee and Kaspersky have developed applications which:
    a. provide real-time protection by scanning all incoming network data for malware and blocking any threats it detects; and
    b. detect and remove any malware products that have already been installed onto the computer by inspecting the contents of the registry, operating system files, and installed programs, and removing items which match a list of known malware.

    Many anti-malware applications are able to detect some software keyloggers and quarantine, disable or cleanse them. However, because keylogging programs may be being used legitimately, anti-spyware software sometimes fails to label malicious installations as malware. As a result anti-keylogger software has been specifically designed to handle this problem. The primary difference between this type of application and conventional anti-virus software is that an anti-keylogger does not make a distinction between a *legitimate* keystroke-logging program and an *illegitimate* keystroke-logging program (such as a virus); hence legitimate keylogging applications, if any are installed, will be immobilised or deleted by these applications.

9. **Ensure physical security**: You need to think about the physical security of your organisation. Unless your organisation has full security, any intruder can simply walk in your office premises to gain whatever information they want. Hence, with technical security, you must also ensure that the physical security mechanisms of your organisation are fully functional and effective.

10. **Perform attack and penetration tests**: These can identify those vulnerable points in the network that can be easily accessed from both external and internal users. After identifying these points, you would be able to thwart attacks from external sources and correct the pitfalls that could become the entry points for intruders to hack into your network. The test must be done from both the internal as well as external perspectives to detect all the vulnerable points. Specialist organisations can be employed to perform 'pen tests'.

11. **The importance of regular and thorough testing based on the results of the impact analysis cannot be over-stated.**

12. Defensive responses to **DDoS attacks** typically involve the use of a combination of attack detection, traffic classification and response tools, aiming to block traffic that they identify as illegitimate and allow traffic that they identify as legitimate. Firewalls can be set up to have simple rules, such as to allow or deny protocols, ports or IP addresses. In the case of a simple attack coming from a small number of unusual IP addresses for instance, one could put up a simple rule to drop all incoming traffic from those attackers. More complex attacks will, however, be hard to block with simple rules such as this.

Across a securities company there will be dozens, if not hundreds, of applications that need to be supported. To have an initial concept of the importance of managing and supporting these applications, one should appreciate that some of these applications are critical to the operational effectiveness of an organisation.

3.2 Cataloguing the Applications

Learning Objective

8.6   Understand the concept of management and support of applications

An effectively managed help desk is a prerequisite for minimising operational risk. If the help desk is being established for the first time, then the following information needs to be collated. This type of information is often known as an **infrastructure catalogue**, and includes full details of all:

- **Users the desk supports** – key details include:
    - name, department, telephone number, email address and physical location;
    - normal working hours and working days.
- **Applications the desk supports** – key details include:
    - name of application;
    - details of its role in the business;
    - name and full contact details of the organisation that is responsible for supporting it. Note that this may be the firm's IT department, or an external vendor. If it is an external vendor, then full details of any **service level agreements** need to be available to the help desk;
    - technical details – is it a PC application such as Word or Excel, or is it a web-based application that does not require installation in a user PC, or is it a client-server application employing a database? If it is a client-server application, what database is used, and what specific servers does it run on?
    - any requirements for specific version numbers for database and operating system software;
    - hours during the day and days of the week on which there is expected to be activity. If there is a great deal of night-time activity in this application, then the desk will need to hold out-of-hours contact details, and perhaps rotas for support staff who may need to be contacted at home;

- an assessment as to how critical the loss of this application for an extended period would be to the business;
    - licence details – the number of simultaneous users, scope of use, volume limits, etc.
- **Hardware the desk supports** – key details include:
    - locations of all servers and routers;
    - whether they are used for production, testing or disaster recovery;
    - which applications are running on each server.

Once the infrastructure catalogue has been built up, IT management needs to decide:

- which applications are 'critical' to the business;
- which applications need to be supported 'around the clock' on normal working days and which need to be supported for shorter periods;
- which applications need to be routinely supported at weekends and on public holidays.

If **round-the-clock support** is required, then what is the best way to achieve it? The following models are commonly used:

- **'Follow the Sun'** – this model is widely used by firms that have operations in more than one time zone, and users accessing the same applications and servers from different countries. During normal European working hours, support for all users worldwide is provided from a European location. When Europe closes, support moves to a North American support centre, and, when North America closes, support is handled by an Asian support centre.
- **Extended working hours** – this model is widely used when a firm is doing business in a single time zone, but is using applications that are working throughout the day and night. A single help desk works in shifts. One shift coincides with normal working hours for the majority of the users, and is more heavily manned than the other shift, which deals only with emergency calls.
- **Partial outsourcing** – if the number of out-of-hours calls are expected to be very few in number but may be critical, then overnight manning of the help desk could be outsourced to a third party specialist firm.

3.3 Managing the Help Desk

Learning Objective

8.7   Understand the function of Service (Help) Desks and Follow-The-Sun Model

3.3.1 Help Desk Functions

As part of its 'business as usual' activity, the department will normally need to set up a help desk to handle requests for assistance from its users. In a large organisation these requests will cover a very wide range of topics, which may be divided into the following categories.

- **Planned administrative or preventative maintenance activities**, such as:
    - provide a new user with a PC and/or appropriate software to run on that PC and/or usernames and passwords to run software applications;

- ○ move one or more PCs or servers or other hardware items within the office;
- ○ upgrade an item of hardware or software at an agreed date in the future, including the latest antivirus software.
- **Unplanned emergency activities**, such as:
  - ○ an item of hardware or an application is not performing correctly and needs to be fixed to enable the user to continue normal daily operations;
  - ○ An item of hardware or software has failed in the recent past and action needs to be taken to recover from the problems that were created.

Such requests are often referred to as **issues**. The role of the help desk is therefore:

1. to receive issues from users;
2. to prioritise them;
3. to pass them to the appropriate individuals for action;
4. to monitor whether the issue has been actioned to the satisfaction of the requestor, and:
   - ○ if they have, to close the issues;
   - ○ if they have not, to escalate them to management;
5. to provide a database of 'Frequently Asked Questions' that can be used by help desk staff in the future to deal with common queries;
6. to provide statistical and trend reports to management about the number of issues, and the severity of issues that are recorded:
   - ○ by different business units;
   - ○ for different applications.

3.3.2 Recording and Actioning Issues

In many firms, issues are now recorded directly into a help desk management system by the users affected. Such systems have business rules that allow for the automatic logging of issues by the user concerned, and also:

- provide a pre-defined series of issue types, priority codes, applications and environments for the reporting user to select from;
- based on the input into these pre-defined lists, automatically assign the problem to the correct individual or section;
- provide facilities for the section dealing with the issue to respond to the requestor by automated email when the issue has been actioned;
- provide facilities for the responder to provide details of the time spent dealing with a particular problem;
- provide facilities for issues of a particular type to follow a particular workflow pattern. For example, an issue that requires a software enhancement needs to be directed to:
  - ○ a business analyst – to decide what the software change needs to be; then
  - ○ a developer – to make the change; then
  - ○ a test analyst – to test the change; then
  - ○ the user who reported the issue – to sign it off.

Because help desk activities are essentially collaborative, many help desk management systems now incorporate social networking capabilities, and increasingly such applications are now based in 'the cloud'. These concepts are discussed more fully in Chapter 10.

The illustration below shows an example of an issue that has been entered into a help desk management system by a user. In this case, the item was entered into the JIRA system developed by Atlassian Software Systems Pty Ltd and is reproduced with Atlassian's permission:

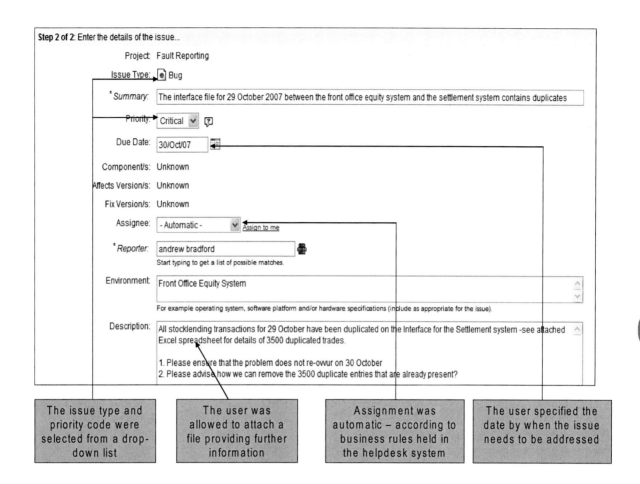

As soon as the user makes the entry in the help desk system, the assignee will receive an email informing him of the new issue. Depending on the nature of the issue, the assignee will take one or more of the following actions:

1. Action it immediately.
2. Diarise it for action at a later date.
3. Respond to the user with requests for clarification.
4. Delegate it to another individual.
5. Provide an estimate for the effort required to handle the issue.
6. Split the issue into two or more issues, or create sub-issues.
7. Attach further documents to the issue.

The assignee records each action taken in the help desk system, and each time he makes an entry an email is automatically generated to the requestor informing him of the current state of the issue. Sometimes there are online screens that permit users to track their outstanding issues.

3.3.3 Service Level Agreements (SLAs) and Key Performance Indicators (KPIs)

Learning Objective

8.8 Know the purpose of service level agreements (SLAs) and key performance indicators (KPIs) (internal and external)

In its role in managing the help desk, the IT department often enters into **Service Level Agreements** with its users and third parties.

A service level agreement (SLA) is that part of a service contract in which a certain level of service is agreed upon. 'Level of service' in this context refers to both the quality of the service and the time deadlines for performing the service. It may also specify penalties to be paid by either party if the level of service provided fails to reach the minimum standards in the agreement for an extended period of time.

The SLA is a fundamental tool from the perspective of both the supplier and the recipient in provision of a service. The quality of the service level agreement is a critical matter as it defines the relationship between all concerned parties.

The SLA itself must be of sufficient detail and scope in relation to the service being offered and the scale thereof. Typical SLA sections are as follows:

- introduction (parties, signatures, service description);
- scope of work (service hours, support);
- performance;
- tracking and reporting (content, frequency);
- problem management (change procedures, escalation);
- compensation and service credits;
- customer duties and responsibilities;
- warranties and remedies;
- security;
- intellectual property rights and confidential information;
- legal compliance and resolution of disputes; and
- termination and signatures.

Internal SLAs are agreements set out between two groups within the same organisation, while **external SLAs** involve external parties. Some securities companies provide a service to an external customer where they are assessed on their compliance with the SLA, while other securities companies might outsource some of their non-essential business to an external vendor who is able to provide an agreed service.

An SLA sets out the expectations of both parties and the method for escalation, if and when issues arise. The SLA should also identify which metrics need to be provided, how they should be reviewed and the consequences or escalation required when certain limits are met or breached. These metrics or **Key Performance Indicators (KPIs)** are often categorised into areas of supportability, recoverability, durability, performance, reliability, functionality, scalability, and flexibility.

The metrics, or KPIs, for a given system or suite of systems that support a business line might be presented in a **dashboard** to give a health evaluation of the IT systems supporting the business. Where an area is below what is expected it will be given a low mark or highlighted by an alert.

Examples of measured values that might be included in a dashboard include:

- availability of the application over a length of time (downtime measurement);
- transaction speeds;
- response times;
- functional errors reported by the system; or
- average number of users or transactions.

Dashboards can be used to initiate discussion around business strategy and ongoing investment required to support the business. **Service Level Management (SLM)** is the management of SLAs to ensure that they are up-to-date and current. The goal of SLM is to maintain and gradually improve the services that are being provided through a continuous cycle of monitoring, reporting and agreeing new targets during periodic reviews.

3.3.4   Support Call Prioritisation

Learning Objective

8.9   Understand prioritisation levels and the responsibilities of support teams

Support teams are often tiered in order that an appropriate resource is assigned to work on relevant incidents. From the perspective of the person with the problem, an appropriate resource might be seen as a person with experience or appropriate specialisation to deal with an incident. An incident will get escalated, based on its urgency, severity or impact. Incidents might also get escalated if they are not resolved within an agreed amount of time. Typically, the service level agreement will outline what metrics need to be recorded and how incidents should be assessed and escalated.

The typical responsibilities of teams providing IT services are as follows:

Level 1 – Help Desk

The level 1 resource is responsible for:

- receiving, recording, prioritising and tracking service calls;
- ensuring that SLA time targets are met;
- monitoring and status-tracking of all incidents;
- escalation and referral to other parts of the organisation;
- first line support; and
- closing incidents with confirmation from the requestor.

If the solutions documented in the repository do not resolve the incident, it is assigned to level 2.

Level 2 – Analyst

The core aspects of an incident should have been obtained by the help desk. If incidents can be easily answered by looking at the problem report management database, they will be sent by level 2 to level 1 with instructions to contact the customer and resolve. Incidents entered by the help desk which do not have the core aspects filled in will also be sent by the analyst back to the help desk for completion. This allows level 2 resources to focus on the analysis of new problems rather than re-investigating known solutions, or those with incomplete information that might lead to a known solution.

Incidents that cannot be resolved by the level 2 resource are then escalated to level 3. When problems previously escalated to the third level return to the analysts, the solution needs to be edited to ensure that it is clear for the purposes of the user and stripped of any internal comments amongst the support lines.

Level 3 – Service Specialists

Service specialists should normally be hidden from the user, letting the analysts handle interaction with the users. Knowing the identity of the level 3 service specialist of the day should not be necessary for the second level support, as level resources should have an internal mechanism to escalate to the right person via impersonal email accounts or service boxes. When a specific problem with a service has been identified, the service (level 3) should inform level 2 (analysts) of problem repercussions and the likely timescale for returning to a normal production environment.

Any major anticipated system changes should be announced by the service to the users and the second level analysts in a timeframe according to the relevant rules, together with the documentation, tools and assistance to handle any additional questions.

The time for service incidents being satisfied should be recorded and any incidents that took an unacceptable amount of time to be resolved might need to be recorded in a specific report to be reviewed by level 4 management.

Level 4 – Management

Through a series of review meetings, the operational aspects of the services being provided can be determined in terms of service level, statistics, issues from problematic cases and overall performance and resourcing. All outstanding escalated problems should be reviewed for status and to ensure that the problem is being given the correct amount of attention. Where one business area has had a greater number of recorded problems per week than deemed acceptable, then a review of support requirements within the business needs to be arranged.

4. Disaster Recovery (DR) and Business Continuity Planning (BCP)

Learning Objective

8.10   Understand the IT implications of disaster recovery (DR) and business continuity planning (BCP) including: planning; risk assessment; priorities for processing and operations; recovery strategies; data collection; written plan; testing criteria and procedures

4.1   Definitions

Business continuity plans are concerned with ensuring that the firm is able to recover from an emergency such as utility disruptions, software failures and hardware failures – some of the key operational risk events defined in Basel II.

Disaster recovery is the process of regaining access to the data, hardware and software necessary to resume critical business operations after a natural or human-induced disaster. A disaster recovery plan (DRP) should also include plans for coping with the unexpected or sudden loss of key personnel. DRP is part of the larger process of business continuity planning (BCP).

A 'disaster' could be any one or more of the following kinds of events, ranked by increasing severity:

1. One or more of the applications that the firm uses to process its business is lost, either as a result of a software or hardware failure. The failure is in one of the firm's own systems, and it is the only firm affected.
2. An external application on which the firm is dependent (such as one provided by an exchange or clearing house system or an information provider's system) is lost, either as a result of a software or hardware failure. Other user firms with which the firm trades are also dependent on this application.
3. The firm is the victim of an event such as fire, flood, or criminal or terrorist-related activity, and has lost access to one of its key buildings. Other neighbouring businesses may also be affected. In locations such as the City of London or downtown Manhattan, where there is a large concentration of investment firms, there is the likelihood that many of the firm's trading parties and critical suppliers may also be affected.

Since 9/11, much attention has been paid to the most severe event. But let us first look at the less dramatic and more common events that are confined to the loss of an individual firm's applications.

4.2   The Disaster Recovery Planning Process

A disaster recovery plan is a comprehensive statement of consistent actions to be taken before, during and after a disaster. The plan should be documented and tested to ensure the continuity of operations and the availability of critical resources in the event of a disaster.

The primary objective of disaster recovery planning is to protect the organisation in the event that all (or part) of its operations and/or computer services are rendered unusable. Preparedness is the key.

The planning process should minimise the disruption of operations and ensure some level of organisational stability and an orderly recovery after a disaster.

Other objectives of disaster recovery planning include:

- providing a sense of security;
- minimising the risk of delays;
- guaranteeing the reliability of standby systems;
- providing a standard for testing the plan;
- ensuring there is a clear communicative plan in the event of an issue; and
- minimising decision-making during a disaster.

The methodology is described below.

4.2.1   Obtain Top Management Commitment

Top management must support and be involved in the development of the disaster recovery planning process. Management should be responsible for co-ordinating the disaster recovery plan and ensuring its effectiveness within the organisation.

Adequate time and resources must be committed to the development and regular (or frequent if you prefer!) testing of an effective plan. Resources could include both financial considerations and the effort of all personnel involved.

4.2.2   Establish a Planning Committee

A planning committee should be appointed to oversee the development, testing and implementation of the plan. The planning committee should include representatives from all functional areas of the organisation. Key committee members should include the operations manager and the data processing manager. The committee also should define the scope of the plan and the frequency of the tests.

4.2.3   Perform a Risk Assessment

The planning committee should prepare a risk analysis and business impact analysis that includes a range of possible disasters, including natural, technical and human threats.

Each functional area of the organisation should be analysed to determine the potential consequence and impact associated with several disaster scenarios. The risk assessment process should also evaluate the safety of critical documents and vital records.

Traditionally, fire has posed the greatest threat to an organisation. Intentional human destruction, however, should also be considered. The plan should provide for the worst-case situation: destruction of the main building.

It is important to assess the impact and consequences resulting from loss of information and services. The planning committee should also analyse the costs related to minimising the potential exposures.

In December 2006 the FSA published its 'Business Continuity Management Practice Guide' (BCMP Guide) which is available from its website (www.fca.org.uk). Among its recommendations for leading practice in this area are the following:

1. Planning considers wide area destruction involving significant loss of staff.
2. Local authority and emergency services plans are taken into account by the firm.
3. Procedures that are agreed with the firm's insurers are included in the plans.

4.2.4 Establish Priorities for Processing and Operations

The critical needs of each department within the organisation should be carefully evaluated in such areas as:

- functional operations;
- key personnel;
- information;
- processing systems;
- service;
- documentation;
- vital records; and
- policies and procedures.

Processing and operations should be analysed to determine the maximum amount of time that the department and organisation can operate without each critical system.

Critical needs are defined as the necessary procedures and equipment required to continue operations should a department, computer centre, main facility or a combination of these be destroyed or become inaccessible.

A method of determining the critical needs of a department is to document all the functions performed by each department. Once the primary functions have been identified, the operations and processes should be ranked in order of priority: essential, important and non-essential.

4.2.5 Determine Recovery Strategies

The most practical alternatives for processing in case of a disaster should be researched and evaluated. It is important to consider all aspects of the organisation, such as:

- facilities;
- hardware;
- software;
- communications;
- data files;
- customer services;
- user operations;
- end-user systems; and
- other processing operations.

Alternatives, dependent upon the evaluation of the criticality of each application, may include:

- **Hot sites** – an approach to maintaining system availability whereby all transactions are routinely written to the production server and the standby server at different locations simultaneously. The standby server is therefore ready to take over the processing load instantaneously, should there be any failure in the production system.
- **Warm sites** – implementing a range of automated procedures to maintain same data on the two servers in the different locations. Typically this involves some form of automatic synchronisation between the databases, such as is provided by **log shipping**. Log shipping essentially consists of automating and integrating the process of backing up, copying and restoring the database from the primary server to the secondary server. This maintains the secondary server's database as an identical copy of the primary server's database apart from a small time latency of between five and 15 minutes.
- **Cold sites** – a cold standby server is a spare server at a standby location that is configured similarly to the primary server and is running the same version of the operating system, database and application software, with all the same service packs applied. If the primary server suffers a failure then the SQL database is restored to the secondary server from the primary's back-up files. The back-up files may not be totally up-to-date, for example they may have been made the previous evening, so there may be a large amount of data that needs to be re-entered. This means that there may be a delay of a few hours before service is restored.

Written agreements for the specific recovery alternatives selected should be prepared, including the following special considerations:

- contract duration;
- termination conditions;
- testing;
- costs;
- special security procedures;
- notification of systems changes;
- hours of operation;
- specific hardware and other equipment required for processing;
- personnel requirements;
- circumstances constituting an emergency;
- process to negotiate extension of service (including clear roles and responsibilities);
- guarantee of compatibility;
- availability;
- non-mainframe resource requirements;
- priorities; and
- other contractual issues.

4.2.6 Perform Data Collection

Recommended data-gathering materials and documentation include:

- back-up position listing;
- critical telephone numbers;
- communications inventory;
- distribution register;

- documentation inventory (covering recovery procedures as well as normal BAU (business as usual) procedures);
- equipment inventory;
- forms inventory;
- insurance policy inventory;
- main computer hardware inventory;
- master call list;
- master vendor list;
- microcomputer hardware and software inventory;
- notification checklist;
- office supply inventory;
- off-site storage location inventory;
- software and data files back-up/retention schedules;
- telephone inventory;
- temporary location specifications; and
- other materials and documentation.

It is extremely helpful to develop pre-formatted forms to facilitate the data-gathering process.

4.2.7   Organise and Document a Written Plan

An outline of the plan's contents should be prepared to guide the development of the detailed procedures. Top management should review and approve the proposed plan. The outline can ultimately be used for the table of contents after final revision. Other benefits of this approach are that it:

- helps to organise the detailed procedures;
- identifies all major steps before the writing begins;
- identifies redundant procedures that only need to be written once; and
- provides a 'road map' for developing the procedures.

A standard format should be developed to facilitate the writing of detailed procedures and the documentation of other information to be included in the plan. This will help ensure that the disaster plan follows a consistent format and allows for ongoing maintenance of the plan. Standardisation is especially important if more than one person is involved in writing the procedures.

The plan should be thoroughly developed, including all detailed procedures to be used before, during and after a disaster. It may not be practical to develop detailed procedures until back-up alternatives have been defined.

The procedures should include methods for maintaining and updating the plan to reflect any significant internal, external or systems changes. The procedures should allow for a regular review of the plan by key personnel within the organisation.

The disaster recovery plan should be structured using a team approach. Specific responsibilities should be assigned to the appropriate team for each functional area of the company.

The structure of the contingency organisation may not be the same as the existing organisation chart. The contingency organisation is usually structured, with teams responsible for major functional areas such as:

- administrative functions;
- facilities;
- logistics;
- user support;
- computer back-up;
- restoration; and
- other important areas.

The management team is especially important because it co-ordinates the recovery process. The team should assess the disaster, activate the recovery plan, and contact team managers and third-party suppliers. The management team also oversees, documents and monitors the recovery process. Management team members should be the final decision-makers in setting priorities, policies and procedures.

Each team has specific responsibilities that must be completed to ensure successful execution of the plan. The teams should have an assigned manager and an alternative in case the team manager is not available. Other team members should also have specific assignments where possible.

4.2.8   Develop Testing Criteria and Procedures

It is essential that the plan be thoroughly tested and evaluated on a regular basis (at least annually). Scenarios to be tested and testing procedures should be documented. The tests will provide the organisation with the assurance that all necessary steps are included in the plan. Other reasons for testing include:

- determining the feasibility and compatibility of back-up facilities and procedures;
- ensuring the plan is realistic;
- identifying areas in the plan that need modification;
- providing training to the team managers and team members;
- demonstrating the ability of the organisation to recover; and
- providing motivation for maintaining and updating the disaster recovery plan.

4.2.9   Test the Plan

After testing procedures have been completed, an initial test of the plan should be performed by conducting a structured walk-through test. The test will provide additional information regarding any further steps that may need to be included, changes in procedures that are not effective, and other appropriate adjustments. The plan should be updated to correct any problems identified during the test. Initially, testing of the plan should be done in sections and after normal business hours to minimise disruption to the overall operations of the organisation.

Types of tests include:

- checklist tests;
- simulation tests;
- parallel tests.
- full interruption tests; and
- cross-industry tests involving suppliers and customers.

Key recommendations about testing in the FSA's BCMP Guide include:

1. Critical suppliers are involved in tests at least annually.
2. The firm should be prepared to supply evidence of its testing to its own customers, suppliers and regulators.

To facilitate these recommendations, most exchanges and clearing houses offer their customers facilities to test whether their back-up facilities are able to communicate successfully with the providers' own systems.

4.2.10 Approve the Plan

Once the disaster recovery plan has been written and tested, the plan should be approved by top management. It is top management's ultimate responsibility that the organisation has a documented and tested plan.

Management is responsible for:

- establishing policies, procedures and responsibilities for comprehensive contingency planning; and
- reviewing and approving the contingency plan annually, documenting such reviews in writing.

If the organisation receives information processing from a service bureau, management must also:

- evaluate the adequacy of contingency plans for its service bureau;
- ensure that its contingency plan is compatible with its service bureau's plan; and
- approve the budget for the disaster recovery (DR) test.

4.2.11 Update the Plan

Whenever new applications are deployed, old applications retired, new business units opened or existing units closed, the plan will require updating. Depending on the nature of the change, it may be necessary to repeat some or all of the steps described in this chapter.

4.3 Conclusion

Disaster recovery planning involves more than just off-site storage or back-up processing. Organisations should also develop written, comprehensive disaster recovery plans that address all the critical operations and functions of the business. The plan should include documented and tested procedures which, if followed, will ensure the ongoing availability of critical resources and the continuity of operations. The plan must be updated whenever there is any change implemented within the organisation.

The probability of a disaster occurring in an organisation is highly uncertain. A disaster recovery plan, however, is similar to liability insurance: it provides a certain level of comfort in knowing that, if a major catastrophe occurs, it will not result in financial disaster. Insurance alone is not adequate because it may not compensate for the incalculable loss of business during the interruption, or the business that never returns.

Learning Objective

8.11   Understand the importance of change control procedures

---

5.1   Definition

One of the responsibilities of the department is to release new software objects and new hardware into the configuration. Changes may be required as a result of process improvement or bug fixes. New releases sometimes cause as many problems as they are designed to solve, and change control procedures are an essential method of minimising this type of risk.

Change control procedures are processes designed to prevent software or hardware objects from being amended without auditability and review of the impact by all interested parties. There are two aspects to change management: the use of version control systems to control access to items that need to be changed; and the development of procedures that ensure that only authorised changes are made to software or hardware items.

5.2   Symptoms of Poor Change Control

Symptoms of poor change control practices include:

- The latest version of source code cannot be found.
- A difficult defect that was fixed at great expense suddenly reappears.
- A developed and tested feature is mysteriously missing.
- A fully tested program suddenly does not work.
- The wrong version of the code was deployed.
- The wrong version of the code was tested.
- There is no traceability between the software requirements, documentation and code.
- Programmers are working on the wrong version of the code.
- The wrong versions of the configuration items are being baselined.
- No one knows which modules comprise the software system delivered to the customer.

5.3   Version Control Systems (VCSs)

Version control systems (VCS) are software applications that manage multiple revisions of the same unit of information. In particular, they:

1. prevent more than one developer working on a change to a program or other software object at the same time (without the other developer knowing);
2. ensure that when a program or other object is selected for modification, there is an audit trail of who is modifying it;
3. ensure that the modifications are being made to the right version of the program.

In the event that the wrong version of an object is released, these applications provide the ability to 'roll back' to a prior version.

Because version control and change management are essentially collaborative activities, many version control systems now incorporate social networking capabilities, and increasingly such applications are now based in 'the cloud'. These concepts are discussed more fully in Chapter 10.

5.4   Software Change Control Procedures

Implementing version control software on its own is not enough to guarantee effective change control. Firms also need to develop appropriate **change control procedures** – business practices that are designed to:

- allow changes to accepted work products to be proposed and evaluated, schedule and quality impact assessed, and the changes approved or rejected for release into production systems in a controlled manner;
- provide a mechanism for management to accept and sign off changes that improve the product overall while rejecting those that degrade it;
- notify all parties materially affected by a proposed revision of the need to accept the new version;
- notify interested parties on the periphery of development regarding change proposals, their assessed impact, and whether the changes were approved or rejected;
- facilitate efficient deployment of changes to environments where they are required.

Many firms hold periodic (often weekly in the case of large organisations with complex configurations) change control meetings to ensure that these aims are achieved. The participants will include representatives of all the business areas affected. Change control meetings may be guided by a change management policy. For example:

1. Many firms do not allow any major changes to critical systems in the last four weeks of their financial year, in order that the production of their annual accounts is not destabilised because of problems with new software.
2. Many firms do not allow any major changes applied to critical systems in the last week of any accounting month. This is to avoid destabilising the preparation of the bank's monthly accounts.

End of Chapter Questions

Think of an answer for each question and refer to the appropriate section for confirmation.

1. List all the things that an IT department can do to mitigate the risks of internal and external fraud.
    Section 2

2. What are four of the risks that need to be managed when introducing business change?
    Section 2.2

3. What is a Botnet?
    Section 3.1

4. List the possible actions that the receiver of an issue might do when an issue is routed to him or her through a help desk management system.
    Section 3.3.2

5. What are the usual responsibilities of a team providing level 3 help desk support?
    Section 3.3.4

6. What is the definition of disaster recovery and how does it differ from business continuity planning?
    Section 4.1

7. List the symptoms of poor change control practice.
    Section 5.2

8. What is the purpose of version control software?
    Section 5.3

9. What is the purpose of software change control procedures?
    Section 5.4

10. Why would a firm have a policy of not accepting major changes to software during the last few weeks of its financial year?
    Section 5.4

Chapter Nine

Managing Business Change

This syllabus area will provide approximately 7 of the 50 examination questions

9

1. Introduction

Learning Objective

9.1   Understand the purpose and benefits of project planning and control

9.2   Understand the importance of project governance

This chapter deals with the processes and procedures that need to be put in place in an investment firm in order to minimise the risks of introducing business change.

Effective IT **project governance** is about ensuring that complex IT projects deliver the value expected of them, rather than being an expensive and embarrassing failure. An appropriate governance framework helps save money by ensuring that all expenditure is appropriate for the risks being tackled.

Project governance is important because, in the global information economy, IT-supported business project management and execution becomes fundamental to an organisation's survival. While successful ICT project delivery should improve competitive positioning, a failed project can place an organisation at a strategic **disadvantage** to its competitors, and is a source of **operational risk**.

Project governance is vital because:

- It ensures that all external and internal roles and responsibilities are documented; in other words, ownership of projects and sub-roles is allocated.
- It provides a decision framework, eg, the programme board can only make certain decisions but other, less material decisions can be delegated to sponsors, suppliers, project managers and so on. Therefore, if decisions need to be made, then clear guidance is provided on who can make these decisions.
- It provides a framework for reporting and tracking, eg, regular weekly reports, monthly programme board meetings, cost reports, etc.
- It allows organisations to assess the impact of various projects on other projects, eg, if Project X is delayed, how does that impact Projects Y and Z?

Modern theory of project governance states that, for each programme or project, a senior executive should be appointed **senior responsible owner**, or **SRO**. In some project management methodologies, the SRO may be known as the **project sponsor**. The SRO is the individual responsible for ensuring that a project or programme of change meets its objectives and delivers the projected benefits. They should be the owner of the overall business change that is being supported by the project. The SRO should ensure that the change maintains its business focus and has clear authority and that the context, including risks, is actively managed. This individual must be senior and must take personal responsibility for successful delivery of the project. They should be recognised as the owner throughout the organisation.

An individual's responsibilities as an SRO should be explicitly included in their personal objectives and the individual should remain in place throughout the project or programme, or alter only when a distinct phase of benefit delivery has been completed.

The SRO should be prepared to take decisions, and should be proactive in providing leadership and direction throughout the life of the project or programme. They should be responsible for ensuring that the organisation can fully exploit the outcome of the change such that the benefits are delivered as a result of that outcome.

The SRO works with programme managers and project managers to develop and implement procedure and practices for project planning and control, and, where applicable, for software development. Some of the common approaches to these issues are discussed below.

2. Software Development Life Cycles (SDLCs)

Learning Objective

9.3 Understand the key stages of a software development life cycle (SDLC) including: project planning; feasibility study; systems analysis; requirements definition; systems design; code generation; development; integration and testing; acceptance; installation; deployment; maintenance

2.1 Introduction

The Software Development Life Cycle (SDLC) is a standardised process of developing information systems or applications through the completion of defined steps or phases. Synonyms include Systems Development Life Cycle, Systems Implementation Life Cycle and Software Implementation Life Cycle (SILC).

The SDLC recognises the following factors:

1. The further the project is from completion, the higher the risk and uncertainty. Risk and doubt decrease as the project moves closer to fulfilling the project vision.
2. Cost and resource requirements are lower at the beginning of a project, but grow as the project progresses. Once the project moves into the final closing process, cost and resource requirements again taper off dramatically. It is important for a project manager to be able to assess how much resource is actively working on their project (in terms of time or cost) so that this risk can be monitored.
3. Changes are easier and more likely at the early phases of the project life cycle than at the completion. Changes at the beginning of the project generally cost less and have lower risk than changes at the end of the project. Therefore, stakeholders need to be happy with project deliverables from the early phases, otherwise there is a risk that in the final phases of the project life cycle additional costs may need to be incurred.

2.2 Standardised SDLC Approaches

There are a number of standardised versions of the SDLC, but many organisations have adapted their own versions. In the standardised UK version, known as the **Systems Life Cycle (SLC)**, the following names are used for each stage:

1. **Terms of Reference** – the management decides what capabilities and objectives it wishes the new system to incorporate.
2. **Feasibility Study** – this asks whether the management's concept of its desired new system is actually an achievable, realistic goal – in terms of money, time and end result. Often, it may be decided simply to update an existing system, rather than to replace one completely.
3. **Fact-Finding and Recording** – how is the current system used? Often questionnaires are used here, but also just monitoring (watching) the staff to see how they work is better, as people will often be reluctant to be entirely honest, through embarrassment, if merely asked about the parts of the existing system they have trouble with and find difficult.
4. **Analysis** – free from any cost or unrealistic constraints, this stage lets minds run wild as 'wonder systems' can be thought-up, though all must incorporate everything asked for by the management in the terms of reference stage.
5. **Design** – designers will produce one or more 'models' of what they see a system eventually looking like, with ideas from the analysis section either used or discarded. A document will be produced with a description of the system, but nothing is specific: eg, they might say 'touchscreen' or 'GUI operating system', but not mention any specific brands.
6. **System Specification** – having generically decided on which software packages to use and which hardware to incorporate, the plan now has to be very specific, choosing exact models, brands and suppliers for each software application and hardware device.
7. **Implementation and Review** – set up and install the new system (including writing any bespoke code required), train staff to use it, then monitor how it operates for initial problems, and then regularly maintain thereafter. During this stage, any old system that was in use will usually be discarded once the new one has proved it is reliable and usable.
8. **Use** – obviously the system needs to be actually used by somebody, otherwise the above process would be completely useless.
9. **Close** – the last step in a system's life cycle is its end, which is most often forgotten when you design the system. The system can be closed, it can be migrated to another (more modern platform), or its data can be migrated into a replacing system.

2.3 Adapting the SDLC for an Individual Organisation's Requirements

Section 2.2 describes the standard UK SDLC. However, many organisations have developed their own customised SDLCs to meet their own particular requirements. Some of these SDLCs, for example, put a great deal of emphasis on the early stages of the project, while some of them put emphasis on the later stages.

To some extent the emphasis varies according to which software development methodologies the organisation uses. These are dealt with in Section 3 of this chapter.

3. Software Development Methodologies

Learning Objective

9.4 Understand the different software development methodologies, including: traditional or waterfall methodologies; iterative/incremental methodologies; other methodologies

---

A **software development process** is a structure imposed on the development of a software product. There are several models for such processes, each describing approaches to a variety of tasks or activities that take place during the process, but the various models can be divided into three categories:

- traditional or waterfall models;
- iterative/incremental models; and
- other models.

3.1 Traditional or Waterfall ModelS

These traditional ways of developing software divide the process into a number of phases, the first of which is requirements-gathering. They are based on the theory that no design or development should start until the requirements:

1. have been gathered from the users;
2. are fully understood by the designers;
3. have been fully documented by the design team; and
4. these documents have been signed off by the users.

They therefore place great emphasis on the requirements-gathering process.

3.1.1 The Basic Waterfall Model

The **waterfall model** was the first methodology and is also known as the **classic life cycle model** or **linear sequence model**.

In the waterfall methodology, there are sequences of phases. Where there is a problem with the previous phase of delivery, the solution is returned to the previous phase and rework occurs before the waterfall continues. This is sometimes known as the 'implied waterfall model' or 'waterfall model with backflow'.

The model maintains that one should move to a phase only when its preceding phase is completed and perfected. The **output** of each phase becomes the **input** of the next phase. It assumes that software development is like constructing a building – start with the foundations, then the walls, then the roof, etc. Phases of development in the waterfall model are discrete, and there is no jumping back and forth or overlap between them.

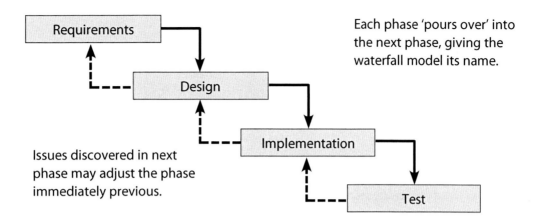

Each phase 'pours over' into the next phase, giving the waterfall model its name.

Issues discovered in next phase may adjust the phase immediately previous.

3.1.2   The Fountain Model

The fountain model recognises that there are opportunities for some phases of the life cycle to occur at the same time or to overlap. Overlap occurs between adjacent phases, and change control processes need to be effective to ensure that work is not undertaken on incorrect assumptions.

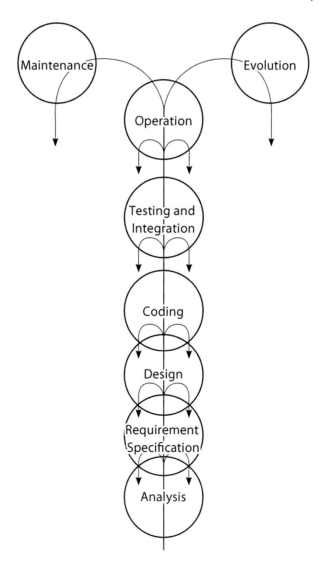

3.1.3 Criticisms of Traditional Methodologies

1. The most prominent criticism revolves around the fact that, very often, customers do not really know what they want up front; rather, what they want emerges out of repeated two-way interactions over the course of the project. For this reason, the waterfall model, with its emphasis on up-front requirements-capture and design, is seen as somewhat unrealistic and unsuitable for the complexities of the real world.
2. Given the uncertain nature of customer needs, estimating time and costs with any degree of accuracy (as the model suggests) is often extremely difficult. In general, therefore, the model is recommended for use only in projects which are relatively stable and where customer needs can be clearly identified at an early stage.
3. The model's implicit assumption is that designs can be feasibly translated into real products; this sometimes runs into problems when developers actually begin implementation. Often, designs that look feasible on paper turn out to be expensive or difficult in practice, requiring a redesign and hence destroying the clear distinctions between phases of the traditional waterfall model.
4. Some critics also point out that the model implies a clear division of labour between, say, 'designers', 'programmers' and 'testers'; in reality, such a division of labour, in many organisations, is neither realistic nor efficient.

Because of these criticisms, some organisations prefer to use iterative/incremental software methodologies.

3.2 Iterative/Incremental Models

Several different iterative/incremental models have been developed to overcome the criticisms of the waterfall model.

Incremental development is a scheduling and staging strategy in which the various parts of the system are developed at different times or rates, and integrated as they are completed. **Iterative development** is a rework scheduling strategy in which time is set aside to revise and improve parts of the system. A typical difference is that the output from an increment is released to users, whereas the output from an iteration is examined for further modification before release.

Common iterative/incremental models include the following.

3.2.1 Prototyping

Prototyping is the process of quickly putting together a working model (a prototype) in order to test various aspects of a design, illustrate ideas or features and gather early user feedback. Prototyping is often treated as an integral part of the system design process, where it is believed to reduce project risk and cost. Often one or more prototypes are made in a process of iterative and incremental development, where each prototype is influenced by the performance of previous designs; in this way problems or deficiencies in design can be corrected.

When the prototype is sufficiently refined and meets the functionality, robustness, manufacturability and other design goals, the product is ready for production. The technology used to build the prototypes is not necessarily the same technology that is used to build the production system.

3.2.2　The Spiral Model

This model of development combines the features of the prototyping model and the waterfall model. The spiral model is intended for large, expensive and complicated projects. Graphically, the spiral model is represented by the following diagram:

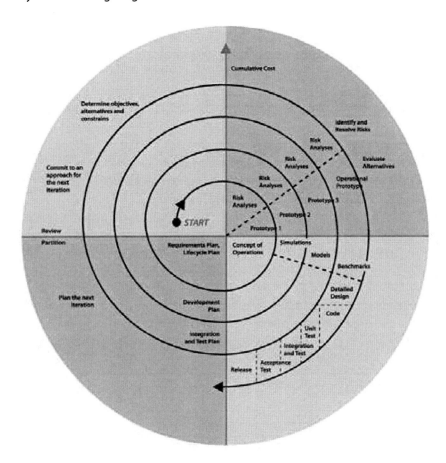

The processes in the spiral model are as follows:

1. The new system requirements are defined in as much detail as possible. This usually involves interviewing a number of users representing all the external or internal users and other aspects of the existing system.
2. A preliminary design is created for the new system.
3. A first prototype of the new system is constructed from the preliminary design. This is usually a scaled-down system, and represents an approximation of the characteristics of the final product.
4. A second prototype is evolved by a fourfold procedure:
    ○   evaluating the first prototype in terms of its strengths, weaknesses, and risks;
    ○   defining the requirements of the second prototype;
    ○   planning and designing the second prototype;
    ○   constructing and testing the second prototype.
5. At the customer's option, the entire project can be aborted if the risk is deemed too great. Risk factors might involve development cost overruns, operating cost miscalculation, or any other factor that could, in the customer's judgment, result in a less-than-satisfactory final product.
6. The existing prototype is evaluated in the same manner as was the previous prototype, and, if necessary, another prototype is developed from it according to the fourfold procedure outlined above.
7. The preceding steps are iterated until the customer is satisfied that the refined prototype represents the final product desired.

8. The final system is constructed, based on the refined prototype.
9. The final system is thoroughly evaluated and tested. Routine maintenance is carried out on a continuing basis to prevent large-scale failures and to minimise downtime.

3.2.3 The Agile Model

The aim of the **agile model** is to minimise risk by developing software in short amounts of time. Software developed during one unit of time is referred to as an **iteration**, which may last from one to four weeks. Each iteration is an entire software project, including planning, requirements analysis, design, coding, testing, and documentation. An iteration may not add enough functionality to warrant releasing the product to market, but the goal is to have an available release (without bugs) that is capable of being deployed at the end of each iteration. At the end of each iteration, the team re-evaluates project priorities.

The agile model emphasises face-to-face communication over written documents. The method produces very little written documentation relative to other methods. This has resulted in criticism of agile methods as being undisciplined. Further criticisms include:

1. There is a lack of formal documentation of both the requirements and the project direction and controls.
2. The ultimate solution may 'drift' from the optimal solution. This also means that it is hard to plan a budget and project end date. This may be caused by the effect of a dominant personality on the team, or by the fact that the users have poorly formed ideas of their needs.
3. Face-to-face communication can be difficult to implement on large projects, or on projects where the team members are geographically dispersed.

For these reasons, agile software development is not usually recommended for:

- large-scale projects involving more than 20 developers;
- projects with mainly inexperienced developers;
- projects where the development teams are geographically dispersed;
- life-critical or mission-critical systems.

3.3 Other Commonly Used Models

3.3.1 Joint Application Development (JAD)

Joint Application Development (JAD) is a methodology that involves the client or end-user in the design and development of an application, through a succession of collaborative workshops called **JAD sessions**.

3.3.2 Rapid Application Development (RAD)

Rapid Application Development (RAD) is a methodology that works on the basis that a prototype can quickly be constructed that looks and acts like the desired product in order to test its usefulness. During the requirements determination phase, the prototype is developed, sometimes using different tools to the proposed final product.

3.3.3 Build and Fix/Fix on Fail

Build and Fix/Fix on Fail is the method of modifying the code until the customer is happy. There is a substantial risk that consumed effort is undertaken without adequate planning and that users request 'fixes' which are actually enhancements.

3.3.4 End-User Development (EUD)

End-User Development (EUD) is a set of activities or techniques that allows individuals, who are non-professional developers, to create or modify a software object. A typical example of EUD is macro-programming in applications such as Microsoft Excel™. End-user development is not limited to programming. Other examples of end-user development include the creation and modification of web pages and the use of applications such as Crystal Reports™ that allow users to create online and printed reports based on Structured Query Language (SQL) queries.

End users may be able to employ their specialised business knowledge directly and quickly – they know the requirements and can implement them without having to explain them to developers.

However, there are often cases where the application's existence is either unknown to the IT department at all, or its place in the configuration is insufficiently understood. As a result, the application:

- may not be included in the business continuity plan;
- may be forgotten about completely if a decision is made to outsource an aspect of processing;
- may not be included in change control procedures, as a result of which a change may be made to another software product on which this application relies that destabilises this application;
- may become unsupportable if the staff member who developed it leaves the firm.

3.3.5 Synchronise and Stabilise

Synchronise and stabilise (or sync and stabilise) is an SDLC in which teams work in parallel on individual application modules. There is a requirement for all teams to synchronise their code with the other teams regularly and debug or stabilise it regularly throughout the development process.

4. Project Management Methodologies

Learning Objective

9.5 Know the following different methodologies used in technology delivery: PRINCE; PMI; ISO

4.1 Introduction

Before we examine project management in more detail, let us first of all try to define a **project**. Some commonly used definitions include the following:

1. A **temporary and one-time endeavour** undertaken to create a unique product or service, which brings about beneficial change or added value.
2. A set of **inter-related and controlled activities** with start and finish dates, undertaken to achieve a unique **objective** conforming to **specific requirements**, including the restraints of **time, cost and resources**.

The properties of being a **temporary and one-time** undertaking contrast with normal operations, which are permanent repetitive functional work carried out to create the same product or service over and over again. Because the objective is to bring about change, it is necessary to define the reasons for and extent of the change (the **requirements**); the **resources** that are available to make the change and the **costs** of those resources; and the **date** on which the change is required (the time constraint).

Project management, in turn, can be described as the discipline of organising and managing resources (eg, people) in such a way that the project is completed within defined scope, quality, time and cost constraints.

There are a number of generally accepted methodologies used by industry and governments to manage projects of all types – these methodologies are just as applicable to, say, the mounting of an important exhibition at an art gallery as they are to building and/or implementing new software in the financial sector. All of these methodologies are designed to reduce project risk, ie, the risks that the project may be delivered late, and/or over budget, and/or that it doesn't deliver the benefits that were expected of it.

The most commonly used methodologies are described below.

4.2   PRINCE

PRINCE stands for **Projects in Controlled Environments** and is a management methodology covering the organisation, management and control of projects. PRINCE was first developed in 1989 by the Central Computer and Telecommunications Agency (CCTA), now part of the Office of Government Commerce (OGC), as a UK government standard for IT project management.

Since its introduction, PRINCE has become widely used in both the public and private sectors throughout the world. Although PRINCE was originally developed for the needs of IT projects, it has also been used on many non-IT projects. The latest version, **PRINCE2**, is a more generic, best practice approach for the management of all types of projects.

The method describes how a project is divided into manageable phases or stages, enabling efficient control of resources and regular progress-monitoring throughout. The various roles and responsibilities for managing a project are fully described and are adaptable to suit the size and complexity of the project and skills of the organisation. The project's business case outlines the justification, commitment and rationale for the deliverables, while the project plan is product-based, which means that there is a focus on delivering results.

The PRINCE2 methodology provides a common language and structure for all interested parties involved in a project, and embodies proven and established best practice in project management. Good PRINCE2 practice encourages:

- a controlled and organised start, middle and end;
- regular reviews of progress against plan and of the business case;
- built-in decision points;
- management control of deviations from plan;
- the involvement of management and stakeholders at the right time and place of the project life cycle;
- good communication channels between stakeholders.

4.2.1 PRINCE2 Process Stages

PRINCE2 divides projects into the following phases:

- **Starting up a project (SU)** – in this process the **project team** is appointed and a **project brief** (describing, in outline, what the project is attempting to achieve and the business justification for doing it) is prepared. In addition, the overall approach to be taken is decided and the next stage of the project is planned. As part of this phase, the **project board, project sponsor** and **project manager** are appointed. The project board is usually chaired by the project sponsor. This is normally the senior executive who instigated the change and is responsible to the business for the success of the project. Other members of the project board will include executives from the various sections of the firm that will either benefit from the project or have a role in delivering it. The project manager is also a member of the project board. The project manager is the individual responsible for delivering the project. Once this work is done, the project board is asked to authorise the next stage, that of initiating the project.

- **Planning (PL)** – PRINCE2 advocates **product-based planning**, which means that the first task when planning is to identify and analyse products. Once the activities required to create these products are identified, it is possible to estimate the effort required for each and then schedule activities into a plan.

- **Initiating a project (IP)** – this process builds on the work of the start-up (SU) activity and the project brief is augmented to form a **business case** – the non-technical reason for the project. The logic of the business case is that whenever resources, such as money or effort, are consumed, they should be in support of the business. An example could be that a software upgrade might improve system performance, but the 'business case' is that better performance would improve customer satisfaction.

- **Directing a project (DP)** – these sub-processes dictate how the project board should control the overall project. It also specifies the way in which the board can give *ad hoc* direction to a project and the way in which a project should be closed down.

- **Controlling a stage (CS)** – PRINCE2 suggests that projects should be broken down into stages and these sub-processes dictate how each individual stage should be controlled. Most fundamentally, this includes the way in which work packages (subsets of a project that can be assigned to a specific party for execution) are authorised. It also specifies the way in which progress should be monitored and how the highlights of the progress should be reported to the project board.

- **Managing product delivery (MP)** – this process specifies the way in which a work package should be accepted, executed and delivered.

- **Managing stage boundaries (SB)** – this process dictates what should be done towards the end of a stage. The fundamental principle of this stage is to ensure that, at the end of each stage, the project stays focused on delivering business benefit. Most obviously, the next stage should be planned and the overall project plan, risk log and business case amended as necessary. The process also covers what should be done for a stage that has gone outside its tolerance levels. Finally, the process dictates how the end of the stage should be reported.

- **Closing a project (CP)** – this process covers the things that should be done at the end of a project. The project should be formally de-commissioned (and resources freed up for allocation to other activities), follow-on actions should be identified and the project itself should be formally evaluated.

4.2.2 PRINCE2 Qualifications

There are two PRINCE2 qualifications: the **foundation examination** certifies that the principles and terminology have been understood, and the **practitioner examination** certifies that the holder exhibits competence to apply PRINCE2 while running and managing a project.

4.3   The Project Management Institute (PMI)

The Project Management Institute (PMI) was formed in 1999 in the US to serve the interests of the project management industry. The PMI is now a global body with over 240,000 members in 160 countries. The premise of the PMI is that the tools and techniques of project management are common, even among the widespread application of projects from the software industry to the construction industry.

4.3.1   The PMBOK Guide

In 1981, the PMI published the first edition of what is now known as *A Guide to the Project Management Body of Knowledge* (**PMBOK Guide**), containing the standards and guidelines of practice that are widely used throughout the profession. PMBOK is divided into two major parts: **project initiation** and **exam essentials**. The project initiation part focuses on developing and executing a project plan and creating, protecting and fulfilling a project scope.

The Guide is process-based, meaning that it describes work as being accomplished by processes. Processes overlap and interact throughout a project or its various phases. Processes are described in terms of:

*   inputs (documents, plans, designs, etc);
*   tools and techniques (mechanisms applied to inputs);
*   outputs (documents, products, etc).

The Guide recognises 44 processes that fall into five basic process groups and nine knowledge areas that are typical of almost all projects. The five process groups are:

1.   initiating;
2.   planning;
3.   executing;
4.   controlling and monitoring; and
5.   closing.

The nine knowledge areas are:

1.   project integration management;
2.   project scope management;
3.   project time management;
4.   project cost management;
5.   project quality management;
6.   project human resource management;
7.   project communications management;
8.   project risk management;
9.   project procurement management.

4.3.2   PMI Qualifications

Membership of the Institute is based upon examination. The Institute offers accredited education programmes, based on PMBOK, in partnership with academic institutions in North America, Europe and Asia, together with a large number of learning tools and publications that are available both to members and non-members.

PMI professional credentials are available which demonstrate that appropriate education or professional experience has been fulfilled, a rigorous examination has been passed and the individual is committed to maintaining their active credentials and agrees to abide by a professional code of conduct.

4.4 ISO Standards

The **International Organization for Standardization (ISO)** was established in 1947 to develop common international standards in many areas. Its members come from over 120 national standards bodies which, through associated accreditation and certification bodies, act as audit organisations in recognising which companies have gained applicable ISO standards. ISO's purpose is to facilitate international trade by providing a single set of standards that people everywhere can recognise and respect. Within the UK there are also some mature British standards that have been developed in parallel, and often adopted by the ISO.

The ISO has provided the following standards that are concerned with project management.

4.4.1 ISO 9000

ISO 9000 includes the following standards:

- **ISO 9000:2000, Quality management systems – fundamentals and vocabulary** – the basics of what quality management systems are; it contains the ISO 9000 series of standards.
- **ISO 9001, Quality management systems – requirements** – provides the requirements that an organisation needs to fulfil in order to achieve customer satisfaction through consistent products and services.

There are many different standards which are referenced in the **ISO 9000 family**. A lot of them do not even carry 'ISO 900x' numbers. For example, parts of the 10,000 range are also considered part of the 9000 family.

ISO 9001 certification has been adopted by thousands of organisations in over one hundred countries and is an internationally recognised quality management tool. It should be noted that, when an organisation claims to be **ISO 9000-compliant**, it actually means that it conforms to ISO 9001:2000.

In order to achieve ISO 9001 certification, the applying organisation is assessed based on an extensive sample of its sites, functions, products, services, and processes and a list of how problems have been made known and resolved by management. An ISO certificate must be renewed at regular intervals, following a review by an independent standards auditor, as recommended by the certification body, usually every three years.

Both internal and external **audits** must occur in a continual process of review and assessment to verify that the system is working as defined and to identify where it can be improved and corrected. The auditing process is typically addressed by performing compliance auditing:

- Tell me what you do (describe the business process).
- Show me where it says that (reference the procedure manuals).
- Prove the results (exhibit evidence in documented records).

As the organisation's ISO maturity improves, the audit should tend to focus on risk, status and importance with increasing judgments on what is effective or not. **ISO 19011** is the standard that should be applied to the auditing of ISO certifications.

One criticism of ISO 9000 is that, although it makes processes more consistent, it also may make it more difficult to improve and readapt processes. In Japan, amid complaints of ISO 9000 undermining world-class thinking, Toyota abandoned the standard in 2000, moving back to its in-house Toyota production system.

• **ISO 9004, Quality management systems – guidelines for performance improvements** – covers continual improvement.

5. Software Testing and Quality Assurance

Learning Objective

9.6 Understand the need for testing and its importance to quality assurance, including: testing strategies; test stages; techniques; cycles; test reporting

5.1 Introduction

Software testing is the process used to measure the quality of developed computer software. Software testing is a value judgment. It is not possible to produce a complex application that is completely free of defects – this would equate to delivering 'perfection', which is something that human beings rarely achieve. The number of defects in a complex application can be large; some of them will be critical and some less so. In addition, an individual product may be implemented within a large number of configurations. For example, many applications used in the investment industry run on both SQLServer™ and Unix databases, and errors may be found in one configuration variable but not others.

The purpose of testing is, therefore, to gain a level of confidence in the software so that the organisation is confident that the software has an **acceptable defect rate**: where defects do exist, they are documented and there are adequate workarounds available to the users.

What constitutes an acceptable defect rate depends on the nature of the software. The level of defects that are acceptable in, say, an arcade game would be completely unacceptable in an application that was used in an operating theatre or in a flight control centre serving a busy airport.

It is necessary, therefore, to grade any problems that may be found during testing. The table overleaf is an example of a problem-grading matrix. Each problem is allocated a severity grade, and the firm that developed the system has a set of rules for deciding how many problems of each grade it will tolerate when it decides whether or not to release the developed software. These rules are normally incorporated into its change control policies (see Chapter 8, Section 5).

Grade	Meaning	Policy
A	An extremely serious problem. An important part of the system does not work as it should, and there are no workarounds available to the users.	This release cannot go into production if there are any Grade A defects outstanding.
B	An important part of the system is not working in the way that was intended, but there are workarounds available so that data can be processed in another way.	This release can go into production if there are a very limited number of Grade B defects outstanding and there is an agreed time frame for their resolution after live date.
C	A minor part of the system is not working in the way that was intended, but there are workarounds available so that data can be processed in another way.	This release can go into production if there are a number of Grade C defects outstanding and there is an agreed time frame for their resolution after live date.
D	Cosmetic error – eg, a spelling mistake in the headings of an input/enquiry screen or printed report.	This release can go into production despite the presence of Grade D defects.

5.1.1 Software Testing Axioms

Because software testing is based on value judgments, it is always worth remembering these seven 'axioms':

1. It is impossible to test a program completely.
2. Software testing is a risk-based exercise.
3. Testing cannot show that bugs don't exist.
4. The more bugs you find, the more bugs there are.
5. Not all the bugs you find will be fixed.
6. Product specifications are never final.
7. If you find a problem that occurs once and you can't repeat it, then you can't fix it.

5.2 Test Stages

During the software development life cycle, applications are usually subject to the following series of tests, normally in this order:

1. **Unit testing** – tests the minimal software component, or module. Each unit (basic component) of the software is tested to verify that the detailed design for the unit has been correctly implemented.
2. **Integration or system integration testing** – exposes defects in the interfaces and interaction between integrated components (modules). Progressively larger groups of tested software components corresponding to elements of the architectural design are integrated and tested until the software works as a system.
3. **Functional testing** – tests at any level (class, module, interface, or system) for proper functionality as defined in the specification.
4. **System testing** – tests a completely integrated system to verify that it meets its requirements.

5. **Volume testing or load testing** – tests a software application for a certain data volume. This may be expressed in a number of ways, such as the size of the database, the number of transactions to be processed for a given time period, the length of time that the user has to wait for the results of an enquiry, or the length of time that an overnight process should take to complete. One form of volume testing that is becoming more common is **breakpoint testing**, ie, piling more and more load onto the system to find out when it actually becomes unusable.

6. **System integration testing** – verifies that a system is integrated to any external or third party systems defined in the system requirements.

7. **User acceptance testing** – conducted by the end user, customer or client to validate whether or not to accept the product. Acceptance testing may be performed as part of the hand-off process between any two phases of development.
   - **Alpha testing** is simulated or actual operational testing by potential users/customers or an independent test team at the developers' site. Alpha testing is often employed for off-the-shelf software as a form of internal acceptance testing before the software goes to beta testing.
   - **Beta testing** comes after alpha testing. Versions of the software, known as beta versions, are released to a limited audience outside the company. The software is released to groups of people, so that further testing can ensure the product has few faults.

8. **Penetration testing** – testing the security elements of a system by simulating an attack from a malicious source.

It should be noted that, although both alpha and beta are referred to as 'testing', they are in fact 'user immersion'. The rigours that are applied are often unsystematic, and many of the basic tenets of the testing process are not used. The alpha and beta period provides insight into environmental and utilisation conditions that can impact the software.

5.2.1   Regression Testing

After modifying software, either for a change in functionality or to fix defects, a regression test re-runs previously successful tests on the modified software to ensure that the modifications haven't unintentionally caused a regression of previous functionality. Regression testing can be performed at any or all of the above test levels.

5.3   Test Techniques

Software may be tested by using any or all of the following techniques:

- **Code walkthrough** – a manual testing technique where program logic is traced manually using a small set of test cases to analyse the programmer's logic and assumptions.
- **White box testing** – in white box testing the tester has access to the source code and can write tests specific to the area of change.
- **Black box, concrete box or functional testing** – in black box testing the tester only accesses the software through the same interfaces that the customer or user would, or through automation of similar interfaces, to confirm the functional specification of the program.
- **Grey box testing** – a technique that uses a combination of black box and white box testing. Grey box testing is not black box testing, because the tester does know some of the internal workings of the software under test. In grey box testing, the tester applies a limited number of test cases to the internal workings of the software under test. In the remaining part of the grey box testing, one takes a black box approach in applying inputs to the software under test and observing the outputs.

- **Smoke, sanity or skim testing** – this is a cursory examination of all of the basic components of a software system without reference to the internal workings to ensure that they hang together. Typically, smoke testing is used to verify a software build. The term originates from the electronics industry where the circuits are laid out and power is applied; if anything starts smoking, there is a problem.
- **Agile testing** – agile software development (described in Section 3.2.3 of this chapter) adheres to a test-driven software development model where the unit tests are written first and fail initially until the code is written. The test harness is continuously updated as new failure conditions are discovered and they are integrated with any regression tests that have been developed. The stages of an agile development cycle are as follows:
  - write the test;
  - write the code;
  - run the automated tests;
  - re-factor;
  - repeat.
- **Handshake or rattle test** – this test aims to prove that it is possible to send and receive communications between two or more systems. Such a test does not prove that the two or more systems can understand one another, just that messages do not get lost en route.

5.4   The Test Cycle

The test cycle usually consists of the following steps:

1. **Requirements analysis** – testing should begin in the requirements phase of the software development life cycle. During the design phase, testers work with developers in determining what aspects of a design are testable and under what parameters those tests work.
2. **Test planning** – the planning stage comprises the development of the test strategy, test bed and test plan(s). These, in turn, comprise the following:
   - The **test strategy** outlines which of the stages (Section 5.2) will be used and which techniques (Section 5.3) will be used.
   - The **test bed** is the definition of the hardware, operating system and database configuration that will be used to perform the testing.
   - The **test plan** allocates resources to the testing, and specifies how issues will be reported, actioned and retested prior to release.
3. **Test development** – in this phase the test scenarios, test cases and test scripts are written.
   - A **test case** is a set of conditions or variables under which testers will determine if a requirement is partially or fully satisfied.
   - They will then prepare a **test script** for each test case. A test script details the inputs that will be made to the application and the expected results of each input.
   - A **test scenario** is a collection of test cases that are connected with each other.

5.5   Test Automation

Traditionally, testing of financial sector applications has been performed by test team members manually entering transactions, running background processes such as the sending of settlement instructions, mark-to-market and interest accrual, and then reviewing the results of this activity by the inspection of reports, enquiries and interface files created by the application. For a large application, this is a highly labour-intensive process that can create bottlenecks. In particular, the resource-hungry nature of this way of working makes it extremely difficult to carry out volume tests and regression tests, because of the very large amount of data entry and inspection that is required by these types of tests.

There are now a large number of software tools on the market that can automate some of these activities. Usually, these tools provide **record and playback features** that allow users to record user actions and replay them back any number of times, comparing actual results to those expected.

In addition to the tools that provide the 'record and playback' facilities there are a number of automation tools available that allow the code to conduct unit tests to determine whether various sections of the code are acting as expected in various circumstances. Test cases describe tests that need to be run on the program to verify that the program runs as expected.

Automated test tools can be expensive to purchase, and can automate only a well-thought-through test script. It is an addition to, not a replacement of, manual testing.

5.6 Test Reporting and Control

In order to execute a test plan, there has to be an agreed methodology for reporting issues, actioning them, retesting them, and either releasing them to the production environment when they pass or re-working the fix if they fail the retest. In addition, the stakeholders will require regular reports of the numbers and severity of issues outstanding. The type of help desk management system that was described in Section 3.2 of Chapter 8 is usually used for these purposes.

5.7 ISO 9126 – The ISO Standard for Software Evaluation

Learning Objective

9.5 Know the following different methodologies used in technology delivery: PRINCE; PMI; ISO

ISO 9126 is an international standard for the evaluation of software. The standard is divided into four parts which address, respectively, the following subjects:

- quality model;
- external metrics;
- internal metrics; and
- quality in use metrics.

The quality model classifies software quality in a structured set of factors as follows:

Functionality	Suitability	Accuracy
Interoperability	Compliance	Security
Reliability	Maturity	Recoverability
Fault tolerance	Usability	Learnability
Understandability	Operability	Efficiency
Time behaviour	Resource behaviour	Maintainability
Stability	Analysability	Changeability
Testability	Portability	Installability
Conformance	Replaceability	Adaptability

Each quality factor can be further divided into attributes which can be verified or measured in the software product. Attributes are not defined in the standard, as they vary between different software products.

The ISO 9126 standard also distinguishes between a defect and a nonconformity, a defect being the non-fulfilment of intended usage requirements while a nonconformity is the non-fulfilment of specified requirements. In a similar distinction, while testing the software product, the user requirements need to be validated and specified requirements verified.

6. Disruptive Innovation

Learning Objective

9.7   Know the impact of disruptive innovations: cloud computing; big data, social networking applications; mobile computing

6.1   What is a Disruptive Innovation?

A disruptive innovation is an innovative technology that improves a product or service in ways that the market does not expect, typically by lowering prices, designing for a different set of consumers or delivering it in a different way. As a result, it creates demand for new types of services and reduces demand for existing services – it therefore disrupts the existing market. Historical examples include the development of low-cost motor vehicles by Henry Ford at the beginning of the 20th century, the invention of the personal computer in the 1980s, and the availability of high-speed internet connections in this century.

The term 'disruptive innovation' was coined by Clayton Christensen in 1997, a Harvard academic, and Christensen defines disruptive innovations as generally being:

Technologically straightforward, consisting of off-the-shelf components put together in a product architecture that was often simpler than prior approaches. They offered less of what customers in established markets wanted and so could rarely be initially employed there. They offered a different package of attributes valued only in emerging markets remote from, and unimportant to, the mainstream.

For example, early automobiles were not a threat to the horse and carriage, because they were too expensive. But when Henry Ford invented the low-cost automobile the existing road transport industry was disrupted to the point of virtual obliteration. Early PCs were not capable of replacing mainframes, so mainframe manufacturers never regarded them as a threat. Twenty years later, however, vast numbers of applications, that in the past would have run on mainframes, now run on servers that use PC architecture which are sold for a fraction of the cost of a mainframe computer.

6.2 Cloud Computing

6.2.1 Definition

Cloud computing (which is also known as **Software as a Service** or **Computing on Demand**) is the provision of IT resources (hardware, software, networks, applications, etc) **on demand** via a network. It has been compared to the supply of electricity and gas, or the provision of telephone, television and postal services. All of these services are presented to the users in a relatively simple way that is easy to understand without the users needing to know how they are provided, what location they are provided from, or what the physical configurations of the systems that deliver the services are.

Anybody who has used services such as Hotmail, Gmail, Google Docs, Facebook, YouTube or Twitter, or has an online blog or a personal website, is using cloud computing. The major providers of cloud computing services include Microsoft, Google, and Amazon Web Services. These three companies individually own computing resources which are far larger than any one financial institution.

The benefits of delivering applications using the vast resources of the cloud are shown in the following diagram:

Cloud Computing versus Traditional Data Centre

Traditional Approach

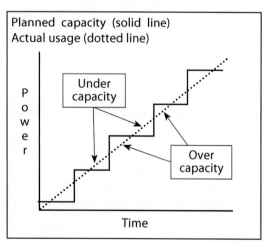

The Cloud

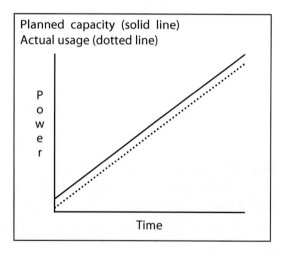

The traditional approach to delivering an application is to build a data centre to house it. Capacity planning can never be precise and, if new servers, networks or software licences need to be purchased because of increased demand, there will always be a lead time to commission them. This means that at any one time the data centre will either be running with excess capacity (which creates additional expense) or inadequate capacity (which results in dissatisfied users). Using the cloud model, the actual capacity that cloud vendors are able to deliver through their enormous data centres is much more closely aligned with actual usage. In effect, an organisation is moving from a fixed/step cost model to a variable one.

6.2.2   Cloud Computing in the Banking and Securities Industry

While it is easy to see how the services provided by the above companies to the personal sector have transformed the way people communicate with each other and share photos, music and videos, and have disrupted the retail markets for music, books and photo processing, the question is: to what extent is 'the cloud' capable of disrupting the markets for financial services software, hardware and networks?

A 2010 survey by PwC revealed that 48% of financial sector firms are using the cloud, and that the main motivation for doing so is to reduce costs (move from a fixed/step cost model to a variable cost model). The same survey revealed that 44% of firms in all industries are entrusting critical applications to cloud providers. One UK fund management firm, which has £6 billion under management, deploys all its computing requirements from cloud providers. The firm claims the benefits of this approach to be as follows:

- Reduced IT costs – they have no significant networks or servers and no internal IT department.
- In particular, they claim to have no project management overheads. They claim that all their software requirements can be sourced from the cloud at a fraction of the cost of internal projects, and that the controls on projects and change programmes that were discussed in earlier chapters are unnecessary, because of the low costs of cloud computing.
- Simpler business recovery plans, as there are no servers or networks to replicate or relocate in the event of not having access to their offices. It is the responsibility of the cloud to define resilience in the cloud.
- A greater ability to match data resource availability with actual demand.
- The whole company is more customer-facing as a result of the previous benefits.

In January 2012, Spanish banking group BBVA announced that it would migrate all email, calendar, word processing and video applications for its 110,000 staff to Google's cloud platform. It was satisfied it could manage this migration after the successful completion of a pilot project involving 7,000 staff members.

6.2.3   Concerns about Cloud Computing

Most of the concerns about the cloud are concerned with data security and related issues, including:

- uncertainty as to whether and how the supplier is complying with the client's data security policies;
- uncertainty about suppliers' skills, training and auditing policies;
- data proximity – the customer will never know whether its data is held in the same databases as that of its competitors, or what dangers this presents;
- because the customers have no knowledge of where the data actually is, they may be unable to answer regulators' questions.

These are also issues on privacy, localisation of data, segregation of data, 'culture' change for CIOs, etc.

6.2.4   Conclusion

Cloud computing has already shown itself to be a disruptive innovation in many retail markets such as books, music and image processing. It now looks as though it will become a disruptive innovation in the banking and securities industries, although the issues mentioned previously will need resolving.

6.3   Big Data

According to the Pepper and Rogers Research Group, every day in the US some 7 billion shares of stock or other securities are traded on various financial exchanges, and fully two-thirds of these trades are executed by computers using algorithms to trade with other computers, without human participation.

Roughly 33,000 discrete trades take place every second on the New York Stock Exchange and of course they must (and do) take place in a particular order, one trade at a time, each trade separated from the next by just a few microseconds.

Financial transactions generate an enormous quantity of data to be stored, processed, and re-processed. But all human activity is now generating such data at an accelerating rate. From investing and retail spending, to web browsing, social media, and mobile phones. IBM, estimates that 90% of all data in use today have been accumulated within just the last two years. This data comes from everywhere: sensors used to gather climate information, posts to social media sites, digital pictures and videos, purchase transaction records and cell phone GPS signals to name a few.

A Gartner research report published in 2001 suggested that problems are created not just by the volume of data being generated, but by the increasing velocity at which it is being created (33,000 ordered trades per second, for instance), as well as by its proliferating variety (think of "unstructured" data such as text documents, videos and pictures, for instance).

However, the growth of very large cloud-based data centres has provided opportunities to store and analyse very large, very complex data sets in ways that only a few years ago would not have been possible. Basically, developers can use statistics from these very large data sets to solve problems in new ways. A trade repository (See Chapter 3) is one example of such a data set. Neither the European nor the US regulators have yet published any information about how they are going to interrogate such data sets, and what routine uses they will make of them. Here are some examples of uses of big data:

Google and Machine Translation

Machine translation has been around in one form or another for decades, but has always lagged far behind translations produced by human experts. Much of the software written to perform machine translation involved defining different languages' grammars and dictionaries, a difficult process whose results were unsatisfactory.

Google's approach was to replace all that with a purely statistical approach. Looking at masses of data in parallel – for instance, over 100 years' worth of both the English and French verbatim reports of speeches in the Canadian Parliament – produced far better translations than the old algorithm-driven method. The bigger the corpus, or body of parallel texts, the better the results.

Tesco PLC and Performance Efficiency

The supermarket chain collected 70 million refrigerator-related data points coming off its units and fed them into a dedicated data warehouse. Those data points were analysed to keep better tabs on performance, gauge when the machines might need to be serviced and do more proactive maintenance to cut down on energy costs.

Macy's Inc. and Real-Time Pricing.

The retailer adjusts pricing in near-real time for 73 million items, based on demand and inventory, using technology from SAS.

6.4   The Growth of Mobile Computing

Devices such as smartphones and tablet computers were originally marketed as consumer devices, but they are increasingly being used in corporate environments. This is part of a disruptive trend where IT becomes decentralised, devices become simpler to use and end-users play a more prominent role.

Businesses are facing a demand from employees who want to use their privately owned devices for tasks such as email, working on business presentations and accessing databases. One of the main challenges involved in allowing employee-owned mobile devices into a corporate environment is separating the business and private information on the device.

Highly portable devices are obviously more at risk of theft and loss than larger devices, but there are other issues about their deployment which affect information security. There are worms and other malware that specifically target these devices, such as the iPhone worm that can steal banking data and enlist these devices in a botnet. A botnet (see Chapter 8, Section 3.1.1, where botnets are described in detail) is a collection of infected computers or 'bots' that have been taken over by hackers (also known as 'bot herders') and are used to perform malicious tasks or functions.

This means that firms need to produce clear and practical guidelines for their staff to follow when they are using a privately owned device. They will also need to:

- enforce the same password controls that apply to company-owned devices;
- restrict the use of certain applications on their networks;
- deploy software that is able to remotely 'wipe' data from stolen devices.

Device suppliers are continually innovating to produce new hardware and software designed to:

- enable differentiation between private and business applications;
- provide separate billing for private and business calls and network use;
- identify users who log into the corporate network from their private device and manage e-data permissions;
- safeguard and, if necessary, 'wipe' data on the devices.

6.5   Social Networks in the Workplace

Many businesses use the major social networking websites such as Facebook and Twitter to interact with customers, and LinkedIn is a major force in recruitment. However, there are now a number of packaged software products that include workplace networking facilities that are designed to enable and encourage collaborative working within the individual firm. These applications are particularly suitable for use by staff members working on change projects, reconciliations and investigations, as well as helpdesk activities.

The features they offer include:

- **File sharing** – with no upload limits, files of any size or type may be shared across the organisation and all content is kept in one secure, central cloud-based location.
- **Document locking** – to ensure that one user does not override changes being made by colleagues, documents may be checked and locked in and out of the application.
- **Version and content tracking** – all comments and feedback from colleagues are in one place. Audit trails are automatically added every time an action takes place against a file.
- **Collaboration** – these applications provide integrated editing tools and commenting options to work with clients and colleagues on content.
- **Anywhere, anytime access** – being cloud-based, applications can be accessed from any location, at any time of day, from conventional PCs as well as smartphones and tablets.

Because these applications are based on the same social networking principles as the consumer sites such as Facebook, they empower employees to invite anyone to contribute to the work in progress. This does present security concerns, however, and firms that intend to deploy such applications need to develop policies and procedures to guide users as to which other staff members, customers or suppliers should be invited to particular groups.

End of Chapter Questions

Think of an answer for each question and refer to the appropriate section for confirmation.

1. List the nine stages of the standard UK software development life cycle.
   Section 2.2

2. What are the four pre-conditions that must have been fulfilled before commencing design and/or development using the waterfall model?
   Section 3.1

3. What are the four main criticisms of the waterfall model of software development?
   Section 3.1.3

4. How does the 'agile' method of software development attempt to reduce development risk?
   Section 3.2.3

5. List the advantages and disadvantages of end-user development.
   Section 3.3.4

6. List the six 'good practice' guidelines of PRINCE2.
   Section 4.2

7. What is the role of a project sponsor?
   Section 4.2.1

8. When completing a defect report as a result of software testing, what is the purpose of a 'severity grade'?
   Section 5.1

9. List the seven 'software testing axioms'.
   Section 5.1.1

10. How does cloud computing apply to the banking and securities industry?
    Section 6.2.2

Chapter Ten

IT Services Procurement

This syllabus area will provide approximately 4 of the 50 examination questions

1. Introduction

This chapter deals with the issues relating to new technologies (Section 2), outsourcing, insourcing and the offshoring of key activities of the securities industry firm (Sections 3 to 5), as well as the vendor selection process for IT packages, projects and services (Section 6).

2. Making the Buy or Build Decision

Learning Objective

10.1   Understand the buy versus build decision

When a new solution is required to resolve a business problem, there is often a decision to be made as to whether to build it internally or to buy a packaged product (by using an external specialist). In some conditions, it is more cost-effective to buy; in others it makes more sense to build the solution in-house.

The overall cost of the solution, whether it is built or bought, should include the cost of delivering the solution to production and the ongoing expenses of the solutions once they become part of business as usual operations. For example, a vendor might build a solution for a very low cost, but the ongoing support and maintenance fees might be high. Equally, an internal team might be able to deliver a solution relatively cheaply, but the entire team might need to be retrained to support the solution in production.

2.1   Possible Reasons to Build

Costs – the cost of an internal development may (or may not) be lower than either the purchase of a software package or the fees paid to external developers.

Expertise – depending on the nature of the product or system being introduced, there may be more expertise within the firm than there is outside the firm.

Competitive advantage and intellectual property rights – if the firm requires an application that will give it some competitive advantage, it might not wish to share the intellectual property with a software vendor that could then sell the application to competitors.

Resource availability – and its effect on the elapsed time to bring the system or product into production.

There is no suitable package, or any suitable package has a large amount of expensive functionality that is not required.

2.2   Possible Reasons to Buy

Business strategy – if the new system or product is not a core application, the firm's internal resources may be better spent on core business software.

Costs – may be lower if there are packaged products available that meet the business needs.

Time – if a packaged application exists, it is likely that it could be implemented more quickly.

Generic solution – many parts of the firm's application architecture consist of elements that are needed by all firms in the same sector. For example, all LSE and SWIFT member firms need communications with the LSE and SWIFT respectively, and all firms, in all sectors, need to perform bank and depot reconciliations. These commodity functions do not usually confer any competitive advantage on a particular firm and, as a result, software vendors that specialise in building the necessary applications have evolved. These vendors usually have more skilled resources available in their areas of expertise than an individual securities firm, and are usually able to deliver packaged products for quick delivery.

In addition, user firms hope to become part of an unofficial 'club' of users of that solution, who are jointly funding its onwards development and maintenance. Smaller firms can benefit from the investment made by larger firms in developing the system, and on large scale projects such as regulatory change, where every firm needs their system to be changed in the same way and at the same time, and it will almost always be cheaper to deliver a solution if all clients contribute towards the development cost.

The build or buy decision is one that needs to be answered very early in a change project as it is fundamental to the approach of how change is to be delivered. The decision may be self-evident at the outset, in which case the reasons for the decision will be included in the project brief at the beginning of the project. In other cases, the build versus buy decision will need research, in which case the project planning phase will include a task to evaluate the alternatives. Until such time as the project steering committee has considered the alternatives, it may not be possible to plan the project any further.

3. Outsourcing

Learning Objective

10.2   Know the advantages and disadvantages of outsourcing

3.1   The Concept of Outsourcing

Outsourcing entered the business lexicon in the 1980s and refers to *'the delegation of non-core operations from internal production to an external entity specialising in the management of that operation'*. For example, ABC Investment Company plc is an investment manager. As such, its core operation could be defined as selecting the correct financial instruments and markets in which to invest (in order to meet the specified investment goals of its customers) and executing transactions as a result of such selections. In order to be able to manage just its core operation, it needs to employ customer account managers, fund managers, investment analysts, economists and dealers.

However, once the investment decisions have been taken, it then needs to employ operations personnel to settle the transactions, accounting staff to account for them, IT staff to select and manage the systems that play a part in making the investment decisions and process the trades, and HR staff and building management staff to manage the people and property.

It is argued that all of these activities are 'non-core' operations, and that some or all of them would best be delegated to an outside supplier whose own core competence lies in the management of one or more of these activities. Almost any non-core activity may be outsourced; some possible examples are shown in the table opposite.

Business Area	Department	Activity	Notes
Front Office	Investment Research	All investment research; or:	
		Economic research for a particular market; eg, US; or for a particular sector, eg, pharmaceuticals	
	Trade Execution	All trade execution; or:	
		Trade execution for a particular market; eg, US; or for a particular sector, eg, pharmaceuticals; or for certain types of financial instrument; eg, FX, derivatives	
Operations	Settlements	All settlement activity, or some of:	Note that when settlement activity is outsourced, the supplier – not the customer – usually takes on the risks of non-payment of debts by the customer's own customer
		Settlement activity for a particular geographical market; eg, US, Japan	
		Settlement activity for particular financial instruments; eg, derivatives, FX, equities	
	Information Technology – 'Production Outsourcing'	All IT activities; or some of:	
		Supply and maintenance of desktop PCs and associated software	
		Provision of business continuity (disaster recovery) back-up site	
		Supply and maintenance of data servers	
		Maintenance and support of specific (existing) business applications	The customer may choose to outsource the management of all its applications, or just outsource the management of some of them, while developing and supporting the others in-house
	Information Technology – 'Innovation Outsourcing'	Development of (specific) new business applications	The customer may choose to outsource the development of all its new applications, or just a single one of them while continuing to develop the others in-house
Administration	HR	All HR activities; or some of:	
		Permanent staff recruitment	
		Temporary staff recruitment	
		Payroll administration	
		Pension and benefit administration	
	Premises	All premises-related activities; or some of:	
		Building maintenance	
		Reception services	
		Catering	

10

Notice that the outsourced IT activities may be divided into two distinct categories. 'Production outsourcing' is concerned with the maintenance and support of software products that have already been developed, while 'innovation outsourcing' is concerned with the development of new applications.

3.2 The Advantages And Disadvantages Of Outsourcing

Outsourcing involves the transference or sharing of the management control and/or decision-making of a business function to an outside supplier. This involves a high degree of two-way information exchange, co-ordination and trust between the outsourcer and its client.

Entering into an outsourcing agreement for a significantly large non-core business area is therefore not a decision to be taken lightly; the investment company needs to take considerable care in the following:

- Selecting a supplier that has the right level of competence in the activity to be outsourced (see Section 6).
- Planning and managing the migration project (see Chapter 9, Section 4).
- Drawing up a service level agreement (SLA) that states quite clearly the scope of the activity to be outsourced, the responsibilities of both the customer and the vendor, the escalation procedures to be adopted when the service level falls below the requirements of the SLA, and any financial penalties that the vendor must pay to the customer if the service level falls below the SLA level for an extended period of time.

3.2.1 Benefits of Outsourcing

A correctly managed outsourcing agreement and migration project should provide the customer with the following benefits.

Specialisation: Enabling a Higher Quality of Service

ABC Investment Company plc is not a specialist IT company. It would normally delegate the management of some, or all, of its IT functions to a company that is a specialist IT company; this company should be able to improve the quality of the service offered because of the following factors.

- It is in a better position to recruit highly skilled staff because it can offer them a career path in their chosen specialisation.
- It has a larger pool of skilled specialist staff to cover for absences and to share problems.
- It has other customers similar to ABC Investment Company and may be able to leverage the experience gained by working with those customers to ABC's benefit.
- It may be in a better position than the customer to replace outdated technologies and working methods.

Specialisation: Enabling Cost Reduction

The specialist IT company should be able to reduce ABC's costs because of the following:

- It has greater bargaining power when negotiating with its own suppliers.
- It has a larger pool of specialist labour, which means that it can provide cover for absences without the expense of recruiting temporary staff.

- It may be able to carry out some or all of the outsourced functions 'offshore' in countries with lower labour unit costs and/or favourable tax regimes and/or weak currencies.
- It may be able to undertake 'joint developments' for more than one customer in the same industry so that the capital cost of a large software development project is shared by more than one customer.

Business Focus: Management is Now Free to Concentrate on its 'Core Operations'

ABC Investment Company's core competence is in fund management. Because it has outsourced some or all of its non-core operations, its management is now free to manage its core business – it is no longer distracted by these activities, so it is able to concentrate on the following:

- improving customer relationships;
- improving the quality of their core business activity;
- extending the range of services offered to its customers – innovation.

Summary of the Advantages

As a result of successful outsourcing, the company should be in a position to deliver new and improved products to customers more quickly and with a lower level of investment.

3.2.2 Possible Disadvantages of Outsourcing

No business decision of any kind just offers benefits. Companies that are considering outsourcing some, or all, of their non-core functions should be aware of the following problems and disadvantages that can, and do, occur in some outsourcing arrangements.

Information Security

When an activity is outsourced, sensitive information about customers, staff, investment decisions and positions, the firm's own financial position and its own intellectual property are passed to third parties. The exact nature of the sensitive information that is passed on depends on the type of activity that is being outsourced. Such information can be misused and, in an extreme example, could be used fraudulently.

As a result of a small number of high-profile fraud cases involving US corporations, NASSCOM (the National Association of Software and Services Companies) in India has attempted to address these fraud concerns by creating the National Skills Registry. This database contains personal and work-related information, enabling employers to verify a staff member's credentials and allowing police to track the background of workers.

Is the Decision to Outsource Reversible?

When an activity is outsourced, the employees that used to carry out the activity either leave the company (often to become employees of the service provider) or are redeployed within the company. If the company wanted to terminate the outsourcing arrangement at some time in the future, then hiring an entire replacement team might be difficult. If the company is unhappy with the service it receives, it may be easier to change outsourcers than to bring the operation back in-house.

Work, Labour and the Economy

Outsourcing – more specifically offshoring in this context – is controversial. Politicians and consumer groups are quick to criticise firms that outsource jobs abroad, or that incorporated in overseas tax havens to avoid paying their fair share of taxes. In the UK, offshoring decisions that involve the creation of large numbers of jobs in offshore centres and/or the loss of large numbers of jobs in the domestic economy sometimes generate negative press. Some UK companies – including some major retail banks – have made promises to customers that all their call centres will remain in the UK.

The Quality of the Service Fails to Live Up to the Customer's Expectations

There are a number of reasons why the service that is delivered might fail to live up to the expectations of the management, staff and/or customers of the company that has outsourced its operations. Many of these issues are preventable, and the techniques and procedures to prevent them are discussed in other learning objectives in this workbook. They include the following:

Problem Description	Section
Poor selection of vendor – the vendor does not have the expertise to carry out the functions.	This chapter, Section 6
Inadequate service level agreement – the SLA either doesn't cover the real requirements of the service or it defines unrealistically high or low levels of service.	This chapter, Section 6
Communication – the SLA has not been properly explained to staff or customers, therefore their expectations are not the same as those of the service provider. They are unsure of what to do when something goes wrong.	This chapter, Section 6
Poor project management – managing the transition from in- to outsourcing is a complex project. It needs to be managed using an accepted project management methodology such as PRINCE, PMI or one of the other standards described here.	Chapter 9, Section 4
Inadequately documented systems and working practices.	This section
Existing systems and working practices are unsuitable for outsourcing.	This section
Inadequately documented development requirements.	This section

Inadequately Documented Systems and Working Practices

When an operation is outsourced, the systems that are used to support it may or may not change, but the working practices always do. There will need to be different procedures for escalating and resolving problems. It is important that the staff of both companies are provided with comprehensive documentation and training in how to use the systems concerned, how to work with normal and exceptional workflows, and how to escalate and resolve problems.

Existing Systems and Working Practices Are Unsuitable for Outsourcing

In an extreme case, it could prove to be the case that a customer's existing systems and working practices are so company-specific and so antiquated that they are basically unsuitable for outsourcing in their current form. In such a case, the outsourcing programme should allow for the replacement of some systems and workflows before the operation is outsourced. Both parties should recognise this problem before taking the decision to outsource.

Inadequately Documented Development Requirements

This is a particular problem for those commissioning software developments that are to be outsourced to an offshore location for the first time. The commissioning company may have had no experience in this method of working before, and the fact that the users can no longer raise or resolve queries by meeting the developers informally and at short notice may come as a culture shock.

For a large outsourced development to be successful, there needs to be very clear and precise documentation of requirements, and very clear procedures for raising queries and raising change requests.

These standards should, of course, be in place for internal developments, as well as outsourced developments, but they become far more critical when development is outsourced, especially if it is outsourced to an offshore location in a remote time zone.

4.   Insourcing

Learning Objective

10.3   Know the advantages and disadvantages of insourcing

4.1   Definition of Insourcing

In this context, insourcing (internal outsourcing) occurs where a company sets up an operation to carry out work that would otherwise have been contracted out. Insourcing often involves the centralisation of activities that have previously been dispersed across a number of business units and geographical territories.

Example

A firm currently has securities settlement operations in every one of its European offices (Amsterdam, London, Frankfurt, Madrid, and Paris), each reporting to the local office manager, who is also responsible for sales and trading in those centres.

Using the insourcing model, the securities firm would set up a single settlements division reporting to its own manager. The settlements division would centralise, where possible, all activities in one location. This location could be in one of the cities where there is a sales and trading office, or it could be in an offshore location.

The settlements division would treat all the sales offices as customers in exactly the same way that an outsourced operation would have done. It would charge them a fee for its services, and would expect to recover its costs by this fee.

In other words, the settlement operation has been outsourced, but the provider of the outsourced service is part of the same company as the customer.

4.2 Advantages of Insourcing over Outsourcing

- Centralisation of the activity provides the opportunities to create:
  - economies of scale;
  - a centre of excellence for the activity being insourced.
- Retention of 'institutional memory'.
- Goals and vision shared with the customer business units.
- Continued employee loyalty/improved career paths.

4.3 Disadvantages of Insourcing over Outsourcing

Unless insourcing is accompanied by offshoring, there are fewer opportunities for cost-saving due to high employment costs in major financial centres.

Outsourcing offers more opportunities for radical change to systems and working practices. With the insourcing model, there is a danger that the firm carries on doing things in the same way that it has always done them.

Senior management may continue to regard the insourced operation as a cost centre; it may have difficulty obtaining budget approval for radical developments.

5. Offshoring, Near-Shoring and Best-Shoring

Learning Objective

10.4   Know the advantages and disadvantages of offshoring, near-shoring, best-shoring

5.1 Definition of Terms

5.1.1 Offshoring

Offshoring is defined as the movement of a business process done at a company in one country to the same or another company in another, different country. It is almost always the case that work is moved due to a lower cost of operations in the new location.

The reasons why costs are lower usually include more than one of the following:

- lower salary rates in the offshore location;
- lower infrastructure costs in the offshore location;
- lower tax rates in the offshore location;
- the offshore location may have a weak currency compared to the onshore location; and
- the possible availability of government grants and other incentives to set up business in the offshore location.

Offshoring is usually – but not always – associated with outsourcing; it is of, course, possible to outsource without offshoring, and to offshore without outsourcing. Some large banks and other companies have formed wholly owned subsidiary companies in India and the Philippines to carry out business processes for their parent company – these companies are, therefore, both insourcing and offshoring.

When we hear the term 'offshoring' we usually think of a business process being moved from, say, the UK or the US to India or the Philippines, several thousand miles and several time zones away. This is classic offshoring, but there are forms of offshoring that have a different model.

5.1.2   Near-Shoring

Near-shoring implies relocation of business processes to (typically) lower-cost foreign locations, but in close geographical proximity. Some common examples include:

- shifting United States-based business processes to Canada or Latin America;
- shifting London-based operations either to a lower-cost European country, such as Hungary, or to a lower-cost part of the UK, such as Northern Ireland;
- shifting German-based operations to countries such as the Czech Republic, Poland or Hungary. These countries have a competitive advantage over their counterparts, the 'classic' outsourcing countries such as India and the Philippines, because German is more widely spoken in these near-shore locations.

Near-shoring is usually more expensive than classic offshoring, so it is usually chosen as an alternative to classic offshoring when any of the following factors becomes important.

1. There is a shortage of resources in the classic offshoring centres that are able to communicate in the customer's native language.
2. The work involves frequent visits to, or by, the customer – in such a situation the costs of air fares might erode the classic offshore centre's usual cost advantages.
3. The work being undertaken has such a strong customer focus or regulations-driven reporting element, and is tied so intrinsically to the business, that it is harder to draw a solid line between it and the rest of the operation.

However, the near-shore centres do not, in general, attract a high proportion of 'innovation outsourcing' work. This is because new application development usually needs a very large number of man-hours, and the 'classic' offshore locations have a significant competitive advantage over the near-shore locations in terms of personnel and premises costs.

5.1.3 Best-Shoring

The idea behind best-shoring is that some services need to be delivered in a location close to the customer, while other services do not. The 'best-shoring' strategy involves tailoring specific customer care needs to locations that are best suited for these functions. It allows the customer to save on the cost of domestically sourcing the work, while at the same time removing the inflexibility of using only one offshore location.

Many of the world's leading consultancy companies, such as Perot Systems and Accenture, as well as many of the large Indian outsourcing companies, have invested in facilities in near-shore locations such as the Czech Republic, Hungary and Northern Ireland, so that they can offer their clients the advantages of best-shoring.

5.2 Advantages and Disadvantages

The following table summarises the advantages and disadvantages of each offshoring methodology, and also lists the typical services that are usually provided through each:

Offshoring Methodology	Advantages	Disadvantages	Typical Work Undertaken
Classic Offshoring	Usually the lowest-cost option Very large numbers of skilled resources are available in the major centres in India and the Philippines Usually the most appropriate location for 'innovation outsourcing', ie, the creation of new business applications. This is because these tasks involve a very large number of man-hours, and hence the low-cost environments of the major development centres in Asia have a considerable advantage over their near-shore competitors	Major time zone differences Travel costs Possible language and cultural barriers – especially if the customer's working language is not English Lack of control	Call centre functions Simple transaction processing Software maintenance Large scale software development/business process re-engineering Research and development Investment analysis
Near-Shoring	Lower time-zone differences Lower travel costs Fewer language and cultural barriers – especially if the customer's working language is not English	Higher cost than classic offshoring The near-shore centre may not have access to the very large numbers of skilled resources available to classic offshoring centres	Call centre functions More complex transaction processing – perhaps involving a strong customer focus or regulations-driven reporting element Any work that involves frequent visits to or from the customer

Best-Shoring	Attempts to provide the benefits of both classic offshoring and near-shoring Highly flexible	More expensive than classic offshoring Fragmentation – the customer may be dealing with service providers in many locations. As a result, this method is suitable only if a large number of functions are to be offshored. Both the customer and the service provider need a management structure capable of handling this fragmentation	All of the above

6. The Vendor Relationship

Learning Objective

10.5   Understand the vendor relationship, including: the vendor selection process; vendor assessment; task order/work order/contract negotiation and finalisation; effective vendor management

6.1   The Vendor Selection Process

Securities industry IT departments are often involved in selecting vendors for IT products and services. The IT department is usually solely responsible for selecting suppliers of PC and server hardware, networks and configuration management software. The department usually works alongside the user departments in selecting vendors of the following:

- packaged application software, such as order management systems, settlement systems and general ledger systems;
- outsourced innovation services, such as bespoke software development;
- some outsourced production services, such as a settlement/transaction processing service that has a high IT content.

This section deals with the principles of vendor assessment for these types of products and services where the IT department will be working alongside the users.

6.2 The Seven Stages of Vendor Assessment

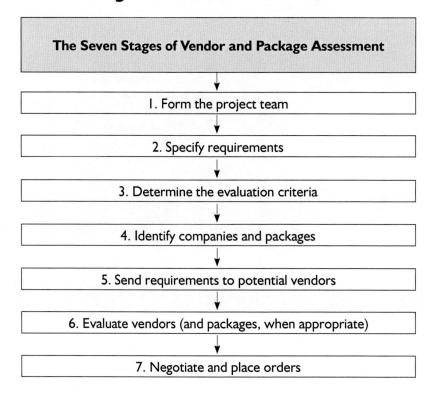

The Seven Stages of Vendor and Package Assessment

1. Form the project team
2. Specify requirements
3. Determine the evaluation criteria
4. Identify companies and packages
5. Send requirements to potential vendors
6. Evaluate vendors (and packages, when appropriate)
7. Negotiate and place orders

6.2.1 Form the Project Team

Assumptions

1. If you are selecting a vendor for a packaged software product, then the company has already made the 'build-versus-buy' decision (refer to Chapter 9, Section 6) and has decided to buy.
2. If you are selecting a vendor for a bespoke development, then the company has already made the 'build-versus-buy' decision (refer to Chapter 9, Section 6) and has decided to build, and also to outsource the build.
3. If you are selecting a vendor for an outsourced production service, then the company has already made the decision to outsource the service.

Project Team Membership

The team needs to consist of representatives from the relevant user departments and the IT department who have relevant expertise in the application being purchased and who have the time to devote to the vendor selection process. Because this process may be quite time-consuming, project team members may need to relinquish some, or all, of their other routine duties. For this reason, the team is often managed by, or its members may include, third-party consultants.

6.2.2 Specify Requirements

The user department's requirements for the system or service need to be gathered. User requirements in this context need to include all of the following:

- Functional requirements of the application or service – 'What does it do?'
- Volume/performance/availability requirements – 'How fast does it do it?'
- Technical constraints – such as permitted or prohibited operating systems, databases, data security requirements, etc.
- Support requirements – 'How do we get help and when can we get it?'
- Budgetary constraints – 'How much will it cost?'
- Delivery date constraints – 'When can we get it?'

These requirements need to be presented in a form that can be used as a **Request for Proposal (RFP)** that will be sent to a list of potential suppliers. An RFP is a statement of intent to purchase, followed by a list of questions covering all of the issues that can be sent to potential vendors for them to reply to in writing. Vendors will need to know the timeline and how the company will make its decision in order to match their capabilities to its needs in the best way. The RFP usually also contains an overview of the current systems infrastructure and a description of the applications that are to be replaced.

Some of the questions asked will be about the cost of the system or service. It is important to phrase these questions in such a way that will trigger detailed information about:

- one-off capital expenditure for the right to use the package or service for a predetermined period;
- one-off capital expenditure for consultancy concerned with essential system enhancements and implementation project activity;
- annual maintenance and support;
- whether the amounts quoted include Value Added Tax (VAT) or other local taxes, or whether these amounts are excluded from the quotation;
- whether the amounts quoted include reimbursement of the vendor's travel and subsistence, or whether these amounts are excluded from the quotation.

6.2.3 Determine Evaluation Criteria

In order to make a reasoned selection, the most important (eg, must-do) requirements must be articulated and the criteria must be prioritised and weighted to allow the suitability of the solutions to be ranked. The financial viability of the vendors and their access to skilled project resources must also be evaluated.

6.2.4 Identify Potential Vendors

Potential vendors may be identified in a number of ways, including:

- internet search engines;
- more specialised online directories – for example, when looking for a vendor who has consulting expertise or package products concerned with SWIFT connectivity, then the SWIFT Partner Solutions Directory (at www.swift.com) lists several hundred vendors under various searchable geographical and functional categories;

- advertisements and editorial items in trade magazines such as *STP Magazine*, the *Securities & Investment Review* and *Futures & Options World*;
- attendance at exhibitions and conferences;
- word of mouth – what vendors have counterparties and competitors used? Have any in-house project team members worked at other companies that have recently had to do the same type of evaluation? If looking for a service connected with a particular stock exchange or clearing house, does the exchange concerned have a list of suitable vendors?

6.2.5 Send Requirements to Potential Vendors

The RFP can then be sent to the vendors identified in the previous stage. If a very large number of potential vendors have been identified, then it might be worth considering sending an abbreviated version of the RFP at this stage, and using the results of that exercise to form a shortlist of vendors to whom the full RFP can be sent. The abbreviated form of an RFP is usually referred to as a **request for information (RFI)**.

As well as asking the questions described in Section 6.2.2, the vendors should also be asked to provide at least three suitable customer references that can be followed up. A suitable reference site is an organisation that is using the same package product or outsourced service in the same industry and geographic region as the one being addressed. If selecting a vendor for a bespoke development, then a suitable reference site is a company in the same geographical region for whom the vendor has recently worked in a similar project.

The vendor should also be asked to supply a copy of its latest audited accounts, and a draft contract for the service or product to be provided.

6.2.6 Evaluate Vendors (and Packages, When Appropriate)

The criteria to be used have already been identified. Vendors should be evaluated against those criteria using all of the following as evidence of the vendors' ability to deliver and commitment to the commissioning company and its project.

Quality of the Answers to the RFP Questions

- Have all the functional, volume/performance and technical questions been answered in an appropriate amount of depth, or were the answers woolly and vague? Did the vendor seek clarification about any of the questions? Are the answers satisfactory?
- Has the vendor confirmed that it is able to deliver on a timely basis?
- Do we now have a clear idea of the level of investment that is needed to purchase this service or package? Is the vendor's quote within budget?

Product Demonstrations

When selecting a **packaged application**, it is essential to have at least one demonstration of the package – preferably more than one – and to ensure that the right project team members and other key personnel are able to attend. It is a good idea to ask the vendor to demonstrate using sample transactions or scenarios that apply to the commissioning organisation.

When selecting a vendor for an **outsourced bespoke development**, then that vendor should be asked to demonstrate something else that it has developed for another company in a similar business area.

When selecting a vendor for an outsourced service, and part of that service involves supplying the commissioning company with, say, transaction entry software, then make sure that this software is demonstrated.

Evaluate the Vendor's Key People

By this time the commissioning company will have had several meetings with the vendor's key personnel. The following questions should be asked:

- Do they act in a professional manner? Are they punctual in attending meetings and do they return calls promptly?
- Do they have sufficient domain expertise in the areas that they are working in? Has the commissioning company met functional and technical experts, or just members of the sales force?

Evaluate the Vendor's Financial Status

A qualified accountant should be asked to evaluate the vendor's audited accounts and raise any concerns. If there are any, they should be raised with the vendor directly and tactfully.

Review the Contract

The contract should be reviewed to see if the terms of the supply of the service are acceptable. Note that, depending upon what type of product or service is being purchased, the contract may not be a single document, but many documents (see Section 6.2.7).

Take up References from Other Users

It is essential to take up references from the reference sites requested in the RFP. This is especially true when commissioning bespoke developments or outsourced services, where there is a limit to what can be learnt from product demonstrations; but it is still necessary to take up references when purchasing a packaged product.

The commissioning company should be very wary of any vendor who cannot supply at least three references that seem relevant, unless purchasing from a start-up company where it may be the first user of the service or product. If the latter is the case, then the principals of the company should be able to supply personal references from previous employers or business associates.

When taking up references, follow these guidelines:

- Visit the reference site – don't just take up references by phone or email.
- Ask questions about the following:
  - Functionality – does the product, bespoke development or service that they use do what the vendor said it would do? Does it do what they expected it to do? In what way has it improved the process in their company?
  - System/service performance – does it handle the volumes that they expected it to?
  - Vendor performance – did the vendor deliver on time and within budget? Are help desk calls usually resolved satisfactorily and promptly?

6.2.7 Negotiate and Place Orders

By now the preferred supplier will be identified. It is now time to negotiate contracts.

Price

The vendor may be prepared to reduce the price that was quoted in the response to the RFP. For concessions on price, it will usually ask for something in return. Typically, the vendor will ask the customer to co-operate in publicity about the latest sale; it will usually ask that the customer agree to its issuing a press release mentioning your company's name; additionally, it may ask for co-operation in producing a case study to be published in the trade press.

Contractual Terms

The contract may not be a single document, but many documents. The following table illustrates the common types of documents that it will be necessary to agree on for various types of purchase:

Document Type	Document Type/Type of Purchase (where this document is used)	Brief Description of Document
Software Licence	Software Package	The document grants the customer the right to use the software package for a given period of time, in return for the payment of a licence fee
		Typically, this document may have restrictions about the use of the package. For example: • The user may only use this product in a given location • The licence may expire after a given number of years • The licence may restrict the number of transactions to be processed in a given day, week or month
Software Maintenance Contract	Software Package	The document obliges the vendor to provide support for the package, in return for payment of a maintenance fee
		Typically, this document may have limitations about the provision of support. For example: • Support may be restricted to telephone support and not include site visits which are charged separately • Support may either be available 24/7, or it may be restricted to normal business hours/days in the country from where it is provided • Support may be restricted to just problem-solving, or it might entitle the user to new releases/upgrades of the package

Development Contract	Outsourced Development Projects/Software Package	This document commits the vendor to develop software specified by the customer, in return for payment of development fees
		Development fees may be charged on a 'time and materials' basis, eg, $1,000 per day, or may be on a fixed price basis, eg, $250,000 for the complete development
		When development fees are charged on a fixed price basis, the scope of the development needs to be agreed at the start, and the contract will cater for variations. Variations are then dealt with by work orders or task orders
Service Contract	Outsourced Business Process	This document describes the work that is to be outsourced to the vendor in return for payment of a services fee by the customer
		Typically, this document may have restrictions about the use of the service. For example: • The user may only use this service in a given location • The service usually refers to trading volumes; there may be a minimum charge for the first, say, 1,000 transactions per day/week/month, and extra transactions will be charged for on a sliding scale
Service Level Agreement	Outsourced Business Process	A service level agreement (SLA) is that part of a service contract in which a certain level of service is agreed upon. Level of service in this context refers to both the quality of the service and the time deadlines for performing the service. It may also specify penalties to be paid by either party if the level of service provided fails to reach the minimum standards in the agreement for an extended period of time
Work Order	Outsourced Development Projects/Outsourced Business Process/ Software Package	In the case of a package, a work order may be used instead of a development contract
		In the case of an outsourced development project, work orders are used mainly to vary the scope of the previously agreed development
		In the case of an outsourced business process, it is used to request the vendor to carry out work that is outside the scope of the original service contract
		It obliges the vendor to carry out the specified work in return for the agreed fee
Task Order	Outsourced Development Projects/Outsourced Business Process/ Software Package	An alternative to a work order
Change Request	Outsourced Development Projects/Outsourced Business Process/ Software Package	An alternative to a work order

10

6.3 Effective Vendor Management

If the firm has selected a vendor for a core application or service, then it will have to work alongside the selected vendor's staff for an extended period, possibly for many years. Assume that the firm has just selected a vendor and a package to replace its core settlement system. The likely activities that the vendor and the customer will need to undertake jointly can be shown by the following (simplified) project plan, which assumes that the new system can go live five months after purchase date. In practice, this period may be shorter or longer depending on the complexity of the project and the availability of the firm's staff to work on it.

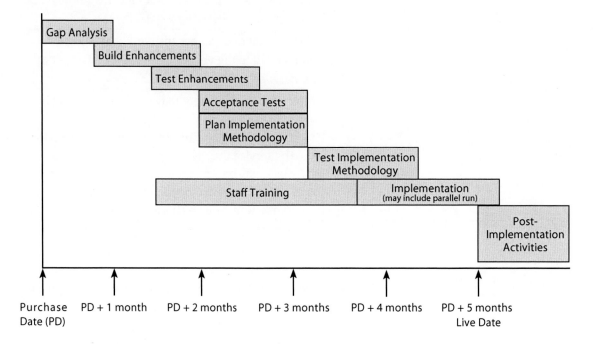

During the period between purchase date and go-live date, both the customer and the vendor may need to commit significant numbers of people to the project. Often, vendor staff may be working full-time at the customers' premises.

Post-implementation activities include, *inter alia*:

- Hand-holding customer staff through the initial 'live' period.
- General help-desk support.
- Delivery of new releases of the vendor's system.
- Specific client-related enhancements.
- Post-implementation review.

These activities usually demand fewer resources, and there may be no need for a full-time vendor presence on-site.

Even if both parties have used best efforts in the vendor selection process, and employed best practice project governance, things can still go wrong with the vendor-client relationship. Some of the causes of poor relations were examined in Section 3.2.2 of this chapter.

Another frequent cause of disputes is the effect of regulatory changes. Take MiFID as an example. These new regulations created the need for major changes to many applications, and in many cases the client firms expected the vendor to fund those changes as part of the maintenance agreement, while the vendor stated that changes of this magnitude were never anticipated when the level of charges was originally negotiated.

6.3.1 Practical Steps Customers Can Take to Pro-Actively Manage Vendors

Maintain strong communication links with all vendors. This can be achieved through regular progress meetings, user groups, vendor presentations and newsletters.

Endeavour to keep acquainted with new enhancements to software and services, to ensure that they are on the right version and communicate any changes required in order to ensure that the system or service meets their ongoing requirements.

Implement regular systems/service 'health checks' to make sure they are getting the most from the software or service and that they are using and maintaining it correctly.

Monitor service level agreements – many organisations will have agreements in place to ensure that levels of service are appropriate to effectively support their business. These should be reviewed regularly with the supplier, to ensure that they are appropriate and that they are being met.

6.3.2 Is Vendor Management an Art or a Science?

Traditionally, it has been seen as an art. However, as configurations become larger and more complex, many firms now use a more formalised approach. There are now vendor management software packages on the market that support this process. They usually automate the administration of contracts and centralise all associated information into one central repository that is globally accessible via a web browser. These products enable organisations to monitor their spending, terminate contracts at the correct time, monitor and track their costs against benefits gained, and ensure that more informed decisions are made based on quantifiable facts and figures.

End of Chapter Questions

Think of an answer for each question and refer to the appropriate section for confirmation.

1. List the reasons why a firm might decide to build an application in-house and the reasons why it might decide to buy a package?
   Section 1

2. List the possible benefits and disadvantages of outsourcing.
   Section 3.2

3. List the reasons why the quality of an outsourced product or service might fail to live up to a customer's expectations.
   Section 3.2.2

4. Define insourcing in your own words.
   Section 4.1

5. List the reasons why the cost of an offshore service is likely to be lower than that of an onshore service.
   Section 5.1.1

6. What are the common reasons for preferring to deliver a product or service by near-shoring instead of classic offshoring?
   Section 5.1.2

7. What is the definition of best-shoring?
   Section 5.1.3

8. List the seven stages of the vendor selection process.
   Section 6.2

9. What document is sent to potential vendors inviting them to reply to written questions about their products or services?
   Section 6.2.2

10. When sending a list of requirements to potential vendors, what other things should you ask them to provide in addition to the answers to your specific questions?
    Section 6.2.2

11. What obligations does a software maintenance contract place on: the software vendor; the customer and what are the typical limitations to such an agreement?
    Section 6.2.7

Glossary and Abbreviations

Glossary

Accounting Explosion Table

A data table that contains the rules for selecting which general ledger account to use for a particular posting.

Accrual

A method of accounting in which each item is entered as it is earned or incurred, regardless of when actual payments are received or made.

Accrued Interest

The interest that has accumulated on a holding since the last interest payment date or start date, up to, but not including, the current date.

ACK/NACK Protocol

This protocol is used by SWIFT to confirm that messages sent by its members have passed network validation and are, therefore, good messages (ACK), or have failed validation (NACK).

Affirmation

The process where a buy-side firm sends a communication to a sell-side firm indicating their agreement to the details of a confirmation received from the sell-side firm.

Agile Model

A methodology to manage the designing and building of software applications.

Algorithmic Trading

The placing of a buy or sell order of a defined quantity into a quantitative model that automatically generates the timing of orders and the size of orders based on goals specified by the parameters and constraints of the algorithm.

Allocation

The process where a buy-side firm sends a communication to a sell-side firm advising the sell-side firm of the details of the investors who are parties to a trade.

Assets

Everything a corporation owns or that is due to it: cash, investments, money due, materials and inventories, which are called current assets; buildings and machinery, which are known as fixed assets; and patents and goodwill, known as intangible assets.

Availability Management

Review of reliability, availability, resilience, maintainability and serviceability of assets such as servers, networks and applications.

Average Price

The average price per unit of a position. If the position is long (ie, positive), then further purchases modify the average price, and sales create P&L but do not modify the average price. If the position is short (ie, negative) then further sales modify the average price, and purchases create P&L but do not modify the average price.

Basel Committee

A committee of central bankers which publishes a set of minimal capital requirements for banks known as the Basel Accord.

Baseline

A declared summary description of the point in a project, indicating original content and stage reached, as a basis for measuring project performance and estimates to complete.

Baseline Control

A system of procedures that allows monitoring and control of the emerging project scope against the scope baseline. Also known as 'Configuration Control'.

Basis Point (BP)

A basis point is a unit that is equal to 1/100th of 1%, and is used to denote the change in a financial instrument. The basis point is commonly used for calculating changes in interest rates, equity indexes and the yield of a fixed-income security. The relationship between percentage changes and basis points can be summarised as follows: 1% change = 100 basis points, and 0.01% = 1 basis point. So, a bond whose yield increases from 5% to 5.5% is said to increase by 50 basis points; or interest rates that have risen 1% are said to have increased by 100 basis points.

Beneficial Owner

A legal term where specific property rights ('use and title') in equity belong to a person even though legal title of the property belongs to another person, the Nominal or Legal Owner.

Best Execution

The process that an investment firm goes through, when executing orders, to obtain the best possible result for its clients taking into account the prices available in various markets, as well as a number of other defined execution factors.

Best-Shoring

The 'Best-Shoring' strategy involves tailoring specific customer care needs to locations that are best suited for these functions. It allows the customer to save on the cost of domestically sourcing the work, while at the same time removing the inflexibility of using only one offshore location.

Bid Price

The highest price that a prospective buyer is willing to pay for a specific security. On the other hand, the offer price, also called the 'ask price', is the lowest price acceptable to a prospective seller of the same security. The highest bid and lowest offer are quoted on most major exchanges, and the difference between the two prices is called the 'spread'.

Bond

A debt instrument issued for a period of more than one year with the purpose of raising capital by borrowing. Governments, states, cities, corporations and many other types of institutions sell bonds. Generally, a bond is a promise to repay the principal along with interest (coupons) on a specified date (maturity).

Book or Trading Book

A portfolio of financial instruments held by a brokerage or bank. The financial instruments in the trading book are purchased or sold to facilitate trading for their customers, to profit from spreads between the bid/ask price, or to hedge against various types of risk. Sometimes this term is used interchangeably with 'position'.

Bourse or Börse

See *Investment Exchange*.

Broker Crossing Network

A network provided by an investment bank which allows the bank's clients to match up and conduct crossing transactions without going through an investment exchange.

Business Case

The business reason for starting a change project.

Business Continuity Plan (BCP)

A plan developed to mitigate different disaster or worst-case scenarios. The BCP will contain agreed workarounds and task lists for those supporting the business process or application during a disaster. The goal of BCP processes is to ensure that IT and other services can be recovered within required, agreed and business-sensitive timescales.

Buy-Side Firms

Fund management institutions that take investment decisions on behalf of investors.

Call Option

See *Option*.

Capacity Management

Review of application sizing, workload, performance, demand and resource management.

Cash Instrument

See *Underlying Instrument*.

Central Counterparty (CCP)

A central counterparty is a financial institution that acts as an intermediary between market participants. This reduces the amount of counterparty risk to which market participants are exposed.

Central Securities Depository (CSD)

A Central Securities Depository (CSD) is an entity holding securities, either in certificated or uncertificated (dematerialised) form, to enable settlement by book entry transfer. In some cases these organisations also carry out centralised comparison and transaction processing such as clearing and custody-type services relating to securities. The physical securities may be immobilised by the depository, or securities may be dematerialised (so that they exist only as electronic records). An International Central Securities Depository (ICSD) is a central securities depository that settles trades in international securities and in various domestic securities, usually through direct or indirect (through local agents) links to local CSDs. Clearstream International Luxembourg (earlier Cedel), Euroclear Bank and SegaInterSettle are considered ICSDs.

Change Control Procedures

A process developed to prevent an item of software or hardware from being amended without auditability and review of the impact by all interested parties.

Chinese Walls

Information barriers implemented within firms to separate and isolate persons who make investment decisions from persons who are privy to undisclosed material information which may influence those decisions.

Clearing House

A financial institution that operates clearing, central counterparty or settlement services.

Client Money

Money belonging to clients which an investment business is holding. It could either be free money or settlement money and, in either case, it must be kept in a bank account separate from the firm's own money.

Cloud Computing

The provision of IT resources (hardware, software, networks and services) on demand via a network. Cloud computing provides software, data access and storage services that do not require end-user knowledge of the physical location and configuration of the system that delivers the services.

Collateral

A security or guarantee (usually an asset) pledged for the repayment of a loan.

Commodity Futures Trading Commission (CFTC)

The CFTC was created in 1974 as an independent agency with the mandate to regulate commodity futures and option markets in the United States. The agency's mandate has been renewed and expanded several times since then, most recently by the Dodd-Frank Wall Street Reform and Consumer Protection Act.

Computer Virus

A malicious software program that can copy itself and infect multiple files on an individual computer, as well as spread from one computer to another.

Confirmation

The process where one party to a trade sends the other party a communication that confirms that the order has been executed, and provides details of the resulting trade.

Consideration

For a securities trade, the amount paid by the buyer and received by the seller. Consideration is the sum of the principal amount, accrued interest, commissions, fees and charges.

Continuity Management

Review of business continuity, risk analysis and risk management, defining assets, threats, vulnerabilities and countermeasures (protection and recovery), development, testing and maintenance of the IT service continuity plan, IT recovery options and management roles.

Contract for Difference (CFD)

An agreement between two parties to exchange the difference between the opening value and the closing value of a particular financial instrument. These are generally short-term contracts. The asset firm's exposure to default by its client is controlled by margin requirements and collateral deposits.

Coupon Date

The interest payment date of a bond.

Coupon Rate

The interest rate of a bond.

Credit Limit

The maximum amount of credit that a bank or other lender will extend to a debtor. In the securities industry, 'debtors' may include clients, counterparties, countries or business sectors. In addition, securities firms usually have limits that they apply to individual traders or trading books.

Credit Rating Agency

A credit rating agency (also called a ratings service) is a company (such as Moody's or Standard and Poor's) that assigns credit ratings, which rate a debtor's ability to pay back debt by making timely interest payments, and which assesses the likelihood of default by the debtor

Credit Risk

The risk associated with one party not fulfilling its contractual obligations at a specific future date.

Critical Path

The series of interdependent project activities, connected end-to-end, which determines the longest path through the project network and, hence, the shortest total duration of the project. The critical path may change from time to time as tasks are completed behind or ahead of schedule.

Crossing

The situation when a broker acts as agent on both sides of a given securities transaction. If the broker has a buy order and an equivalent sell order, it can 'cross' the orders. Under MiFID rules, crossing is only permitted if it results in best execution. Broker crossing networks are a form of MTF.

Custodian Bank

A bank, agent, or other organisation responsible for safeguarding a firm's or individual's financial assets. The role of a custodian in such a case would be the following: to hold in safe keeping assets, such as equities and bonds; to arrange settlement of any purchases and sales of such securities; to collect information on and income from such assets (dividends in the case of equities and interest in the case of bonds); to provide information on the underlying companies and their annual general meetings; to manage cash transactions; to perform foreign exchange transactions where required; and to provide regular reporting on all their activities to their clients.

Cyber-Espionage

The theft of valuable information about products, services, patents, designs and other intellectual property, when it is facilitated by hacking or other forms of computer crime.

Dark Pools

'Dark pools' is the name given to applications and trading platforms that allow traders to buy or sell large orders without running the risk that other traders will work out what is going on and put the price up, or down, to take advantage of the order. They have been criticised for their lack of transparency and because the inevitable fragmentation of trading could lead to less efficient pricing in traditional open stock exchanges.

Dashboard

A digital dashboard, also known as an enterprise dashboard or executive dashboard, is a business management tool used to ascertain the status (or 'health') of a business enterprise through visual key business indicators. Digital dashboards use visual, at-a-glance displays of data pulled from disparate business systems to provide warnings, action notices, next steps and summaries of business conditions.

Data Dictionary

A centralised repository of information about data such as meaning, relationships to other data, origin, usage, and format.

Data Protection Act 1998

This Act details how personal data should be managed to protect its integrity and to protect the rights of the persons concerned.

Data Replication

The process of sharing information so as to ensure consistency between redundant resources, such as software or hardware components, to improve reliability, fault-tolerance or accessibility.

Deliverable

The physical outcome of a task resulting from applying defined processes to a set of inputs. A deliverable is a measurable, tangible, verifiable item produced as part of a project.

Delivery versus Payment (DvP)

The simultaneous and irrevocable delivery of securities by a seller and payment of sale proceeds by a purchaser of securities on settlement date.

Depot

The account with a settlement agent which is used to record transactions and balances in security quantities.

Derivative Instrument

A financial contract whose value depends upon the value of an underlying instrument or asset (typically a commodity, bond, equity or currency, or a combination of these). Three classes of financial products fall under the heading of derivatives: derivative securities; exchange-traded derivatives; and over-the-counter (OTC) derivatives.

Designated Investment Exchange (DIE)

An overseas exchange that does not carry on a regulated activity in the UK and is not a regulated market. Overseas exchanges may apply to the FSA to be included on the FSA's list of designated investment exchanges.

Deutsche Börse Group

Owner and operator of the Frankfurt Stock Exchange, as well as Clearstream and the Eurex derivatives exchange.

Digital Certificate

An electronic 'credit card' that establishes your credentials when doing business or other transactions on the web. It is issued by a certification authority (CA). It contains your name, a serial number, expiration date, a copy of the certificate holder's public key (used for encrypting messages and digital signatures) and the digital signature of the certificate-issuing authority so that a recipient can verify that the certificate is real.

Direct Market Access

The automated process of routing a securities order directly to an execution venue, therefore avoiding intervention by a third party. Execution venues include exchanges, alternative trading systems and electronic communication networks.

Disintermediation

The elimination of intermediaries in the supply chain; also referred to as 'cutting out the middle men'.

Disruptive Innovation

An innovative technology which improves a product or service in ways that the market does not expect, typically by lowering price or designing for a different set of consumers.

Distributed Denial of Service (DDoS) Attack

A denial-of-service attack (DoS attack) or distributed denial-of-service attack (DDoS attack) is an attempt (usually by criminals) to make a computer or network resource unavailable to its intended users.

Distributed System

A configuration which contains a number of hardware elements which are connected by some transmission technology.

Dodd-Frank

The Dodd-Frank Wall Street Reform and Consumer Protection Act is a United States law that was signed in July 2010 and will be implemented in stages beginning in 2012. It is the most significant change to financial regulation in the United States since the 1930s. Dodd-Frank's consequences include the requirements for Legal Entity Identifiers (LEIs) and trade repositories.

DvP or DVP

See *Delivery versus Payment*.

Economic and Monetary Union (EMU)

On 1 January 1999, the euro became the official currency for eleven participating countries in the European Union (EU). In 2001, Greece also adopted the euro as its official currency. From that date forward, the respective foreign exchange operations, new public debt and all stocks and bonds on all stock exchanges in the participating member areas were quoted or issued in euros. Euro banknotes were first made available three years later. The euro is now used by 17 EU member states.

End-User Development

A methodology to manage the designing and building of software applications.

Equity

Ownership interest in a corporation in the form of common or preferred stocks or shares.

Euroclear Bank

An ICSD for the international bond market.

Euroclear UK & Ireland Limited (EUI)

The central securities depository for the UK and Ireland.

Euronext

Owner and operator of the Amsterdam, Brussels, Lisbon and Paris stock exchanges, as well as the NYSE Liffe futures exchange in London. Part of the New York Stock Exchange (NYSE) group.

EUROSETS

A trading system operated by the London Stock Exchange (LSE).

European Markets Infrastructure Regulations (EMIR)

A set of regulations for the European Economic Area that is being finalised in 2012.

European Securities Markets Authority (ESMA)

An independent EU regulator that contributes to safeguarding the stability of the EU's financial system by ensuring the integrity, transparency, efficiency and orderly functioning of securities markets, as well as enhancing investor protection.

Financial Conduct Authority (FCA)

A UK regulator that took over the business conduct regulatory activities of the Financial Services Authority in 2013. The FCA focuses on regulation of all firms in retail and wholesale financial markets, as well as the infrastructure that supports these markets. In effect it has responsibility for firms that do not fall under the scope of the Prudential Regulatory Authority (PRA) (approximately 25,000 firms). The FCA's role includes supervision of investment exchanges and monitoring firms' compliance with the Market Abuse Directive, with powers to investigate and prosecute insider dealing.

Financial Control Department (FCD)

The department of the securities firm that is responsible for managing the financial resources of the business.

Financial Policy Committee (FPC)

A committee established within the Bank of England, with responsibility for 'macro-prudential' regulation, or regulation of the stability and resilience of the financial system as a whole. This committee works alongside the two UK regulators, the Prudential Regulatory Authority (PRA) and the Financial Conduct Authority (FCA).

Financial Services and Markets Act 2000 (FSMA)

The Financial Services and Markets Act 2000 introduced a new structure for the regulation of the financial services industry in the UK which came into effect from midnight on 30 November 2001. It established a new regulatory regime, empowering the Financial Services Authority (FSA) with broad responsibility for both the prudential and business conduct regulation of firms within the financial services industry.

Financial Services Authority (FSA)

Between 2001 and 2012, the FSA was the sole UK regulator for the financial services industry. In 2013 the FSA was superseded by two new regulators, the Prudential Regulation Authority (PRA) and the Financial Conduct Authority (FCA).

FIX Protocol

The Financial Interface eXchange (FIX) protocol was initiated in 1992 by a group of institutions and brokers interested in streamlining their trading processes. It is an open message standard controlled by no single entity, that can be structured to match the business requirements of each firm.

Foreign Account Tax Compliance Act (FATCA)

An act passed by the United States government in 2010 designed to combat tax evasion by US persons holding investments in offshore accounts.

Follow-the-Sun Model

A method of running a help desk where an incident that is reported during one time zone will continue to be worked on and handed over to others around the clock until it is resolved ready for the requestor to sign off and close on their return to the office.

Foreign Exchange

The simultaneous buying of one currency and selling of another, either for spot (ie, immediate) settlement, or for forward settlement (ie, settlement at a later date).

Foreign Financial Institution (FFI)

An organisation such as a securities or investment firm that, while not a resident of the United States, still has to comply with certain regulations of the US Foreign Accounts Tax Compliance Act (FATCA).

Fountain Model

A methodology to manage the designing and building of software applications.

FpML (Financial products Markup Language)

An XML message standard for the OTC derivatives industry.

Free of Payment (FoP)

A term used in a settlement instruction where the movement of cash and the movement of securities are NOT inextricably linked to one another. In other words, FoP is the opposite of Delivery-versus-Payment (DvP).

Future or Futures Contract

A standardised, transferable, exchange-traded contract that requires delivery of an asset, commodity, bond, share, currency or stock index (the underlying instrument), at a specified price, on a specified future date.

General Clearing Member (GCM)

A futures and options exchange member that is also a member of the exchange's clearing house, and which clears trades done by other exchange members, who are known as non-clearing members.

General Ledger

The general ledger, sometimes known as the nominal ledger, is the main accounting record of a business which uses the double-entry book keeping convention. It will usually include accounts for such items as current assets, fixed assets, liabilities, revenue and expense items, gains and losses.

Hacking

The process of gaining unauthorised access to computer systems for the purpose of stealing and/or corrupting data.

Hedging

The purchase or sale of a commodity, security or other financial instrument for the purpose of offsetting the profit or loss of another security or investment. Thus, any loss on the original investment will be hedged, or offset, by a corresponding profit from the hedging instrument.

Help Desk

A section of the IT department that takes requests from users to deal with systems problems and/ or out-of-the-ordinary requests, logs them, prioritises them, and hands them on to the appropriate individuals for action.

HM Revenue & Customs (HMRC)

The tax-collecting agency of the UK government.

Hybrid System

A stock exchange trading system that uses both an order queue and market makers.

Identity Fraud

The process of stealing personal information so that the criminal is able to pose as the person or organisation whose identity has been stolen.

Innovation Outsourcing

The development of new business applications by an outsource provider.

Insider Dealing

Illegal share dealings by employees or directors of a company where they have used confidential price-sensitive information for their own gain or for the gain of their associates.

Insourcing

Insourcing (internal outsourcing) occurs where a company sets up an operation to carry out work that would otherwise have been contracted out.

It usually implies the centralisation of a service that would have previously been decentralised, and may also imply that the insourced service is now provided offshore.

Internal Revenue Service (IRS)

The tax-collecting agency of the US government,

International Capital Markets Association (ICMA)

A Swiss-based organisation with the status of a designated investment exchange in the UK. The ICMA promotes by-laws, statutes, rules and recommendations for market practices in the bond markets.

International Central Securities Depository (ICSD)

See *Central Securities Depository*.

International Organization for Standardization (ISO)

A United Nations-sponsored organisation that sets international standards that can be used in any type of business, which are accepted around the world as proof that a business can provide assured quality.

Investment Exchange

A corporation or mutual organisation which provides facilities for brokers and traders to trade company stocks and other securities, including bonds, derivatives and physical commodities such as precious metals and agricultural products.

Investment Services Directive (ISD)

A European Commission Directive issued in 1993. It specified that, if a firm had been authorised by one member state to provide investment services, then this single authorisation enabled the firm to provide those same investment services via a 'passport' in other member states without further authorisation. The originating state providing authorisation is commonly referred to as the 'home' state, whereas other states where investment services are offered are known as 'host' states. MiFID superseded the ISD in November 2007.

IP Protocol

The internet protocol suite is the set of communications protocols that implement the protocol stack on which the internet runs. It is sometimes called the TCP/IP protocol suite, after the two most important protocols in it: the Transmission Control Protocol (TCP) and the Internet Protocol (IP), which were also contained within the first two defined.

ISDA

The International Swaps and Derivatives Association.

ISDA Master Agreement

A standardised contract (drafted by ISDA) to enter into OTC derivatives transactions. This means it contains general terms and conditions (such as provisions relating to payment netting, tax gross-up, tax representations, basic corporate representations, basic covenants, events of default and termination) but does not, by itself, include details of any specific derivatives transactions the parties may enter into. The ISDA Master Agreement is a pre-printed form which will not be amended itself (save for writing in the names of the parties on the front and signature pages). However, it also has a manually produced schedule in which the parties are required to select certain options and may modify sections of the Master Agreement if desired.

ISIN

The International Securities Identification number, a code that represents, for example, Sony Corporation ordinary shares. If the security is listed on more than one exchange, there is only one ISIN code. Most custodians and clearing houses identify securities by the ISIN code on messages.

ISO28000

A methodology to manage projects of any kind, including those related to software development and implementation.

IT Infrastructure Library (ITIL)

The ITIL was created by the UK government to act as a standard for best practice in the provision of IT service. It is a methodology that has been embraced by the securities industry as well as other scrutinised institutions such as the government and listed companies.

Iterative/Incremental

A methodology to manage the designing and building of software applications.

Joint Application Development (JAD)

A methodology to manage the designing and building of software applications.

Key Performance Indicators

Critical items in a Service Level Agreement (SLA) that are capable of being measured.

LCH.Clearnet Limited

A recognised clearing house that operates central counterparty services for a number of exchanges and markets, including the LSE and LME.

Liabilities

All the claims against a corporation. Liabilities include accounts, wages and salaries payable; dividends declared payable; accrued taxes payable; and fixed or long-term liabilities, such as mortgage bonds, debentures and bank loans.

LIFFE CONNECT®

A trading system operated by NYSE Liffe.

London Stock Exchange (LSE)

The largest formal market for securities in the UK; the LSE facilitates deals in equities, bonds and some derivatives such as exchange-traded funds and covered warrants.

Long Position

See *Position*.

MA-CUG
(Member Administered Closed User Groups)

Companies not eligible for the Standardised Corporate Environment (SCORE) model can join SWIFT by registering in a closed user group set up and managed by their financial institution (ie, the financial institution elects which customers can participate). Within the MA-CUG, a corporate can communicate only with its bank, which decides which kinds of messages and files (payments, treasury, reporting, securities) can be exchanged. If a corporate wishes to communicate with several banks it can register in multiple MA-CUGs, resulting in similar multi-banking capabilities as SCORE.

Malware

Malware (short for malicious software) is software which is designed to gain surreptitious access to computer systems in order to disrupt normal operation or gather private information that may be used illegally.

Margin

The cash or collateral that a holder of a position in securities or in exchange-traded derivatives is required to post to cover potential adverse movements in the value of the position.

Mark-to-Market (MTM)

An accounting procedure by which assets are 'marked', or recorded, at their current market value, which may be higher or lower than their purchase price or book value.

Market Abuse

An offence introduced by FSMA 2000 judged on what a 'regular user' would view as a failure to observe the required standards. The offence includes abuse of information, misleading the market and distortion of the market.

Market Maker

A sell-side firm that has accepted the obligation to quote both a buy and a sell price in a financial instrument or commodity, hoping to make a profit on the turn or the bid/offer spread.

Markit BOAT

A new venture launched in 2006 to provide regulatory trade reporting and data services for participants as a result of MiFID. Now owned by Markit and entitled Markit BOAT.

Matching Engine

A form of trade agreement where both parties input their trade details to the matching engine database. The matching engine then compares the two trade reports and provides them to both parties in real time.

Maturity Ladder

A form of cash flow projection.

MiFID

The Markets in Financial Instruments Directive (MiFID) introduced a single market and regulatory regime for investment services across the member states of the EEA in 2007.

Milestone

A significant event in a project, usually completion of a major deliverable, at a given point in time.

Money Laundering

The process of turning 'dirty' money (money derived from criminal activities) into 'clean' money (money that appears to be legitimate).

Multilateral Trading Facility (MTF)

A term introduced by MiFID which describes a system that brings together multiple parties that are interested in buying and selling financial instruments, and enables them to do so.

Near-Shoring

A form of offshoring where the business process is relocated to lower-cost foreign locations but these locations are in close geographical proximity to the customer's country of business.

Nominal Ledger

See *General Ledger*.

Nominal Owner

A person or group that holds title to a security or piece of real estate but is not the true beneficial owner.

Non-Clearing Member

A firm that is a member of a futures and options exchange but not its associated clearing house. The non-clearing member relies on general clearing members to clear its trades on the relevant exchanges.

Non-Disclosure Agreement (NDA)

A legal contract between the parties that outlines confidential materials or knowledge which the parties wish to share with one another for certain purposes but wish to restrict from generalised use. In other words it is a contract through which the parties agree not to disclose information covered by the agreement. An NDA creates a confidential relationship between the parties to protect any type of trade secret.

Nostro

The account with a settlement agent which is used to record transactions and balances in cash amounts. Nostro means 'our account with you'.

Novation

The substitution of one party to a contract by another party; in particular novation occurs at the point when the central counterparty assumes the responsibility to settle a trade.

Objective

A concise statement (or statements) of what a project is to achieve.

Offer Price

The lowest price acceptable to a prospective seller of a specific security. The highest bid and lowest offer are quoted on most major exchanges; and the difference between the two prices is called the 'spread'.

Offshoring

Offshoring is defined as the movement of a business process performed by a company in one country to the same or another company in another, different country. Almost always work is moved to benefit from the lower cost of operations in the new location.

Operational Risk

The risk of loss resulting from inadequate or failed internal processes, people and systems or from external events.

Option or Options Contract

A call option gives the buyer (or holder) the right (but NOT the obligation) to purchase the underlying instrument at a specified price on or before a given date. A put option on the other hand gives the buyer (or holder) the right (but NOT the obligation) to sell the underlying instrument at a specified price on or before a given date.

Order-Driven System

An exchange trading system that does not rely on market makers. A member firm who wishes to buy a given financial instrument at a given price submits an order to the system, while at the same time other member firms who wish to sell submit sell orders to the system.

OTC (Over-the-Counter) Market

A decentralised market for financial instruments not listed on an exchange where market participants trade over the telephone, fax or electronic network. There is no central exchange providing a trading system. CCPs, however, may exist.

Outsourcing

The delegation of non-core operations from internal production to an external entity specialising in the management of that operation.

Phishing

A type of cybercrime designed to trick computer users into disclosing personal financial details.

Planning for Procurement

The process of identifying what, if any, parts of a project or delivery should be obtained from resources outside the organisation.

Platform

An online service designed to enable both financial advisers and retail investors to manage their investment portfolios.

Portfolio

In the context of software development, a portfolio is a suite of projects being undertaken by a function. In the context of investment management, a portfolio is a collection of investments held by an institution or a private individual. The term is sometimes also used as an alternative to 'book' or 'trading book'.

Position

The net total of all the purchases of a security, less all the sales of the same security. When the position is positive it is said to be a 'long' position, when it is negative it is said to be a 'short' position. Sometimes this term is used interchangeably with 'book' or 'trading book'.

Primary Market

The process of bringing securities to the market and raising funds for the issuer.

PRINCE

A methodology to manage projects of any kind, including those related to software development and implementation.

Production Outsourcing

The maintenance and support of IT applications that have already been developed.

Programme

A group of projects that is managed together.

Project

A set of inter-related and controlled activities, with start and finish dates, undertaken to achieve a unique objective conforming to specific requirements, including the restraints of time, cost and resources.

Project Brief

A document produced in the early stages of a project that describes, in outline, what the project is attempting to achieve and the business justification for doing it.

Project Management

The discipline of organising and managing resources (eg, people) in such a way that the project is completed within defined scope, quality, time and cost constraints.

Project Management Institute (PMI)

Similar to PRINCE, another methodology to manage projects of any kind, including those related to software development and implementation.

Project Manager

The individual responsible for delivering a project.

Project Sponsor

Normally, the senior executive that instigated a business change and who is responsible to the business for the success of a project. See also *Senior Responsible Owner*.

Prudential Regulation Authority (PRA)

Since 2013, the Prudential Regulation Authority (PRA) has been the UK regulator responsible for prudential regulation of financial firms that manage significant risks on their balance sheets – in other words, it will be responsible for the regulation and supervision of 'significant' individual firms including all deposit-taking institutions, insurers and other prudentially significant firms.

PTM Levy

A charge automatically imposed on investors, and collected by their brokers, when they sell or buy shares with an aggregate value in excess of £10,000. The charge is £1, and the money raised goes to finance the Panel on Takeovers and Mergers (PTM).

Put Option

See *Option*.

Quote-Driven Systems

A stock exchange trading system where some of the exchange's member firms take on the obligation of always making a two-way price in each of the stocks in which they make markets. These firms are, therefore known as 'market makers'.

Rapid Application Development (RAD)

A methodology to manage the designing and building of software applications.

Realised P&L

Profit and loss that arises as a result of selling securities and other assets.

Recognised Clearing House (RCH)

A clearing house that is recognised as such by the FSA.

Recognised Investment Exchange (RIE)

An investment exchange in the UK that is recognised by the FSA.

Recognised Overseas Investment Exchange (ROIE)

An investment exchange located outside the UK that admits UK firms as members and is recognised by the FSA.

Reference Data

Information about the firm, its trading parties, clients and the instruments it trades. Alternatively defined as the store of information that is used to determine the appropriate actions necessary to ensure successful processing of a trade. Also known as **static data**.

Reference Data Repository

A system that consolidates the firm's view of reference data and feeds it to all the other systems in the configuration.

Regulatory Trade Reporting

Broker-dealers authorised by the FSA have an obligation to report all trades executed by them to the FSA.

Relational Database

A collection of data items organised as a set of formally described tables from which data can be accessed or reassembled in many different ways without having to reorganise the database tables.

Repo

Repos – sale and repurchase agreements – are transactions where Party A lends money to Party B providing that Party B provides Party A with collateral in the form of government bonds.

Request for Proposal (RFP)

A request for proposal (referred to as an RFP) is an invitation for suppliers, through a bidding process, to bid on a specific product or service. An RFP is usually part of a complex sales process, also known as 'enterprise sales'.

Sale and Repurchase Agreement

See *Repo*.

Scamming

A low-tech alternative to phishing, it is usually carried out by phone. The caller simply invents a plausible story to persuade the recipient to disclose confidential information that belongs to either the target itself or to customers of the target.

SCORE

The Standardised Corporate Environment (SCORE) is based on a closed user group, administered by SWIFT, where corporates can interact with any number of financial institutions with whom they have a relationship.

Secondary Market

The marketplace for trading in existing securities.

Securities

Equities and Bonds.

SEDOL Code

SEDOL stands for Stock Exchange Daily Official List, a list of security identifiers used in the UK and Ireland for clearing purposes. The codes are assigned by the London Stock Exchange, on request by the security issuer. SEDOLs serve as the ISIN for all securities issued in the UK and are, therefore, part of the security's ISIN as well. Although SEDOL was to have been superseded by ISIN, problems with the ISIN system have since forced a reversal of this decision. In particular, a single ISIN is used to identify the shares of a company no matter what exchange it is being traded on, making it impossible to specify a trade on a particular exchange or currency. For instance, until 2009 DaimlerChrysler shares were traded on 22 different exchanges worldwide, and priced in five different currencies. An expanded ISIN standard is currently being formulated to address this problem.

Sell-Side Firms

Investment banks and stock exchange firms that execute orders on behalf of investors.

Senior Responsible Owner (SRO)

The executive responsible for ensuring that a project or programme of change meets its objectives and delivers the projected benefits. See also *Project Sponsor*.

Service Level Agreement (SLA)

A service level agreement (SLA) is that part of a service contract in which a certain level of service is agreed upon. Level of service in this context refers to both the quality of the service and the time deadlines for performing the service. It may also specify penalties to be paid by either party if the level of service provided fails to reach the minimum standards in the agreement for an extended period of time.

Service Level Management (SLM)

Definition of a service catalogue; identifying, negotiating, monitoring and reviewing service level agreements (SLAs).

Settle within Tolerance

In determining whether instructions match, the settlement agent usually has the ability to 'settle within tolerance'. That is to say, that if the instructions match in every respect apart from a minor difference in the cash consideration, then the agent will settle the trade using the cash figure supplied by the seller.

Settlement Agents

CSDs, ICSDs and custodian banks may be collectively referred to as 'settlement agents'.

Settlement Date

The date that a deal actually does settle, as distinct from value date, which is the date upon which it should settle.

Shareholders' Equity

Assets less liabilities.

Short Position

See *Position*.

Software as a Service

See *Cloud Computing*.

Software Development Life Cycle (SDLC)

A process of developing information systems or applications through the completion of defined steps or phases.

Software Maintenance

Software maintenance is an ongoing process, and it includes the continuing support of end users, the correction of errors and updates of the software over time.

SPAN

Standard Portfolio Analysis of Risk (SPAN) is a system for calculating initial margin requirements for futures and options on futures. It was developed by the Chicago Mercantile Exchange in 1988. SPAN is a portfolio margining method that uses grid simulation. It calculates the likely loss in a set of derivative positions (also called a portfolio) and sets this value as the initial margin payable by the firm holding the portfolio. In this manner, SPAN provides for offsets between correlated positions and enhances margining efficiency.

Spiral Model

A methodology to manage the designing and building of software applications.

Spread

The difference between the bid and offer prices.

Static Data

See *Reference Data*.

Stamp Duty

A UK tax payable by buyers (but not sellers) of most equity shares listed on the UK markets.

Standard Settlement Instructions (SSIs)

Reference data that provides details of the settlement agents used by both the firm and its clients.

Stock Exchange

See *Investment Exchange*.

Stock Exchange Automated Quotations (SEAQ)

A trading system operated by the LSE.

Stock Exchange Electronic Trading System (SETS)

A trading system operated by the London Stock Exchange. See also *SETSqx*.

Stock Lending

The process of the lending of securities by one party to another. The terms of the loan will be governed by a 'Securities Lending Agreement' which requires that the borrower provides the lender with collateral, in the form of cash, other securities or a letter of credit of value equal to or greater than the loaned securities. As payment for the loan, the parties negotiate a fee, quoted as an annualised percentage of the value of the loaned securities. If the agreed form of collateral is cash, then the fee may be quoted as a 'rebate', meaning that the lender will earn all of the interest which accrues on the cash collateral, and will 'rebate' an agreed rate of interest to the borrower.

Stock Lending Intermediary (SLI)

A specialist intermediary that provides liquidity to the stock lending and repo markets.

Stock Record

A system of double-entry book-keeping that accounts on one side for the ownership of securities, and on the other side for the location of the stock.

Structured Query Language (SQL)

The standard user and application program interface to a relational database.

Straight-Through Processing (STP)

Working practices and systems that enable transactions to move seamlessly through the processing cycle, without manual intervention or redundant handling.

Swaps

Derivative products that are used to alter the exposure of investment portfolios, or any series of cash flows. The most common kind of swap is an interest rate swap.

SWIFT

The Society for Worldwide Interbank Financial Telecommunication (SWIFT) is an industry-owned utility that operates a secure telecommunications network, and also designs message standards for communications between market players.

SWIFT Gateway

A term used to describe software applications that are used to access the SWIFT network and which have SWIFTNet Link embedded within them.

SWIFTAlliance

A SWIFT Gateway product supplied by SWIFT.

SWIFTNet Link

A suite of software products, developed by SWIFT that ensures technical interoperability between SWIFT users by providing the minimal functionality required to communicate over these services. It is supplied both to SWIFT member firms directly, and also to software vendors who are able to embed it in their own products.

SWIFTNet PKI

The security component of SWIFTNet Link that uses digital certificates to provide the highest levels of authentication of institutions, end-users and servers.

Systematic Internaliser

Under MiFID rules, a firm that executes orders from its clients against its own book, or against orders from other clients.

Trade Agreement

The processes of trade confirmation, affirmation and allocation.

Trade Date

The date that a deal is carried out.

Trading Book

See *Book*.

Trojan virus

A Trojan, or Trojan horse virus, is a computer program that appears to be legitimate but it actually results in unauthorised access to the victim computer's files.

Underlying Instrument

An underlying instrument is a security (such as a stock) or other type of financial product (such as a stock index or a commodity/asset) whose value determines the value of a derivative investment or product. For example, if you own a stock option, the stock you have the right to buy or sell according to the terms of that option is the option's underlying instrument. Underlying instruments may also be called underlying product, underlying interest, underlying investment or the cash instrument.

Unrealised P&L

Profit & loss (P&L) that arises as a result of the mark-to-market process.

Value at Risk (VaR)

Value at risk is a measure of how the market value of an asset or of a portfolio of assets is likely to decrease over a certain time period (usually over one day or ten days) under usual conditions. It is typically used by securities trading houses or investment banks to measure the market risk of their asset portfolios (market value at risk), but is actually a very general concept that has broad application.

Value Date

The date that a deal is expected to settle, ie, the date that the seller delivers securities and the buyer pays for them.

Virus

See Computer Virus

Waterfall Model

A methodology to manage the designing and building of software applications.

XBRL

Extensible Business Reporting Language. An XML message standard for exchanging information about corporate data such as balance sheets and profit and loss accounts between the company concerned and its auditors, regulators, customers, research analysts and other interested parties.

XML

A flexible way to create common information formats and share both the format and the data on the world wide web, intranets, and elsewhere. XML is a formal recommendation from the World Wide Web Consortium (W3C) similar to the language of today's web pages, the Hypertext Markup Language (HTML).

ABBREVIATIONS

AMA	Advanced Measurement Approach (Basel II)		**DDoS**	Distributed Denial of Service (attacks)
API	Application Programming Interface		**DEX**	Data Exchange Manual
BAU	Business as Usual		**DEX**	Data Exchange Manual
BCBS	Basel Committee on Banking Supervision		**DIE**	Designated Investment Exchange
BCP	Business Continuity Planning		**DMA**	Direct Market Access
BIC	Bank Identifier Code		**DR**	Disaster Recovery
BIS	Bank for International Settlements		**DRP**	Disaster Recovery Plan
CCTA	Central Computer and Telecommunications Agency		**DvP**	Delivery-versus-Payment
CD	Certificate of Deposit		**ECN**	Electronic Communication Network
CDR	Committed Data Rate		**EEA**	European Economic Area
CFD	Contract for Difference		**EMU**	European Monetary Union
CGT	Capital Gains Tax		**ETC**	Electronic Trade Confirmation
CJA	Criminal Justice Act 1993		**EU**	European Union
CLS	Continuous Linked Settlement		**EUD**	End-User Development
CP	Consultation Paper		**FCA**	Financial Conduct Authority
CCP	Central Counterparty		**FCD**	Financial Control Department
CRD	Capital Requirements Directive		**FIFO**	First-In-First-Out
CRM	Customer Relationship Management		**FIX**	Financial Interface eXchange
CSD	Central Securities Depository		**FoP**	Free of Payment
CTB	Change the Bank		**FpML**	Financial Products Markup Language
DBV	Deliveries by Value		**FSA**	Financial Services Authority
DoS	Denial of Service (attacks)		**FSAP**	Financial Services Action Plan
			FSMA	Financial Services and Markets Act 2000
			FTP	File Transfer Protocol

GCM	General Clearing Member		**KYC**	Know Your Customer
GSTPA	Global Straight-Through Processing Association		**LEI**	Legal Entity Identifier
HTML	Hypertext Markup Language		**LIFO**	Last-In-First-Out
HR	Human Resources		**LME**	London Metal Exchange
ICSD	International Central Securities Depository		**LSE**	London Stock Exchange
ICMA	International Capital Markets Association		**MA-CUG**	Member-Administered Closed User Groups
IP	Internet Protocol		**MiFID**	Markets in Financial Instruments Directive
IPO	Initial Public Offer		**MIS**	Management Information Systems
ISA	Individual Savings Account		**MTF**	Multilateral Trading Facility
ISD	Investment Services Directive or Intended Settlement Date		**NASSCOM**	National Association of Software and Services Companies (India)
ISDA	International Swaps and Derivatives Association		**NCM**	Non-Clearing Member
ISIN	International Securities Identification Number		**NDA**	Non-Disclosure Agreement
			NYSE	New York Stock Exchange
ISLA	International Securities Lending Association		**OGC**	Office of Government Commerce
ISO	International Organization for Standardization		**OTC**	Over-the-Counter
			P&L	Profit & Loss
IT	Information Technology		**PCAOB**	Public Company Accounting Oversight Board
ITIL	Information Technology Infrastructure Library		**PDCA**	Plan-Do-Check-Act
JAD	Joint Application Development		**PKI**	Public Key Infrastructure
JMLSG	Joint Money Laundering Steering Group		**PMI**	Project Management Institute
			POCA	Proceeds of Crime Act 2002
JRD	Joint Requirements Development		**PRA**	Prudential Regulation Authority
KPI	Key Performance Indicator		**PRINCE**	Projects in Controlled Environments

PTM	Panel on Takeovers and Mergers	**SOW**	Statement of Work
RAD	Rapid Application Development	**SOX/Sarbox**	Sarbanes-Oxley
RCH	Recognised Clearing House	**SPAN**	Standardised Portfolio Analysis of Risk
RFI	Request for Information	**SQL**	Structured Query Language
RFP	Request for Proposal	**SSI**	Standard Settlement Instructions
RIC	Thomson Reuters Instrument Code	**STP**	Straight-Through Processing
RIE	Recognised Investment Exchange	**SUT**	System Under Test
ROIE	Recognised Overseas Investment Exchange	**SWIFT**	Society for Worldwide Interbank Financial Telecommunication
SC4	Securities and Related Financial Instruments Sub-Committee	**SYSC**	Systems and Controls
		TCP	Transmission Control Protocol
SCM	Software Configuration Management	**TCP/IP**	Transmission Control Protocol/ Internet Protocol
SCORE	Standardised Corporate Environment		
SDLC	Software Development Life Cycle	**TFM**	Transaction Flow Monitor (from ESTPA)
SDRT	Stamp Duty Reserve Tax	**TPS**	Transactions Per Second
SEC	Securities Exchange Commission (US)		
SEDOL	Stock Exchange Daily Official List	**TWIST**	Transaction Workflow Innovation Standards Team
SLA	Service Level Agreement, or Securities Lending Agreement	**UAT**	User Acceptance Testing
		VaR	Value-at-Risk
SLI	Specialised Lending Intermediary	**W3C**	World Wide Web Consortium
SLM	Service Level Management		
		WG4	Working Group Four
SMPG	Securities Market Practice Group		
		XBRL	Extensible Business Reporting Language
SOCPA	Serious Organised Crime and Police Act 2005		

Multiple Choice Questions

Multiple Choice Questions

The following additional questions have been compiled to reflect as closely as possible the examination standard you will experience in your examination. Please note, however, they are not the CISI examination questions themselves.

Tick one answer for each question. When you have completed all questions, refer to the end of this section for the answers.

1. Which of the following statements most accurately describes the purpose of a Maturity Ladder?
    A. It provides the firm with a cash flow projection for the following business day
    B. It tells them whether they should use stock loans or repos to attract funding
    C. It tells them which bank accounts are currently overdrawn
    D. It provides the firm with information that shows them how much funding they need, or the excess funds that are available at each individual nostro account

2. When a sell-side firm acts as principal, its revenue consists of:
    A. Commission
    B. The difference between the buying price and the selling price
    C. A specially negotiated fee
    D. A fixed percentage of the deal value

3. Which of the following statements best describes a stock lending transaction?
    A. A transaction where Party A lends money to Party B, providing that Party B provides Party A with collateral in the form of government bonds.
    B. A transaction where Party A lends securities to Party B, providing that Party B supplies Party A with collateral in the form of cash, other securities or a letter of credit.
    C. A transaction where one party lends or borrows securities from a specialised stock-lending intermediary
    D. A transaction where a market maker instructs Euroclear to make a delivery by value

4. Which of the following is a form of iterative/incremental software development?
    A. Waterfall model
    B. End user development
    C. Fountain model
    D. Agile model

5. Which of the following is a statutory objective of the Financial Conduct Authority?

    A. Promote the safety and soundness of the firms that it regulates

    B. For insurers, to contribute to the securing of an appropriate degree of protection for policyholders

    C. Ensuring that investors do not lose money

    D. Ensuring that the financial markets function well

6. Mark-to-market is?

    A. A measure of how the market value of an asset or of a portfolio of assets is likely to decrease over a certain time period

    B. The calculation of realised trading profit

    C. A method of calculating an investor's liability to capital gains tax

    D. A method of recording the value of assets at their current market value

7. With which element of IT performance would you associate the following risks: duplication, delivery risk, complexity risk, 'scope creep'?

    A. Maintaining business as usual

    B. Disaster recovery

    C. Database management

    D. Introducing business change

8. Data proximity is a concern that many firms have about cloud computing. Data proximity means that:

    A. The firm's data may be held on the same premises as that of a competitor

    B. The firm does not know where the data is held

    C. The firm's data may be held on the same database as that of a competitor

    D. The firm is unable to tell its regulator where its data is held

9. A sell-side firm is obliged by which regulations to have in place a 'best execution' policy in relation to trades undertaken for its clients?

    A. Pillar I of Basel II

    B. MiFID   MiFID III NEW

    C. The Capital Adequacy Directive

    D. Pillar III of Basel II

10. DaimlerChrysler shares are listed on stock exchanges in seven countries. How many ISIN codes are allocated to DaimlerChrysler shares?

    A. One
    B. Seven
    C. Four
    D. Three

11. Which ONE of the following is a wholesale market activity associated with an investment bank?

    A. Execution-only stockbroking
    B. Life assurance
    C. Mergers and acquisitions
    D. Private banking

12. Why would a firm implement a Reference Data Repository?

    A. To allow clients to access their own records
    B. To be able to use a matching engine
    C. To cut software development and maintenance costs
    D. To ensure consistency of data across applications

13. What role does a matching engine play in the trade agreement process?

    A. It sends a confirmation of each trade to a retail investor so they can match the details to their own records
    B. It matches the details of an OTC trade agreement with the standard ISDA Master Agreement
    C. It matches transactions and balances in the depot account with those in the nostro account
    D. It matches the details reported by the two parties to a trade made on an investment exchange

14. Financial products Markup Language is:

    A. An XML message standard for the financial sector
    B. A message standard for the OTC derivatives industry
    C. An XML message standard for the OTC derivatives industry
    D. A new SWIFT message standard for the OTC derivatives Industry

15. Pillar I of Basel II calculates a firm's minimum overall capital ratio as the capital requirement divided by the sum of its exposure to which three risks?

    A. Operational + market + credit
    B. Market + credit + systemic
    C. Operational + market + systemic
    D. Market + credit + liquidity

16. You have made the decision to outsource the development of a new business application. Which of the following is likely to be the most suitable method of outsourcing this work?

    A. Near-shoring
    B. Inshoring
    C. Offshoring
    D. Best-shoring

17. Which of these items is not contained in the header message of a SWIFT FIN (MT series) message?

    A. The first transaction record
    B. The destination BIC code
    C. The sender's BIC code
    D. The message type

18. The source code for a particular application cannot be found. Which of the following techniques have been developed to prevent this type of problem?

    A. Software development life cycle
    B. Change control methodology
    C. Availability management
    D. Service level management

19. User acceptance testing is carried out to ensure?

    A. That users understand how to use the new software
    B. That all defects are identified and, if there are defects, then these defects are acceptable to the user community
    C. That the software conforms to the agreed specifications without exception
    D. That the software will provide the necessary throughput rate

20. Which of the following is the ISO standard for software evaluation?

    A. ISO 9000
    B. ISO 9001   *PROJECT MANAGEMENT*
    C. ISO 9001:2000
    D. ISO 9126   *ISO 9126*

21. The term 'consideration' is used for both equity trades and bond trades. Bond trades have an extra component used in calculating the consideration, in addition to those relating to equity trades. What is this extra component?

    A. Maturity date
    B. Maturity value
    C. Trade currency
    D. Accrued interest

22. What is the minimum frequency of production of periodic statements of account for retail clients of an investment firm?

    A. Every three months

    B. Every six months   *SEMI ANNUAL*

    C. Annually

    D. As often as the client requests it

23. What is the main function of a trade repository?

    A. To collect records of OTC derivatives trades in order to provide regulators with information about firms' risk exposure

    B. To store records of securities trades in order that a regulator can periodically check firms' compliance with conduct of business regulations

    C. To fulfil the reporting and transparency requirements of multilateral trading facilities and broker crossing networks under MiFID

    D. To store records of all securities trades so that regulators can monitor the markets to rack insider dealing and other forms of market abuse

24. Which regulator has the responsibility to enhance the protection of investors and reinforce stable and well-functioning financial markets in the European Union?

    A. The Basel Committee

    B. The European Securities Markets Authority   *ESMA*

    C. The European System of Financial Supervision

    D. The European Banking Authority

25. When stock is loaned, the lender loses the ownership rights to which one of the following?

    A. Dividend proceeds

    B. Voting rights

    C. Corporate action proceeds

    D. Coupon proceeds

26. Which of the following items of information usually shown on a general ledger account report is NOT reference data about the account concerned?

    A. The name of the account

    B. The currency of the account

    C. The date of the opening balance of the account   *BALANCE INFO ITEM*

    D. A unique alphanumeric code that identifies the account

27. Which of the following services is NOT provided by LCH.Clearnet Ltd?

    A. Novation

    B. Central counterparty

    C. Management of credit risk

    D. Processing of corporate actions on behalf of members   *Custodians*

28. In an equity trade, the number of shares multiplied by the price of the share is known as the:

    A. Consideration

    B. Principal amount

    C. Trade quantity

    D. Trade extension

29. You are told that the price of a sterling-denominated bond is 87. Does this mean:

    A. £87 per bond

    B. £87 per £1000 face value of the bond

    C. 87 pence per bond

    D. 87% of face value

30. Market makers play a key role in which type of order-handling system within an investment exchange?

    A. Quote-driven system   *MM*

    B. Order-driven system

    C. Algorithmic trading system

    D. Multilateral trading facility

31. In relation to disaster recovery, what is 'log shipping'?

    A. An automated procedure for backing up databases on two servers in different locations

    B. An approach to maintaining system availability whereby all transactions are written to the production server and a standby server at different locations simultaneously

    C. Maintaining a spare server at a standby location that is configured similarly to the primary server and is running the same version of the operating system, database and application software, with all the same service packs applied

    D. A testing method aimed at determining the feasibility and compatibility of back-up facilities and procedures and ranking critical needs and functions

32. Regression testing is:

    A. A cursory examination of all of the basic components of a software system without reference to the internal workings to ensure that they hang together

    B. A technique of black box testing where the input values are set to the extreme ends of, and just outside of, the input domains to evaluate the cause and handling of errors during system functionality

C. A phase where the current functionality of the software is tested to ensure that any new changes have not caused an impact

D. A software testing technique where the inputs of a program are loaded with random data – if there are fails then possible defects have been identified

33. A firm that holds a position with a central counterparty is asked to supply collateral to the CCP when:

A. The market value of its positions with the CCP show potential losses

B. It starts to trade with a new counterparty

C. The market value of its positions with the CCP show potential profits

D. It develops a new interface to the CCP's systems

34. Which of the following is NOT an example of reference data?

A. Security name

B. Public holiday calendar   *STATIC FACTS*

C. Exchange rate to base currency

D. Base currency

35. Before a buy-side firm places an order, what must it ensure, in order to fulfil its requirement for what is known as 'pre-trade compliance'?

A. That the trade is in line with the firm's conflicts of interest policy

B. That full disclosure on fees, commissions and transaction charges has been made to the client

C. That the investment is compatible with the investor's time horizon and risk appetite

D. That the investment complies with MiFID requirements on best execution

36. Which of the following statements about the MT500 series of messages is true?

A. It deals with securities messages and is based on ISO 7775

B. It deals with foreign exchange and money market messages and is based on ISO 15022

C. It deals with foreign exchange and money market messages and is based on ISO 7775

D. It deals with securities messages and is based on ISO 15022

37. A firm wants to transfer personal data overseas. How does it ensure compliance with the Data Protection Act 1998?

A. Check whether the country has signed a reciprocal arrangement

B. Seek the views of the affected individuals on the proposed action

C. Ensure the country has an adequate level of protection for the data   *PRINCIPAL 8*

D. Categorise the sensitivity of the data before it is transferred

38. Which of the following trade agreement methods is normally used in the foreign exchange market?

    A. Use of a matching engine

    B. Confirmation, affirmation and allocation

    C. Mutual exchange of confirmations *FX/MM/OTC/SWAPS*

    D. SWIFT messaging

39. Structured Query Language is a programming language designed to: *SQL*

    A. Insert, update, delete or query data transmitted by a real-time messaging layer

    B. Insert, update, delete or query data held in a relational database

    C. Produce queries about unmatched items to ensure consistency in a distributed system

    D. Ensure consistency within a server network by improving fault tolerance and reliability

40. The Dodd-Frank Act of the United States required US regulated financial firms to report OTC derivative trades to trade repositories. Which item of European legislation imposes the same requirement on EEA regulated firms?

    A. The Foreign Account Tax Compliance Act (FATCA)

    B. The European Capital Adequacy Directive

    C. The Data Protection Act 1998

    D. The Sarbanes-Oxley Act 2002 ✓

41. Which of the following market practices is NOT designed to mitigate credit risk?

    A. EMIR

    B. MiFID *ALL MITIGATE RISK*

    C. MiFID II

    D. The Capital Requirements Directive *CRD*

42. Which of the following is the most accurate description of a digital 'dashboard'?

    A. A digital display of a business's profit and loss account

    B. A business management tool used to visually ascertain the status of a business enterprise by reporting on key performance indicators *KPIs*

    C. A digital display showing the value of a client's holdings

    D. A business management tool used to give a visual snapshot of the performance of servers and networks

43. The purpose of vendor management software packages is to:

    A. Plan meetings with vendors

    B. Automate the administration of contracts and centralise information

    C. Evaluate the financial status of potential vendors and chart comparison tables

    D. Monitor service level agreements

44. Which of the following models assumes that software development is a sequential process – the first job must complete before the second job may be started?

    A. End user development

    B. Agile model

    C. Waterfall model

    D. Spiral model

45. What is the primary objective of FATCA?

    A. SEC registration

    B. To identify US-resident holders of US investments

    C. To replace the QI regime

    D. To identify US residents investing in offshore accounts   2010/13

46. Which of the following statements most accurately describes the circumstances when a settlement agent will settle a trade?

    A. When the seller's instructions match the buyer's instructions

    B. When the seller has the stock to deliver, the buyer has sufficient cash or collateral to pay for it and the seller's instructions match the buyer's instructions

    C. When value date has been reached, the seller has the stock to deliver, the buyer has sufficient cash or collateral to pay for it and the seller's instructions match the buyer's instructions

    D. When value date has been reached and the seller has the stock to deliver

47. What is the purpose of an explosion table?

    A. It allows users to select to which general ledger accounts individual entries are posted

    B. It allows users to set up and maintain individual general ledger accounts

    C. It allows users to set up and maintain individual sub-accounts for each security, currency and currency

    D. It allows firms to use the double-entry book-keeping convention to record stock quantities and balances

48. Allocation is the process of:

    A. A sell-side firm sending a confirmation to a fund manager

    B. A fund manager indicating agreement to a confirmation received from a sell-side firm

    C. A fund manager advising the sell-side firm of the identities of investors

    D. A buy-side firm sending a confirmation to a sell-side firm

49. When managing a help desk, which of the following is normally a level 1 responsibility?

    A. Analysing a customer's problem and proposing a solution   L2

    B. Informing analysts of problem repercussions and the likely timescale to return to a normal production environment *L3 SERVICE SPECIALIST*

C. Reviewing the status of problems that have been escalated *L4 MANAGEMENT*

D. Monitoring and status-tracking of all incidents

50. Which of the following is a key principle of STP?

A. Trade processing should consist of logical stages which all happen simultaneously

B. Clerical staff should all be trained in the same system and their input should be cross-checked by a single manager

C. A transaction, once entered into a firm's system, should never have to be rekeyed, and an automated interface between systems should avoid errors caused by manual entry

D. The only time clerical intervention is needed is when making a record of a trade after it has completed satisfactorily

Answers to Multiple Choice Questions

Q1. **Answer:** **D Chapter 6, Section 3**

Once instructions have been sent out regarding a trade, both parties have to ensure that they will have the cash available to pay for their purchases, and the stock available to deliver for their sales. Therefore, most settlement systems incorporate a cash flow projection module that shows them how much funding they need. Sometimes this module is referred to as a maturity ladder.

Q2. **Answer:** **B Chapter 4, Section 3.2.1**

A sell-side firm has to decide whether to fill an order as agent or as principal. It has to make its decision according to MiFID rules. If it is filling the order as agent, then it will forward the order to an investment exchange and charge the investor a commission. If it is filling it as principal, then it will (assuming the order is to buy) sell the investor the required quantity of the instrument from its own 'book' or position. The opposite is true if the order is to sell: the sell-side firm will buy the stock from the investor and add it to its own position or book. In the case of principal orders, the sell-side firm's revenue consists of the difference between the buying price and the selling price, instead of a commission.

Q3. **Answer:** **B Chapter 6, Section 2**

The business purpose of a stock loan is to enable one party to lend securities to another. The transaction has a start leg and an end leg. On the value date of the start leg, the lender delivers securities to the borrower in exchange for cash or other collateral. The purpose of the collateral is to provide the lender with security in case the borrower does not return the securities that were borrowed. On the value date of the end leg, the securities are returned to the borrower and the collateral is returned to the lender.

Q4. **Answer:** **D Chapter 9, Section 3**

Several different iterative/incremental models have been developed to overcome the criticisms of the waterfall model. Incremental development is a scheduling and staging strategy in which the various parts of the system are developed at different times or rates, and integrated as they are completed. Iterative development is a rework scheduling strategy in which time is set aside to revise and improve parts of the system. A typical difference is that the output from an increment is released to users, whereas the output from an iteration is examined for further modification before release. Common iterative/incremental models include prototyping, the Spiral Model and the Agile Model.

Q5. **Answer:** **D Chapter 2, Section 1.2**

The Financial Conduct Authority focuses on regulation of all firms in retail and wholesale financial markets, as well as the infrastructure that supports these markets. It has responsibility for firms that do not fall under the PRA's scope (approximately 25,000 firms). The FCA's role includes:

- supervision of investment exchanges and monitoring firms' compliance with the Market Abuse Directive;
- powers to investigate and prosecute insider dealing;
- responsibility for overseeing the Financial Ombudsman Service (FOS), the Consumer Financial Education Body (CFEB) and the Financial Services Compensation Scheme (FSCS);
- working closely with the FPC and PRA.

Its statutory objective is to ensure that the relevant markets function well.

Q6.   **Answer:**   **D   Chapter 4, Section 5.2.1**

Mark-to-market is an accounting procedure by which assets are 'marked', or recorded, at their current market value, which may be higher or lower than their purchase price or book value. As a result of a mark-to-market calculation, all investments are valued in the dealing system at their current market value, and all profits and losses that result from price rises or falls are recognised on the day that they happen.

Q7.   **Answer:**   **D   Chapter 8, Section 2**

Risks that need to be managed when delivering business change within the IT function include: risk of 'reinventing the wheel' – ie, implementing duplicate systems; delivery risk – ie, delivering late, or not delivering what is required; complexity risk – ie, the end solution becomes so complex that it increases cost and impacts delivery; scope expansion risk – ie, the scope grows and grows and grows (also known as 'scope creep').

Q8.   **Answer:**   **C   Chapter 9, Section 6.2**

Most of the concerns about the cloud are concerned with data security and related issues, including data proximity – the customer will never know whether its data is held in the same databases as that of its competitors, or what dangers this presents.

Q9.   **Answer:**   **B   Chapter 2, Section 1.3**

Article 21 of the MiFID regulations places an obligation on the sell-side firm to get the lowest available price for its customer when the customer is buying, and the highest available price when the customer is selling. This is known as 'best execution'.

Q10.   **Answer:**   **A   Chapter 5, Section 1.4**

An ISIN code is a code that represents one company's ordinary shares. Even if the security is listed on more than one exchange, there is only one ISIN code.

Q11.   **Answer: C**   **Chapter 1, Section 2.2**

Investment banks provide advice to, and arrange finance for, companies who want to float on the stock market, to raise additional finance by issuing further shares or bonds, or carry out mergers and acquisitions. They also provide services for those who might want to invest in shares and bonds, for example pension funds and asset managers.

Q12.   **Answer:**   **D   Chapter 5, Section 1.3**

One of the problems involved in managing the IT infrastructure of a large institution is that there may be a large number of individual business application systems in the configuration, all of which hold some of this large amount of reference data, and some of the information may be duplicated across the different systems. Where there is duplication of reference data, there is a danger that errors creep in. To overcome these issues, some firms have built separate reference data repositories (RDRs) that take in data from reliable sources, such as Bloomberg or Thomson Reuters, as well as manually updated reference data, and then feed this to all the other systems in the configuration.

Q13.   **Answer:**   **D   Chapter 5, Section 2.2**

Matching engines provide a level of automation to the trade agreement process. They are provided by investment exchanges and clearing houses to automate the process of confirmation-matching between member firms. Both parties input their trade details, and the matching engine compares the two trade reports. It also sends reports to the regulator.

Q14.   **Answer:**   **C   Chapter 6, Section 5.7**

FpML (Financial products Markup Language) is an XML message standard for the OTC derivatives industry. The standard is managed by the ISDA on behalf of a community of investment banks that make a market in OTC derivatives. The standard is freely licensed, so any firm that trades the instruments that it supports may use it in their own software.

Q15.   **Answer:**   **A   Chapter 2, Section 1.5**

The first pillar of Basel II provides improved risk-sensitivity in the way that capital requirements are calculated for three major components of risk that a bank faces: credit risk, market risk and operational risk. Other risks, such as liquidity and systemic risks, are not considered fully quantifiable at this stage.

Q16.   **Answer:**   **C   Chapter 10, Section 5**

'Innovation outsourcing' work, including new application development, usually needs a very large number of man-hours, and the 'classic' offshore locations have a significant competitive advantage over near-shore and other locations in terms of personnel and premises costs.

Q17.   **Answer:**   **A   Chapter 6, Section 5.4.3**

Within the header line of a FIN message you will see three things: the BIC code of the receiver; the message type; and the BIC code of the sender.

Q18.   **Answer:**   **B   Chapter 8, Section 5**

Changes may be required as a result of process improvement or bug fixes. New software releases sometimes cause as many problems as they are designed to solve, and change control procedures are an essential method of minimising this type of risk. These procedures are processes designed to prevent software or hardware objects from being amended without auditability and review of the impact by all interested parties. Symptoms of poor change control practices include:

- The latest version of source code cannot be found.
- The wrong version of the code was deployed.
- The wrong version of the code was tested.
- There is no traceability between the software requirements, documentation and code.
- Programmers are working on the wrong version of the code.

Q19.   **Answer:**   **B   Chapter 9, Section 5**

Software testing is a value judgment. It is not possible to produce a complex application that is completely free of defects. The number of defects in a complex application can be large; some of them will be critical and some less so. The purpose of testing is, therefore, to gain a level of confidence in the software so that the organisation is confident that the software has an acceptable defect rate; where defects do exist they are documented and there are adequate work rounds available to the users. User acceptance testing is conducted by the end-user, customer, or client to validate whether or not to accept the product.

Q20.   **Answer:**   **D   Chapter 9, Section 5.7**

ISO 9126 is an international standard for the evaluation of software. The other three ISO standards are concerned with project management (see Section 4.4).

Q21.   **Answer: D**   **Chapter 1, Section 3.2.4**

The trade elements of a bond trade are slightly more complicated, because of the effect of interest or coupon on the trade elements. Bond issuers usually pay coupons annually or semi-annually. The coupon is paid to the investor who holds the bond on the record date. Even if that investor only bought the bond a few days before record date, it will receive from the issuer the coupon for the entire coupon period, and the investor that held the bond for the earlier part of the coupon period will receive nothing. For this reason, when bonds are bought and sold on the secondary market, the accrued interest on the bond for the coupon period is also bought and sold at the same time.

Q22.   **Answer:**   **B   Chapter 5, Section 4**

Statements must be sent to clients every six months, but the client is entitled to insist on one being sent every three months. Where there are no transactions in the period, an annual statement is permitted.

Q23.   **Answer:**   **A   Chapter 3, Section 3.6**

A trade repository or swap data repository is an entity that centrally collects and maintains the records of OTC derivatives. The purpose of this is to provide regulators with visibility into risk exposures by firm and counterparty

Q24.   **Answer:**   **B   Chapter 2, Section 1.3**

The European System of Financial Supervision is an institutional architecture of the EU's framework of financial supervision created in response to the financial crisis of 2007/08. First proposed by the European Commission in 2009, it replaced three existing Committees of Supervisors with three new authorities, called European Supervisory Authorities (ESAs): a European Banking Authority (EBA); a European Insurance and Occupational Pensions Authority (EIOPA); and a European Securities and Markets Authority (ESMA).

ESMA's mission is to enhance the protection of investors and reinforce stable and well-functioning financial markets in the European Union. As an independent institution, ESMA achieves this mission by building a single rule book for EU financial markets and ensuring its consistent application and supervision across the EU.

ESMA contributes to the supervision of financial services firms with a pan-European reach, either through direct supervision or through the active co-ordination of national supervisory activity.

Q25.　　**Answer: B**　　**Chapter 6, Section 2.2.1**

Under UK law, the borrower of the securities becomes the nominal owner of them. The rights of the lender are protected, however, as it remains the beneficial owner. What this means in practice is that the borrower receives all dividends, coupons and any other corporate action proceeds that are paid during the period of the loan, but in effect holds the assets in trust for the lender, and has an obligation to repay any proceeds received of this kind to the lender. However, the borrower also acquires (and therefore the lender loses) the right to vote at company meetings, which is how hedge funds are able to use borrowed stock to influence the companies whose shares have been borrowed.

Q26.　　**Answer:**　　**C　Chapter 7, Section 3.2**

The information that is held in an IT system about an individual general ledger account should include reference data items, balance information items and transaction information items. Reference data items include a unique alphanumeric code to identify the account; the name of the account; a code to represent the type of the account, ie, bank account, expense account, etc; and the identity of the currency in which postings are made for this account. The date of the opening balance is a balance information item.

Q27.　　**Answer:**　　**D　Chapter 3, Section 3.4**

Processing corporate actions is one of the functions of the provider of the settlement and custody services, LCH.Clearnet is a central counterparty that does not provide a settlement and custody service.

Q28.　　**Answer: B**　　**Chapter 1, Section 3.2.4**

The number or shares multiplied by the price is known as the principal amount.

Q29.　　**Answer:**　　**D　Chapter 5, Section 1.4.3**

Some shares are traded in whole currency units, but some are traded in penny units. Hence 'buy 100 @ 98' may mean either 98.00 or 0.98 per share. A bond price, on the other hand, is a percentage of face value, hence 'buy 1,000 @ 98' means buy 1,000 @ 98% of 1,000.

Q30.　　**Answer:**　　**A　Chapter 3, Section 2.3**

A quote-driven system is one where some of the exchange's member firms take on the obligation of always making a two-way price in each of the stocks in which they make markets. These firms are known as market makers.

Q31.　　**Answer:**　　**A　Chapter 8, Section 4.2.5**

Dependent upon the evaluation of the criticality of each application, disaster recovery plans for sites designated 'warm' will involve implementing a range of automated procedures to maintain same data on two servers in the different locations. Typically this involves some form of automatic synchronisation between the databases, such as is provided by log shipping. Log shipping essentially consists of automating and integrating the process of backing up, copying and restoring the database from the primary server to the secondary server. This maintains the secondary server's database as an identical copy of the primary server's database apart from a small time latency of between five and 15 minutes.

Q32.   Answer: C   Chapter 9, Section 5.2.1

After modifying software, either for a change in functionality or to fix defects, a regression test re-runs previously successful tests on the modified software to ensure that the modifications haven't unintentionally caused a regression of previous functionality. Regression testing can be performed at any or all test levels.

Q33.   Answer: A   Chapter 3, Section 3.4.1

Whenever a member firm's positions show potential losses it must make a margin payment to the clearing house. In this way the clearing house is protected against default by the member firm. As an alternative to paying the margin call in cash, the member firm may choose to deposit securities with a value exceeding the amount of the margin call with the clearing house. The cash or securities used to meet the call are known as collateral.

Q34.   Answer: C   Chapter 5, Section 1

The exchange rate is not static as it changes regularly; reference data refers to essentially static facts.

Q35.   Answer: C   Chapter 4, Section 3.1.1

Before a buy-side firm places an order on behalf of its client, it needs to ensure that the order is compatible with the client's investment objectives. These include time horizon, risk appetite, and any other considerations that the investor has made the firm aware of. This is known as pre-trade compliance.

Q36.   Answer: D   Chapter 6, Sections 5.4.1 & 5.4.2

The messages that will commonly be used by securities firms will be found in the MT100, 200, 300 and 900 series (for managing firms' cash activities) and the MT500 series (for managing firms' securities business). The ISO standard that governs all the series, except for the MT500 series, is ISO 7775. This standard was developed during the 1980s. In the late 1990s SWIFT and its members realised that the original ISO 7775 messages were too restrictive, did not reflect the full complexity of modern trading instruments, and were still too ambiguous to ensure that full STP could be achieved. Thus was born the ISO 15022 standard, based on a data dictionary approach.

Q37.   Answer: C   Chapter 2, Section 2.1

Principle 8 of the Data Protection Act states that personal data shall not be transferred to a country or territory outside the EEA, unless that country or territory ensures an adequate level of protection in relation to the processing of personal data.

Q38.   Answer: C   Chapter 5, Section 2.1

When the sell-side firm is dealing with a market counterparty, there are two possible practices: mutual exchange of confirmations; or use of a matching engine. The mutual exchange of confirmations method of trade agreement is used extensively in matching confirmations for foreign exchange and money market trades, as well as trades in OTC derivatives, such as swaps.

Q39.   **Answer:**   **B   Chapter 8, Section 1.2.4**

In 2010, the European Commission published its final proposal for the European Market Infrastructure Regulation (EMIR), which sets out to increase stability within OTC derivative markets. The scope of the regulation is very similar to that of the US Dodd-Frank legislation which is covered in Section 5.2 of this workbook.

The regulation introduces:

- a reporting obligation for OTC derivatives; this involves the use of trade repositories which are discussed in Chapter 4. This obligation went live in February 2014;
- a clearing obligation for eligible OTC derivatives;
- measures to reduce counterparty credit risk and operational risk for bilaterally cleared OTC derivatives;
- common rules for central counterparties (CCPs) and for trade repositories; and
- rules on the establishment of interoperability between CCPs.

Q40.   **Answer:**   **D   Chapter 2, Section 5.1**

The Sarbanes-Oxley Act 2002 (also known as the Public Company Accounting Reform and Investor Protection Act and commonly called SOX) is a US federal law enacted on 30 July 2002. SOX established a new quasi-public agency, the Public Company Accounting Oversight board (PCAOB). Through PCAOB, the US Securities Exchange Commission (SEC) has the power to regulate securities companies, or require them to adopt rules to protect investors and the public interest.

Q41.   **Answer:**   **D   Chapter 4, Sections 5.1 & 5.2.2**

Credit risk is the risk associated with one party not fulfilling its contractual obligations to another party at a specific future date. Market risk is the risk that the value of the investments owned by the investor might decline. Value-at-Risk (VaR) is a measure of how the market value of an asset or of a portfolio of assets is likely to decrease over a certain time period (usually over one or ten days) under usual conditions. It is typically used by security houses or investment banks to measure the market risk of their asset portfolios.

Q42.   **Answer:**   **B   Chapter 8, Section 3.2.3**

KPIs for a given system or suite of systems that support a business line can be presented in a 'dashboard' to give a health evaluation of the IT systems supporting the business. Where an area is below what is expected it will be given a low mark or highlighted by an alert. Dashboards can be used to initiate discussion around business strategy and ongoing investment required to support the business.

Q43.   **Answer:**   **B   Chapter 10, Section 6.3.2**

Traditionally, vendor management has been seen as an art, not a science. However, as configurations become larger and more complex, many firms now use a more formalised approach. There are now vendor management software packages on the market that support this process. They usually automate the administration of contracts and centralise all associated information into one central repository that is globally accessible via a web browser. These products enable organisations to monitor their spending, terminate contracts at the correct time, monitor and track their costs against benefits gained and ensure that more informed decisions are made based on quantifiable facts and figures.

Q44. **Answer:** **C Chapter 9, Section 3.1.1**

In the waterfall methodology, there are sequences of phases where the output of each phase becomes the input of the next. Where there is a problem with the previous phase of delivery, the solution is returned to the previous phase and rework occurs before the waterfall continues.

Q45. **Answer:** **D Chapter 2, Section 5.3**

FATCA was enacted in March 2010 and comes into force in January 2013. It is an important development in US efforts to combat tax evasion by US persons holding investments in offshore accounts.

Q46. **Answer:** **C Chapter 6, Section 1.5.1**

The settlement agent will settle a trade provided that:

- value date has been reached;
- the seller has the stock to deliver;
- the buyer has the cash or credit to pay for it; and
- the seller's instructions match the buyer's instructions.

Q47. **Answer:** **A Chapter 7, Section 3.2.2**

Most systems build the business rules for a decision of which account to post to by using an 'explosion table' similar to the one illustrated in the Section 3.2.2 of Chapter 7.

Q48. **Answer:** **C Chapter 4, Section 3.3**

As part of the order flow process, the fund manager will check the confirmation received from the sell-side firm. If it disagrees with the details, it takes the matter up with the sell-side firm, otherwise it is said to affirm the confirmation. At the same time, the fund manager also advises the sell-side firm of the allocation details of this order. The fund manager itself has placed this order on behalf of its own clients (or funds) – there may be just one of them or there may be many. At this stage the fund manager notifies the sell-side firm of the details of who its clients are and how many shares are to be allocated to each client.

Q49. **Answer:** **D Chapter 8, Section 3.2.4**

The level 1 resource is responsible for: receiving, recording, prioritising and tracking service calls; monitoring and status-tracking of all incidents; escalation and referral to other parts of the organisation; first line support; and closing incidents with confirmation from the requestor. Answer A is level 2 (analyst); answer B is level 3 (service specialist), and answer C is the responsibility of level 4 (management).

Q50. **Answer: C Chapter 1, Section 4**

One of the most important principles of straight-through processing (STP) is that the transaction is entered into the firm's systems only once. As most investment firms need to record the transaction into more than one system, there need to be automated interfaces between all systems that need to store records of the order or trade. Clerical intervention should only be to manage by exception, ie, when something goes wrong. The stages should happen in logical order, not simultaneously.

Syllabus Learning Map

Syllabus Unit/ Element		Chapter/ Section
Element 1	**Information Technology In The Securities Industry**	**Chapter 1**
1.1	**Know the role of the following participants within the financial services industry:** • retail banks and building societies • investment banks • pension funds • insurance companies • fund managers • stockbrokers/wealth managers/platforms/IFAs • custodians • third party administrators (TPAs)	2
1.2	**Know the elements of a secondary market equity trade**	3.2.4
1.3	**Know the elements of a secondary market bond trade**	3.2.4
1.4	**Understand the concept of straight-through processing**	4

Syllabus Unit/ Element		Chapter/ Section
Element 2	**The Regulatory Framework**	**Chapter 2**
2.1	Understand the need for regulation	1.1
2.2	Know the function of UK and European regulators in the financial services industry	1.2
2.3	Know the regulatory objectives of MiFID/MiFID II	1.4
2.4	Know the significance of the Data Protection Act 1998 • Principles • Non-compliance	2
2.5	Know the significance to IT of the following rules: • Client Asset Sourcebook (CASS) • Conduct of Business Sourcebook (COB) • Senior Management Arrangements, Systems and Controls (SYSC)	2.4
2.6	Know the regulatory objectives of Basel II/III	1.6
2.7	Know the regulatory objectives of Dodd-Frank	4.1
2.8	Know the regulatory objectives of the Foreign Account Tax Compliance Act (FATCA)	4.2
2.9	Know the regulatory objectives of the European Markets Infrastructure Regulation (EMIR)	1.5

Syllabus Unit/ Element		Chapter/ Section
Element 3	**IT And The Functional Flow Of Financial Instruments**	Chapter 3
3.1	Understand the function and connectivity of investment exchanges, multilateral trading facilities and broker-crossing networks: • Classification • Economic functions • Order handling systems • Connectivity	2
3.2	Understand the function and connectivity of clearing houses: • Recognised clearing houses • Settlement and custody services • Central Counterparty services	3
3.3	Know the function and connectivity of Trade Data Repositories	3.6
3.4	Understand the functionality of external real time information sources: • Pre-trade price and liquidity discovery • Analytics • Post-trade information dissemination	4
Element 4	**The Role Of IT In The Front Office**	Chapter 4
4.1	Understand the investment decision support process	2
4.2	Understand the IT support requirements of order placing and filling, including: • Order entry (agency, principal and 3rd party orders) • Pre-trade compliance • Best execution • Treating Customers Fairly • Transaction capture • Client connectivity including Direct Market Access • Communication via electronic media • Pooling, allocation and aggregation of a single order across two or more investors/funds • Dealing Systems • Charges, fees and expenses	3
4.3	Understand the purpose and consequences of algorithmic trading	4
4.4	Understand the basic IT characteristics of risk mitigation for the following front office functions: • Risk management • Transaction capture • Best execution	5

Syllabus Unit/ Element		Chapter/ Section
Element 5	**The Role Of IT In The Pre-Settlement Phase**	Chapter 5
5.1	Understand the IT alignment to Pre-Settlement Phase Key Risk Indicators, including: • Reference data • Standard settlement instructions • Client and Counterparty Agreements	1
5.2	Understand the IT implications of the Trade Agreement Process	2
5.3	Understand the role of matching engines	2.2
5.4	Understand the IT requirements for reporting to regulators: • wholesale vs retail	3
5.5	Understand the IT requirements for reporting to customers: • wholesale vs retail	4

Syllabus Unit/ Element		Chapter/ Section
Element 6	**The Role Of IT In The Settlement And Post-Settlement Phases**	
6.1	Understand the IT support requirements of transaction instructions	1
6.2	Understand the purposes of stock lending and repos, their IT implications and the importance of segregation	2
6.3	Understand the IT requirements for cash funding (positioning)	3
6.4	Understand the function of IT within the settlement process: • Front office systems • Back office systems • Financial control systems	4
6.5	Know the function of the following standards: • SWIFT • FIX • FpML • XBRL	5
6.6	Understand the function of IT within post-settlement reconciliation procedures, including: • Reconciliation requirements and record keeping • Ensuring cash and stock movements are recorded • Journal movements • Corporate actions (including dividends, bonus issues and rights issues)	6

Syllabus Unit/ Element		Chapter/ Section
Element 7	**The Impact Of IT On Financial Control**	**Chapter 7**
7.1	Know the role of the financial control function	1
7.2	Understand the relationship between the front office, settlement systems and the financial control function	2
7.3	Know the purpose of the general ledger	3
7.4	Know the components of a general ledger account	3.2
7.5	Know how account selection parameters are maintained	3.2.2
7.6	Know the purpose of the stock record	4
Element 8	**IT Management**	**Chapter 8**
8.1	Know the typical roles and responsibilities within the IT department	1.1
8.2	Know the typical building blocks of an IT infrastructure	1.2
8.3	Understand the roles and uses of relational databases, distributed systems and real-time messaging	1.2
8.4	Understand the IT governance relating to: • Measuring IT performance • Managing and monitoring risk • Managing change • Benefits realisation	2
8.5	Know the common methods of securing data against hacking, phishing, scamming and spyware	3.1
8.6	Understand the concept of management and support of applications	3.2
8.7	Understand the function of Service (Help) Desks and Follow-The-Sun Model	3.3
8.8	Know the purpose of Service Level Agreements (SLAs) and Key Performance Indicators (internal and external)	3.3.3
8.9	Understand prioritisation levels and the responsibilities of support teams	3.3.4
8.10	Understand the IT implications of Disaster Recovery (DR) and Business Continuity Planning (BCP): • Planning • Risk assessment • Priorities for processing and operations • Recovery strategies • Data collection • Written plan • Testing criteria and procedures	4
8.11	Understand the importance of change control procedures	5

Syllabus Unit/ Element		Chapter/ Section
Element 9	**Managing Business Change**	**Chapter 9**
9.1	Understand the purpose and benefits of project planning and control	1
9.2	Understand the importance of project governance	1
9.3	Understand the key stages of a Software Development Life Cycle (SDLC) including: • Project planning • Feasibility study • Systems analysis • Requirements definition • Systems design • Code generation • Development • Integration and testing • Acceptance, installation, deployment • Maintenance	2
9.4	Understand the different software development methodologies, including: • Traditional or Waterfall methodologies • Iterative/incremental methodologies • Other methodologies	3
9.5	Know the following different methodologies used in technology delivery: • PRINCE • PMI • ISO	4
9.6	Understand the need for testing and its importance to quality assurance, including: • Testing strategies • Test stages • Techniques • Cycles • Test reporting	5
9.7	Know the impact of disruptive innovation: • cloud computing • big data • social networking • mobile computing	6

Syllabus Unit/ Element		Chapter/ Section
Element 10	**IT Services Procurement**	**Chapter 10**
10.1	Understand the Buy Versus Build decision	2
10.2	Know the advantages and disadvantages of outsourcing	3
10.3	Know the advantages and disadvantages of insourcing	4
10.4	Know the advantages and disadvantages of offshoring, near-shoring, best-shoring	5
10.5	Understand the vendor relationship, including: • The vendor selection process • Vendor assessment • Task order/ work order / contract negotiation and finalisation • Effective vendor management	6

Examination Specification

Each examination paper is constructed from a specification that determines the weightings that will be given to each element. The specification is given below.

It is important to note that the numbers quoted may vary slightly from examination to examination as there is some flexibility to ensure that each examination has a consistent level of difficulty. However, the number of questions tested in each element should not change by more than plus or minus 2.

Element Number	Element	Questions
1	Information Technology in the Securities Industry	4
2	The Regulatory Framework for IT	6
3	IT and the Functional Flow of Financial Instruments	4
4	The Role of IT in the Front Office	4
5	The Role of IT in the Pre-Settlement Phase	5
6	The Role of IT in the Settlement and Post-Settlement Phases	5
7	The Impact of IT on Financial Control	5
8	IT Management	6
9	Managing Business Change	7
10	IT Services Procurement	4
Total		**50**

CISI Associate (ACSI) Membership can work for you...

Studying for a CISI qualification is hard work and we're sure you're putting in plenty of hours, but don't lose sight of your goal!

This is just the first step in your career; there is much more to achieve!

The securities and investments industry attracts ambitious and driven individuals. You're probably one yourself and that's great, but on the other hand you're almost certainly surrounded by lots of other people with similar ambitions.

So how can you stay one step ahead during these uncertain times?

Entry Criteria:

Pass in either:

- Investment Operations Certificate (IOC), IFQ, ICWIM, Capital Markets in, eg, Securities, Derivatives, Advanced Certificates; or
- one CISI Diploma/Masters in Wealth Management paper

Joining Fee: £25 or free if applying via prefilled application form   **Annual Subscription (pro rata):** £125

Using your new CISI qualification* to become an Associate (ACSI) member of the Chartered Institute for Securities & Investment could well be the next important career move you make this year, and help you maintain your competence.

Join our global network of over 40,000 financial services professionals and start enjoying both the professional and personal benefits that CISI membership offers. Once you become a member you can use the prestigious ACSI designation after your name and even work towards becoming personally chartered.

* ie, Investment Operations Certificate (IOC), IFQ, ICWIM, Capital Markets

Benefits in Summary...

- Use of the CISI CPD Scheme
- Unlimited free CPD seminars, webcasts, podcasts and online training tools
- Highly recognised designatory letters
- Unlimited free attendance at CISI Professional Forums
- CISI publications including *S&I Review* and *Change – The Regulatory Update*
- 20% discount on all CISI conferences and training courses
- Invitation to CISI Annual Lecture
- Select Benefits – our exclusive personal benefits portfolio

The ACSI designation will provide you with access to a range of member benefits, including Professional Refresher where there are currently over 60 modules available on subjects including Behavioural Finance, Cybercrime and Conduct Risk. CISI TV is also available to members, allowing you to catch up on the latest CISI events, whilst earning valuable CPD hours.

Plus many other networking opportunities which could be invaluable for your career.

Revision Express Interactive

You've bought the workbook... now test your knowledge before your exam.

Revision Express Interactive is an engaging online study tool to be used in conjunction with CISI workbooks. It contains exercises and revision questions.

Key Features of Revision Express Interactive:
- Examination-focused – the content of Revision Express Interactive covers the key points of the syllabus
- Questions throughout to reaffirm understanding of the subject
- Special end-of-module practice exam to reflect as closely as possible the standard you will experience in your exam (please note, however, they are not the CISI exam questions themselves)
- Interactive exercises throughout
- Extensive glossary of terms
- Useful associated website links
- Allows you to study whenever you like

IMPORTANT: The questions contained in Revision Express Interactive elearning products are designed as aids to revision, and should not be seen in any way as mock exams.

Price per elearning module: £35
Price when purchased with the CISI workbook: £100 (normal price: £110)

To purchase Revision Express Interactive:

call our Customer Support Centre on:
+44 20 7645 0777

or visit CISI Online Bookshop at:
cisi.org/bookshop

For more information on our elearning products, contact our Customer Support Centre on +44 20 7645 0777, or visit our website at cisi.org/study

Professional Refresher

Self-testing elearning modules to refresh your knowledge, meet regulatory and firm requirements, and earn CPD hours.

Professional Refresher is a training solution to help you remain up-to-date with industry developments, maintain regulatory compliance and demonstrate continuing learning.

This popular online learning tool allows self-administered refresher testing on a variety of topics, including the latest regulatory changes.

There are currently over 70 modules available which address UK and international issues. Modules are reviewed by practitioners frequently and new topics are added to the suite on a regular basis.

Benefits to firms:
- Learning and tests can form part of business T&C programme
- Learning and tests kept up-to-date and accurate by the CISI
- Relevant and useful – devised by industry practitioners
- Access to individual results available as part of management overview facility, 'Super User'
- Records of staff training can be produced for internal use and external audits
- Cost-effective – no additional charge for CISI members
- Available to non-members

Benefits to individuals:
- Comprehensive selection of topics across industry sectors
- Modules are frequently reviewed and updated by industry experts
- New topics introduced regularly
- Free for members
- Successfully passed modules are recorded in your CPD log as Active Learning
- Counts as structured learning for RDR purposes
- On completion of a module, a certificate can be printed out for your own records

The full suite of Professional Refresher modules is free to CISI members or £250 for non-members. Modules are also available individually. To view a full list of Professional Refresher modules visit:

cisi.org/refresher

If you or your firm would like to find out more contact our Client Relationship Management team:

+ 44 20 7645 0670
crm@cisi.org

For more information on our elearning products, contact our Customer Support Centre on +44 20 7645 0777, or visit our website at cisi.org/study

Professional Refresher

Free to CISI members

Top 5

SCORM COMPLIANT

Integrity & Ethics
- High Level View
- Ethical Behaviour
- An Ethical Approach
- Compliance vs Ethics

Anti-Money Laundering
- Introduction to Money Laundering
- UK Legislation and Regulation
- Money Laundering Regulations 2007
- Proceeds of Crime Act 2002
- Terrorist Financing
- Suspicious Activity Reporting
- Money Laundering Reporting Officer
- Sanctions

Financial Crime
- What Is Financial Crime?
- Insider Dealing and Market Abuse Introduction, Legislation, Offences and Rules
- Money Laundering Legislation, Regulations, Financial Sanctions and Reporting Requirements
- Money Laundering and the Role of the MLRO

Information Security and Data Protection
- Information Security: The Key Issues
- Latest Cybercrime Developments
- The Lessons From High-Profile Cases
- Key Identity Issues: Know Your Customer
- Implementing the Data Protection Act 1998
- The Next Decade: Predictions For The Future

UK Bribery Act
- Background to the Act
- The Offences
- What the Offences Cover
- When Has an Offence Been Committed?
- The Defences Against Charges of Bribery
- The Penalties

Conduct Rules
- Application and Overview
- Individual Conduct Rules – FCA & PRA
- Senior Management Conduct Rules
- Obligations on Firms

Pensions Advice
- Advice or Guidance?
- Advice During Accumulation
- Defined Contribution Pension Freedoms
- Transfers and Decumulation
- Problems with Accessing New Freedoms

Retirement Planning
- Pensions and Provisions
- Money In
- Money Out

Financial Planning (An introduction)
- Related Activities
- The Financial Plan
- Cash Flow Planning and Modelling
- Behavioural Finance and Financial Planning
- Risk
- The Regulatory Framework
- The Future Landscape

Senior Managers and Certification Regime
- Definitions
- Obligations
- Certification
- Conduct Rules
- Scope of the Rules
- Conclusion and Future Developments

Operations

Best Execution
- What Is Best Execution?
- Achieving Best Execution
- Order Execution Policies
- Information to Clients & Client Consent
- Monitoring, the Rules, and Instructions
- Best Execution for Specific Types of Firms

Approved Persons Regime
- The Basis of the Regime
- Fitness and Propriety
- The Controlled Functions
- Principles for Approved Persons
- The Code of Practice for Approved Persons

Corporate Actions
- Corporate Structure and Finance
- Life Cycle of an Event
- Mandatory Events
- Voluntary Events

Wealth

Client Assets and Client Money
- Protecting Client Assets and Client Money
- Ring-Fencing Client Assets and Client Money
- Due Diligence of Custodians
- Reconciliations
- Records and Accounts
- CASS Oversight

Investment Principles and Risk
- Diversification
- Factfind and Risk Profiling
- Investment Management
- Modern Portfolio Theory and Investing Styles
- Direct and Indirect Investments
- Socially Responsible Investment
- Collective Investments
- Investment Trusts
- Dealing in Debt Securities and Equities

Banking Standards
- Introduction and Background
- Strengthening Individual Accountability
- Reforming Corporate Governance
- Securing Better Outcomes for Consumers
- Enhancing Financial Stability

Suitability of Client Investments
- Assessing Suitability
- Risk Profiling
- Establishing Risk Appetite
- Obtaining Customer Information
- Suitable Questions and Answers
- Making Suitable Investment Selections
- Guidance, Reports and Record Keeping

International

Foreign Account Tax Compliance Act (FATCA)
- Foreign Financial Institutions
- Due Diligence Requirements
- Reporting
- Compliance

MiFID II
- The Organisations Covered by MiFID
- The Products Subject to MiFID's Guidelines
- The Origins of MiFID II
- The Products Covered by MiFID II
- Levels 1, 2, and 3 Implementation

UCITS
- The Original UCITS Directive
- UCITS III
- UCITS IV
- Non-UCITS Funds
- Future Developments

cisi.org/refresher

Feedback to the CISI

Have you found this workbook to be a valuable aid to your studies? We would like your views, so please email us at learningresources@cisi.org with any thoughts, ideas or comments.

Accredited Training Partners

Support for examination students studying for the Chartered Institute for Securities & Investment (CISI) Qualifications is provided by several Accredited Training Partners (ATPs), including Fitch Learning and BPP. The CISI's ATPs offer a range of face-to-face training courses, distance learning programmes, their own learning resources and study packs which have been accredited by the CISI. The CISI works in close collaboration with its ATPs to ensure they are kept informed of changes to CISI examinations so they can build them into their own courses and study packs.

CISI Workbook Specialists Wanted

Workbook Authors

Experienced freelance authors with finance experience, and who have published work in their area of specialism, are sought. Responsibilities include:
- Updating workbooks in line with new syllabuses and any industry developments
- Ensuring that the syllabus is fully covered

Workbook Reviewers

Individuals with a high-level knowledge of the subject area are sought. Responsibilities include:
- Highlighting any inconsistencies against the syllabus
- Assessing the author's interpretation of the workbook

Workbook Technical Reviewers

Technical reviewers provide a detailed review of the workbook and bring the review comments to the panel. Responsibilities include:
- Cross-checking the workbook against the syllabus
- Ensuring sufficient coverage of each learning objective

Workbook Proofreaders

Proofreaders are needed to proof workbooks both grammatically and also in terms of the format and layout. Responsibilities include:
- Checking for spelling and grammar mistakes
- Checking for formatting inconsistencies

If you are interested in becoming a CISI external specialist call:
+44 20 7645 0609

or email:
externalspecialists@cisi.org

For bookings, orders, membership and general enquiries please contact our Customer Support Centre on +44 20 7645 0777, or visit our website at cisi.org